"Shibley and Holt, collaborating as psyc
a tool which empowers mental health
work with immigrants, their families, and counsel on a variety of immigration benefits, including cases in the immigration courts. Drawing from their personal experiences to give practical instruction, this book provides important advice to novice and seasoned professionals alike on best practices for working with clients and their attorneys."

—**Allen Orr Jr.,** President, American Immigration Lawyers Association

"Psychological evaluations are extremely important for torture survivors who are asylum seekers in the U.S. immigration system. This book guides clinicians to develop valuable expertise when conducting these much-needed psychological evaluations. Caring, knowledgeable licensed mental health professionals who provide this specialized service would find it not only rewarding but also life changing."

—**Kathi Anderson**, Executive Director, Survivors of Torture, International

Conducting Immigration Evaluations

This book prepares mental health professionals to conduct a thorough psychological assessment of individuals involved in immigration proceedings and present the results in a professional report. Written by a licensed clinical psychologist with input from an attorney certified in Immigration and Nationality Law, the book uses clear language that makes it accessible to experienced and novice therapists alike.

Chapters present a basic legal understanding of various types of immigration cases and detail the process of conducting the clinical interview, choosing the psychological instruments appropriate for each case, and writing the report. The book also covers practical considerations such as testifying in immigration court and expanding your practice to include immigration evaluations. Vignettes and sample reports link theory to real-world situations, drawing from the authors' many years of combined experience.

This book is an essential guide for clinicians who want to assist the diverse and often disempowered population of immigrants and their families.

Mariela G. Shibley is a clinical and forensic psychologist with a private practice in San Diego, California. She specializes in conducting psychological evaluations for the United States Citizenship and Immigration Services and Immigration Court.

Matthew G. Holt, Esq., is a certified specialist in Immigration and Nationality Law by the California State Bar and the managing attorney of a comprehensive immigration law firm headquartered in San Diego, California.

Conducting Immigration Evaluations

A Practical Guide for Mental
Health Professionals

Mariela G. Shibley
with Matthew G. Holt
Foreword by Celia J. Falicov

Routledge
Taylor & Francis Group

NEW YORK AND LONDON

Cover credit: © Shutterstock

First published 2022
by Routledge
605 Third Avenue, New York, NY 10158

and by Routledge
4 Park Square, Milton Park, Abingdon, Oxon, OX14 4RN

Routledge is an imprint of the Taylor & Francis Group, an informa business

© 2022 Mariela G. Shibley and Matthew G. Holt

Library of Congress Cataloging-in-Publication Data
A catalog record for this title has been requested

ISBN: 978-0-367-69000-7 (hbk)
ISBN: 978-0-367-68998-8 (pbk)
ISBN: 978-1-003-13997-3 (ebk)

DOI: 10.4324/9781003139973

Typeset in Bembo
by Newgen Publishing UK

Contents

About the Authors

Mariela G. Shibley, Psy.D.

Dr. Mariela G. Shibley is a clinical and forensic psychologist with a private practice in San Diego, California. A native of Buenos Aires, Argentina, she immigrated to the United States in 1991. She received her professional training from the University of California, Los Angeles, and the California School of Professional Psychology at Alliant International University, San Diego. She then completed her postdoctoral training in psychoanalytic psychotherapy at the Institute of Contemporary Psychoanalysis and the San Diego Psychoanalytic Center (SDPC), where she is currently concluding a five-year advanced training program in adult psychoanalysis.

Driven by her own experiences as an immigrant, Dr. Shibley specializes in issues around acculturation, immigration, and trauma. Since 2007 she has conducted and supervised over 2,000 psychological evaluations for U.S. Citizenship and Immigration Services and Immigration Court. She provides court testimony, training, and education on immigration and mental health and is a regular guest speaker at conferences of the American Immigration Lawyers Association (AILA).

Dr. Shibley supervises mental health professionals working within her private practice, and she is the founder of PsychEvalCoach, an online training program that teaches those in the mental health field how to conduct immigration evaluations. In addition, she is a volunteer clinical instructor in the Department of Family Medicine and Public Health at the University of California, San Diego, providing therapeutic services to undocumented individuals through the UCSD Free Clinics. She is adjunct faculty at the California School of Professional Psychology at Alliant International University, and she has taught doctoral level classes at the California School of Forensic Studies and at Argosy University in San Diego. Dr. Shibley is an active member of the San Diego Psychological Association, where she is serving on the Board of Directors (for the second time), is a core member of the Forensic Committee, and the former chairperson of the Ethics Committee.

A fierce advocate for self-care, Dr. Shibley enjoys spending time with her family, traveling, and nurturing decades-long friendships.

Matthew G. Holt, Esq.

Mr. Holt is a certified specialist in Immigration and Nationality Law by the California State Bar and the managing attorney of a multi-office comprehensive immigration law firm in San Diego, California. He is a past member of the American Immigration Lawyers Association's Board of Governors and the current chair of the San Diego County Bar Association's Immigration Section. Since 2007, he has dedicated his law practice exclusively to representing and defending immigrants, their families, and their employers before the U.S. Department of Justice, U.S. Citizenship and Immigration Services, U.S. Department of State, and federal courts. He has represented thousands of foreign nationals in their immigration cases in all aspects of US immigration law and successfully won hundreds of trials in the immigration courts. Based on his experience and solution-based approach to complex immigration problems, he is a regularly invited speaker at conferences all over the United States, and his firm regularly contributes to various media outlets.

In his free time, Mr. Holt enjoys spending time with his family, surfing, snowboarding, hiking, playing cards and board games, and travelling. He also volunteers at a local community shelter, engages in local political issues, and coaches youth soccer.

Foreword

Since ancient times, in many cultures around the world, there has existed a social norm—sometimes codified into law—that when outsiders flee to a new land in a desperate attempt to survive, they will not be turned away. For most immigrants, migration is not a choice but a matter of survival. Threats to their survival can arise from many sources: persecution due to race, religion, gender and gender identity, nationality, political engagement, hunger, and scarcity of opportunity. Even behind what is considered "voluntary" migration driven by poverty, other forms of violence may lurk, including economic exploitation, intimate partner violence, and human trafficking.

At various historical periods, that ancient humanitarian promise of the right to be protected has been encumbered by political vicissitudes that make the possibility of permanent relocation of immigrants and asylum seekers a complex, often impenetrable process. The limitations have been also due to a lack of policies about the specific needs of various types of immigration cases and the order of procedures that need to be put into motion to help the plight of immigrant individuals and families who are torn apart, are victims of battering, or are traumatized by crimes.

A positive development in the modern scenario of human migration to the United States has been the inclusion of human rights thinking in policies about legality. This development reached its most concerted efforts after World War II with the codification of the Universal Declaration of Human Rights into law. In recent decades, the increased awareness about the need for order and clarity in the processes for obtaining legal permanent residency has gradually led to the inclusion of mental health professionals as evaluators of the merits that can warrant the protection of immigrants and asylum seekers.

Today, many immigrants and asylum seekers require a comprehensive psychological evaluation in support of their immigration applications. Immigration judges and the United States Citizenship and Immigration Services adjudicators have significant leeway in determining whether someone's case qualifies under the law or not, with adjudicators varying widely in their decisions about similar cases. The decision is often quite subjective, with the "credibility" of the applicant being a key determining factor. A well-written psychological evaluation can be a critically persuasive type of evidence and a determining factor in the decision made by the adjudicator.

Despite the urgent need for conducting immigration-related psychological evaluations and for testifying in immigration court, few mental health professionals receive a relevant conceptual base and a hands-on training in graduate school. Unprepared for this task, those interested in learning these clinical practices usually take short courses or brief webinars that may not impart sufficient knowledge and appropriate resources.

The publication of Dr. Shibley's book is a most timely and crucial contribution to conducting psychological evaluations in support of immigration applications and could be utilized as an essential textbook and practical guide to both teachers and students in doctoral and master-level programs. Dr. Shibley is a clinical and forensic psychologist with extensive experience in conducting psychological evaluations for US Citizenship and Immigration Services. Mr. Holt is an attorney certified specialist in Immigration and Nationality Law. They have collaborated to produce a remarkable comprehensive roadmap for navigating an exhaustive array of categories of immigration appeals, and for conducting the psychological evaluations required to support them. Eligibility requirements for each type of immigration relief ranging from victims of torture, violence against women, the trauma of violent crime, or the hardship involved in removal of family members are spelled in outline form with didactic clarity of what needs to be proven, what factors are in favor of or against the right to remain, and what adjudicators will look for in a report.

Reading and learning from this book, mental health professionals will feel confident in conducting clinical interviews and using relevant psychological measures or instruments. They will also obtain in-depth guidelines on how to write a clear and compelling report that can yield effective results. Vivid—and often moving—clinical illustrations capture compelling narrative details that guide the reader toward the angles to explore, the details to examine, and the arguments to utilize in the pursuit of accurate evaluations of each case.

From my vantage point as a clinical psychologist and family therapist specialized on the psychological impact of immigration experiences, I am aware that immigrants, both authorized and unauthorized, as well as asylum seekers and their families, are the most misunderstood and often among the most vulnerable populations in many institutional settings. One of the many ethical and cutting-edge contributions of this very well-written book is its approach to the cultural differences often present in the individuals applying for legal residence status. Rather than presenting the prevailing "cultural competence" approach which too often includes a list of stereotypical characteristics to evaluate clients from diverse cultural backgrounds, this book encourages mental health professionals to be open-minded. This includes showing curiosity and respect, inquiring about the variability in worldviews, beliefs, or customs, even among immigrants of the same nationality or language but also between themselves, their professional concepts, and their immigrant clients. Pairing cultural competence with cultural humility, what I would call non-stereotyped "cultural attunement," the work presented in this book recognizes that our personal and professional views are not culture free or neutral, and therefore, we may err when applying our own cultural views as the standard of judgment toward immigrants' cultures.

Two other considerations about culture are worth mentioning. One is the attention to the many subtleties of linguistic aspects, including an excellent list of recommendations for the use of interpreters for clients of limited English command and their predicted match or mismatch with clients. The other includes specific recommendations for diagnostic and psychological assessment instruments that hold cross-cultural validity, easing the obstacles to this usually ignored need.

Rarely does immigration status affect only a single individual. Over five million children, most being US citizens, live in "mixed status" families, which means that one or more members in the same family are undocumented. Often the impact of deporting the undocumented spouse, parent, grandparent or sibling, or other crucial relatives of the remaining family members that legally hold citizenship, is ignored. Children and families are often left destitute when breadwinners are detained. Too often the remaining parent must leave a job in order to care for the children, thus pushing families deeper into poverty. Spouses and family members left behind may not speak English or understand the system well enough to avail themselves of what limited help might be available. The effect on individuals and families is devastating to their health and well-being. These issues are considered in the chapter on "appraisal of exceptional and extremely unusual hardship in cancelation of removal," in which the details of the assessment process are described, focusing on family dynamics, attachment styles, and the intricacies of evaluating the children involved.

Throughout my many years of experience working with immigrant families, I have learned that their health and mental health are affected in multiple ways by the stress, trauma, and marginalization often brought about by immigration. I believe in the positive effects of psychotherapy to help cope with some of their stressors relying on their strengths. But precisely because I am constantly aware of the issues affecting immigrant families' mental health, I have come to the realization that for many immigrants the most dramatic transformation of their lives usually does not come from psychotherapy. Rather, the act of obtaining legal permanent residency can have the largest ripple effect of positive consequences for the individual and their primary family relationships. These consequences include protections against economic exploitation of unscrupulous employers, domestic violence by partners, seeking police protection when faced with other forms of violence, access to health care, education, employment, housing, and social services. And perhaps the most deeply emotional benefit of a stable life is allowing children and parents to remain living together rather than being torn apart by separations.

This book offers a path to social justice toward a diverse and often disempowered, under-resourced large population. It is a testament to fundamental human rights for immigrants and asylum seekers in the United States. Most importantly, it will inspire mental health professionals to expand their practices by devoting their time and expertise to engage in the worthy task of helping immigrant individuals and families in vulnerable communities to gain a path toward US citizenship.

Celia Jaes Falicov, PhD

Author of *Latino Families in Therapy*, 2d edition (2014), New York, Guilford Press and coauthor of *Diversity and Multiculturalism in Clinical Supervision* (2014), Washington, DC, APA Publications.

Acknowledgments

I first want to thank Routledge for inviting me to write this book. I want to thank Glenn Lipson for relentlessly encouraging me to pursue this project and helping me along the way, Richard Levak for taking the time to review my proposal, and Celia Falicov for her invaluable guidance, support, generosity, and inspiration. I am forever grateful to my dear mentors of the forensic committee, who continuously hold my hand and inspire me to immerse myself deeper into this amazing field, and my colleagues and friends who remind me constantly the importance of our work.

A big thank-you to Matt Holt for accepting my invitation to partake in this project and for helping me get to where I am today. I believe I still have the very first report I wrote for one of your clients, where in unforgiving red ink you graciously whipped me into place. To my team at Shibley Psychology, current and past, your devotion and enthusiasm propel me to keep learning and refining our craft. Priscilla Posada-Pedrin, your unwaveringly positive disposition and unmeasurable help never go unnoticed. To the hundreds of clients who trusted me to accompany them through their uphill battles and the attorneys who referred them and taught me a thing or two in the process, I would not be writing this book if not for you.

Lastly, my profound gratitude to my husband Greg, who lifted me up every time I felt I might crumble. Words cannot convey how grateful I am for your invaluable contributions, consistent reassurance, and unconditional support.

~ MGS

Echoing the gratitude expressed by Mariela Shibley above, I'd like to thank my family and firm for putting up with me and the odd hours I had to keep to contribute to this book amidst dramatic changes in US immigration law leading up to, and then resulting from, a national election.

I also thank you, the readers, for incorporating immigration evaluations into your practice. The American Dream lives on in part because people embrace that dream from abroad and make their way here to pursue it. Like in any other time since our nation's founding, huddled masses are yearning to breathe free, and they need your help. Every day, US citizen children come home to find one of their parents has been removed to a distant land, foreign nationals seek protection through asylum, victims of trafficking and sexual assault apply for visas set up by our legislature to protect them, and domestic violence survivors find a way out through immigration procedure. As an immigration lawyer, I know how vital mental health professionals can be to all of them. So, thank you for taking a step toward leaning into this work.

Last but not least, I'd like to thank the tireless, brilliant, and brave Mariela Shibley for bringing me into this collaboration to build the book she wished she had when she flung herself into this field and for now so brightly shining her light as a much-needed teacher and mentor.

~ MGH

Introduction

Although there are a handful of books and book chapters on conducting psychological evaluations for immigration court and United States Citizenship and Immigration Services (USCIS), most are aimed toward forensic evaluators and licensed psychologists. Some focus mostly on conducting assessments for immigration court while others are little more than a regurgitation of the USCIS Policy Manual. My intention with this publication is to write for all mental health providers who are interested in entering or furthering their education in this arena.

Because having a pretty good understanding of the legal concepts driving an evaluation is key, I invited Matthew Holt, Esq., an attorney and certified specialist in immigration and nationality law, to contribute his exhaustive knowledge and experience. The result is a book that provides the reader with a thorough background of each immigration case followed by methodical guidelines for conducting psychological evaluations of those involved in different types of immigration processes.

I open the book by delineating the main differences between immigration evaluations and other types of psychological assessments. Although under the umbrella of forensic practice, immigration evaluations differ in many ways from what a forensic examiner is accustomed to doing. I highlight the significance of the referral question (i.e., the psycholegal issue that the evaluator is being asked to address), I describe how the roles of client, evaluator, and adjudicator differ from what is characteristic of other types of psychological evaluations, and I focus on some ethical issues to consider when delving into this type of work.

In Chapters 2, 3, 4, 5, and 6, Mr. Holt explains the intricacies and complexities inherent in immigration law and provides the readers with useful information to place the evaluations in context. With minimal legal jargon, these chapters describe the various forms of immigration relief available to foreign nationals, who qualifies for the relief, what they need to demonstrate to receive the requested benefits, and how a mental health professional can be helpful— and at times instrumental—for substantiating the applicant's or respondent's petition and for assisting the trier of fact in determining the outcome of a case.

As a psychologist who has conducted over a thousand immigration evaluations and trained and supervised dozens of mental health professionals

DOI: 10.4324/9781003139973-1

doing this type of work, I am able to home in on the essential factors to be explored and what the central focus of the evaluation should be. Fictional vignettes inspired by real cases serve to demonstrate how to gather the required information via an interview and psychological measures and what to include in the written report. Samples of the various types of reports are included in the Appendices.

Chapter 7 is exclusively devoted to report writing, including principles for effective report organization, selection of content that will meet legal demands, and writing styles that promote effective communication. It also provides suggestions for simplifying the report writing process, which is oftentimes what mental health professionals find the most challenging.

Mental health professionals are sometimes requested to testify as expert witnesses in immigration court. Although many clinicians dread the thought of appearing in front of a judge, Mr. Holt and I attempt to alleviate this fear by describing the ins and outs of providing expert testimony in immigration court—which is quite different from federal and state courts. In Chapter 8, we discuss the standards for admissibility, what qualifies someone as an expert, and limitations to experts' opinions. We also describe appropriate courtroom communication, withstanding cross-examination, and avoiding diminished credibility.

When working with foreign nationals, considering the complexity and intersectionality among their cultural identities in relation to one's own is critically important to the assessment process. Everyone has differing worldviews, customs, and belief systems, and being curious and open to learning about others' experiences is key. Chapter 9 discusses cultural competency with particular emphasis on cultural humility and the process of acculturation. It focuses on the intersection between culture and trauma and the importance of employing culturally sensitive assessment measures and procedures. It also explores the function of a native tongue versus a second language when discussing emotionally charged material and provides suggestions for successfully working with professional interpreters.

The most common question I am asked in my presentations on conducting immigration evaluations is how to put these skills into practice, and yet that is the one thing that I have never come across in any other writings on the subject! Chapter 10 goes over all the details for marketing one's services and building stable referral sources, working with immigration attorneys and community-based organizations, setting fees, and developing a streamlined process for carrying out these evaluations—both in person and via telehealth. The chapter closes by highlighting the importance of self-care and furthering one's education in this field.

It is my hope that this book will inspire and encourage fellow mental health professionals to partake in this rewarding area of practice. I have grown both personally and professionally by doing this work, as it has taught me to appreciate privileges I used to take for granted while giving voice to so many who suffer in silence.

1 What Is Unique about Immigration Evaluations?

Mariela G. Shibley, Psy.D.

According to the Pew Research Center (2020), there were 44.8 million foreign-born people living in the United States in 2018. This represents a record 13.7% of the total population, a percentage that has more than quadrupled since the 1960s. The number of immigrants living in the United States is projected to almost double from the 2018 figure by 2065. The Migration Policy Institute estimates that one in seven US residents is a foreign national (FN), many of whom reside in mixed-status households (Capps et al., 2020). A mixed-status household (or a mixed-status family) is one whose members include people with different citizenship or varying immigration statuses—a common case being where the parents are undocumented (i.e., residing in the United States without permission) and the children are US citizens (USCs). The National Immigration Law Center (NILC) reported that the number of mixed-status families is growing (2014). As of 2012, more than a quarter of young children in the United States were children of immigrants, and over 90% of these children were USCs. Pew Research Center (2020) also identifies the US states with the highest immigrant populations as California, Texas, New York, Florida, New Jersey, and Illinois. Mental health professionals (MHPs) working in these states, especially those who speak a second language, often come across a request to conduct an evaluation for someone involved in immigration proceedings, whether as the direct treating provider or as an evaluator.

Conducting psychological evaluations for immigration court or the United States Citizenship and Immigration Services (USCIS), although falling under the umbrella of forensic work, is a relatively new area of practice (Barber-Rioja & Garcia-Mansilla, 2019; Evans & Hass, 2018; Frumkin & Friedland, 1995; Meyers, 2020). Consequently, most MHPs interested in this field have never received specific training in graduate school for these evaluations and struggle to find adequate guidance from a knowledgeable mentor or supervisor. Given the expected increase in FNs seeking to apply for and receive immigration benefits, however, there is more of a need than ever for MHPs qualified and willing to conduct evaluations in immigration cases (often referred to simply as "immigration evaluations"). This book is meant to empower MHPs to take part in this meaningful and transformative work as a compliment to their practice.

DOI: 10.4324/9781003139973-2

Psychological evaluations come in many forms. There are, for instance, psychodiagnostic evaluations used to assess psychiatric symptoms within a clinical context to arrive at a diagnosis, treatment recommendations, and prognosis. Neuropsychological evaluations, to take another example, examine brain functions and how they impact behavior. Forensic evaluations help to determine custody arrangements, competency, criminal responsibility, and other legal issues. All of these evaluations share a common set of basic steps: a review of available records, a clinical interview, the administration of psychometric tests, the gathering of relevant collateral information, and the presentation of findings in a written report.

Immigration evaluations are one type of forensic evaluation and work in much the same way. What differentiates them from other types of psychological evaluations are (1) the referral question to be addressed in the report, (2) which MHPs can conduct the evaluation, (3) who retains the services of the evaluator, (4) who receives the written report, and (5) what the report will be used for. All of these will be considered in the sections that follow. I will also discuss some ethical considerations when doing this type of work.

The Referral Question

The referral question guides the evaluation, and the purpose of the report is to answer that question. In a forensic case, the referral question might be to determine whether the evaluee is competent to stand trial, to assess criminal responsibility, or to explain their unlawful behaviors within the context of their background history. In a personal injury case, the purpose of a psychological evaluation might be to explain the psychological impact of having been the victim of an accident, to provide a diagnosis, and to determine the client's prognosis. In a child custody case, evaluators are tasked with determining parents' suitability for caring for their children. In immigration cases, the referral questions typically depend on the type of immigration process an individual is involved in. The general themes include present or prospective hardship to children, spouses, and parents caused by imposed and prolonged separation from one another; the extent to which a traumatic event or events affected the client; the identification of abuse in a familial relationship; or the presence of mitigating factors.

As with all forensic cases, it is crucial that the report is guided by the psycholegal question because deviating from that might, at best, render the report useless, and at worst, jeopardize the client's case. This is especially important in immigration evaluations for FNs and their family members. For example, cancellation of removal is a common form of relief for FNs without legal status in the United States who are facing a potential removal order—previously known as a deportation order or exclusion order—from an immigration judge (IJ). As explained in much greater detail in Chapter 3, the basic premise is that the FN must show good moral character and continuous physical presence for a 10-year period, a lack of disqualifying criminal history, and that their child(ren), spouse, or parent will suffer—individually or in the aggregate—an "exceptional and extremely unusual" hardship if the FN is ordered removed. For this form of relief, the IJ will only consider hardship to the aforementioned family members who are lawful permanent residents (LPRs) or USCs. Thus, an evaluation of a spouse who is protected under Deferred Action for Childhood Arrivals (DACA)—although she is legally entitled to remain in the United States, has a work permit and social security card, and cannot be removed—would be of little direct value because she is neither an LPR nor a USC. Similarly, an evaluation of an applicant's adult son or daughter, regardless of what findings come from it, would be of no use if the form of relief only considers hardship to the applicant's child, defined as a son or daughter under 21 years of age at the time of the trial. Unfortunately, there are countless examples of a well-written immigration report having little to no value because it does not answer the correct psycholegal question. Therefore, as you strive to help people understand and receive support for their immigration cases, it is critical to frame your report around the correct question. As you immerse yourself deeper in the work, you will build up your understanding of what to look for and ask about as you shape your report.

One cannot assume what the referral question is solely based on the information provided by the person requesting to be evaluated or their family member facilitating the introduction. For example, a person might call requesting a psychological evaluation because their attorney told them it would help their case but when asked what type of immigration process they are involved in, the caller is not sure. You could ask the caller a series of questions to help you determine whether it is for an inadmissibility waiver, a petition under the Violence Against Women Act (VAWA), a U visa, a court case involving cancellation of removal, or something else, but sometimes the information they give you is either insufficient or incorrect—not because they are being deceitful, but because they really do not know.

Confusing a case needing a provisional waiver with a case seeking cancellation of removal is the most common mistake. Although the referral question is basically the same—how a separation from a loved one or a relocation in order to stay together would affect the qualifying relative (more on this below)—the differences lie in who can and should be evaluated, who the audience will be, whether you may be called as an expert witness, and the varying degrees of burden of proof. More on all of this is detailed in the chapters to follow.

The consequences of miscommunication can be even more severe when, say, you believe the evaluation is for cancellation of removal to be provided to an IJ but is actually meant to support a petition to USCIS for relief under the VAWA. Imagine the very real possibility of a woman calling to say she needs an evaluation for her son for her to be able to stay in this country. Operating under the belief that the case centers on cancellation of removal and hardship to the son if his mother, who lacks lawful immigration status, is removed from the country, you schedule the evaluation. Over the course of the evaluation, however, it becomes evident that the son also lacks lawful immigration status, he has been a victim of abuse perpetrated by his step-father (the woman's USC husband), and they are therefore applying for relief under VAWA. Had the focus been on how the mother's removal from the United States would affect the son, the report would have been of only minor relevance to the adjudicator. The moral of the story is this: always clarify the referral question, and, whenever possible, consult with the referring attorney regarding the form of relief and the psycholegal elements to be addressed in the evaluation.

The Evaluator

Generally speaking, when thinking of psychological evaluations one might assume that it is only licensed psychologists who can do them, but most immigration evaluations can be performed by all kinds of MHPs—provided they are adequately trained in conducting such evaluations, of course. Although some states or licensing boards restrict counselors, social workers, and marriage and family therapists from conducting certain types of mental health assessments in certain contexts, almost all individuals who are independently licensed to diagnose and treat mental disorders and who have knowledge, training, and experience of conducting psychological evaluations can perform immigration evaluations.[1] More about this is presented at the end of this chapter.

It is possible that one of your therapy patients becomes involved in immigration proceedings and asks you to write a report to be included with their legal paperwork. Unfortunately, doing so would constitute a dual relationship, which is against the codes of ethics of pretty much every mental health profession. For example, the Specialty Guidelines for Forensic Psychologists specifically state, "Providing forensic and therapeutic psychological services to the same individual or closely related individuals involves multiple relationships that may impair objectivity and/or cause exploitation or other harm …" (American Psychological Association, 2017. Guideline 4.02.01: Therapeutic-Forensic Role Conflicts), as the roles of a treating therapist and a forensic evaluator are "irreconcilable" (Greenberg & Shuman, 1997). Gordon (2016) went as far as suggesting that the testimony of an MHP who is both the evaluator and the treating provider should not be admitted in court. In other words, evaluating a patient whom you also treat with regular therapy sessions compromises the integrity of the evaluation and places you at risk of committing an ethical violation.

One could argue that since the therapist and the patient have already established rapport, the therapist knows the patient's background history and can make thorough clinical observations. This is a common misconception among immigration adjudicators, who by and large lack the training and ethical guidance MHPs receive. In fact, treating therapists performing evaluations of their own patients would obliterate the therapist's neutrality and objectivity, rendering a report biased. USCIS, the branch within the US Department of Homeland Security (USDHS) primarily responsible for the administration of immigration benefits, has repeatedly expressed that an evaluation based on only one or a handful of sessions is of limited evidentiary value. Research, however, has demonstrated that such evaluations are actually associated with favorable outcomes. McLawsen et al. (2011) studied thousands of decisions by the Administrative Appeals Office (AAO), the department within USCIS that reviews adjudications of benefit applications, to determine the degree to which expert testimony (i.e., a psychological evaluation) influences the adjudicator's determination of whether an applicant had met the extreme hardship standard. They concluded that an ongoing relationship between an MHP and the applicant did not necessarily yield more favorable outcomes compared to MHPs who only saw the applicant for a one-time psychological evaluation. This is why it is useful to explain somewhere in the report that even though you are not the treating provider, you have been adequately trained to answer the psycholegal question, and it may even be helpful to explain the appropriateness of you providing a report in lieu of the treating provider. As you will see in the various report samples provided in the Appendices, I always include that clarification at the beginning of the report.

Not being able to evaluate your client does not mean that you cannot be helpful with their immigration case. As a matter of fact, McLawsen et al. (2011) also found that applicants who had received some form of mental health treatment in the past had higher rates of success in their appeals than applicants who never received such treatment. This is consistent with Hake and Banks's (2005) findings which concluded that applicants who had a history of mental health treatment had better success in their hardship waivers. A treating provider may still be immensely helpful for a waiver applicant by writing an affidavit, or letter, of support or otherwise providing proof of ongoing care to demonstrate the existence of treatment or to further bolster the findings in a report or evaluation. This does not in any way constitute a dual relationship, and as long as your client is the one requesting the letter, there is no breach of confidentiality. Many MHPs are wary about writing any letters or documents for their clients, fearing that doing so will increase the likelihood of being dragged into a legal proceeding, but that is highly unlikely in immigration court. If your client is requesting that you write a letter about their treatment to help with their immigration case, it is up to you to provide that type of assistance and whether you charge for it. I always go over the letter with my patient, and if there is anything in it that they would prefer to keep private, I remove it. If the patient requests that I send the letter directly to their attorney, I have the patient sign a release of information. A sample of an affidavit of support is included in the Appendices.

When it comes to immigration evaluations, the number of visits required as part of the psychological evaluation process is debatable. Some clinicians prefer to spread an evaluation over three or four visits. Since extensive testing is sometimes called for, it may not be feasible for the client or evaluator to do everything the same day. Many evaluations, however, can be carried out in just one visit. I have found this to be more convenient for the clients, who often travel far to come in for the evaluation and struggle to fit even a single visit into their busy schedules. A thorough clinical interview can be easily carried out in one day, provided that the client is able to withstand a three-to-four-hour appointment. An exception might be when the examinee has experienced severe trauma and getting into the details of such trauma is emotionally overwhelming. In such cases, it is often necessary to slow the pace of the interview and perhaps split it into separate visits. Note that even though we are performing the role of an evaluator, which precludes us from providing therapy, we are still compassionate human beings who have adequate skills to help those in crisis. There have been many times when I had to intervene and engage the client in anxiety-reducing exercises to help them regulate their overwhelming emotions. As you probably already know, empathy and patience are key in these situations, as is maintaining some degree of flexibility in your evaluation process.

Forensic evaluators are often thought of as cold and pragmatic, as opposed to the warm and sympathetic image of the psychotherapist. When conducting immigration evaluations, it is important to be somewhere in the middle of that. I remember attending a conference for forensic psychologists where one of the lectures was on "Therapeutic Evaluations." As I sat there and listened to the presenter describe how the evaluator should offer tissues if the evaluee starts to cry and to intersperse empathic comments throughout the interview, I was utterly confused. Isn't that what any person would do? Apparently not—so much so, in fact, that a lecture on being human was warranted (and well-attended!). Therapists develop a working relationship with their patients, which has, of course, been found to determine a positive treatment outcome (Flückiger et al., 2018). The goal of treatment is to make the patient feel better, among other things; a psychological evaluation does not include treatment, but neither does it preclude empathy.

The difference between an initial therapy session and a psychological evaluation is nicely outlined by Fontes (2008). Some of the contrasting characteristics can be summarized as follows:

1 There is a clear purpose of the interaction. It is not merely a social exchange.
2 There is an inherent hierarchical organization to the relationship, whereby the evaluator holds more of a sense of authority.
3 In general, the evaluator asks the questions and structures the process of the assessment while the client responds accordingly. This results in a one-direction flow of information.
4 While the client is free to discuss as much or as little about what transpired during the evaluation as they deem comfortable, the evaluator is bound to confidentiality guidelines as determined by their profession.

This is why it is very important to make sure the evaluee is aware of the process and purpose of the evaluation, which can absolutely be carried out in a supportive and welcoming environment with a warm and compassionate demeanor. Many times, clients mention how much better they feel after having talked about very painful memories, which is very rewarding to hear. Having compassion is essential in this type of work, especially when working with individuals who have suffered trauma or are prone to discrimination. As long as you are not blurring the line between providing treatment and conducting an evaluation, go ahead and be your warm, kind self—and make sure to have tissues and water or tea at hand!

The Client

In contrast to a forensic evaluation, where the client is usually the attorney or the court, in an immigration evaluation the client is typically the person being evaluated. An attorney or community-based organization likely facilitated the referral, but the person reaching out and paying for it is the evaluee or close family member. Although some might argue that receiving payment directly from the client somehow diminishes the evaluator's neutrality, the same could be said for an evaluator getting paid by the client's attorney, who is clearly advocating for their client. The client and the attorney both want the evaluation to help their case. Therefore, the only time when one can avoid the assumption that the evaluator is biased is when the evaluation is ordered by a judge or a government attorney, which is rarely the case in immigration court because the burden is always on the FN to prove they are both eligible and deserving of whatever immigration benefit they seek. The important thing is always to maintain objectivity and neutrality, regardless of who is requesting your services or paying your fees. No report, case, or client is worth your integrity and reputation. If a client or an attorney wants you to "find" something to help the case that just is not there, be respectful, but hold your ground. You are not part of the legal team.

Not surprisingly, there are some reasonable but incorrect assumptions that may hold a practitioner back from wading into immigration evaluations. Let us touch on those now.

Assumption # 1: The person seeking the evaluation lives abroad. The person seeking assistance, generally, already lives in the United States.

Assumption # 2: The client being evaluated is the aspiring immigrant. Again, no. While an FN may receive the evaluation in certain cases, such as those involving benefits under VAWA, an asylum seeker or refugee, or victims of crime pursuing a U or T visa, it is not so in many other cases. For instance, when attempting to waive a ground of inadmissibility with USCIS or prove hardship to an IJ, the person who needs the evaluation will usually be a USC or LPR spouse, child, or parent.

Assumption # 3: The evaluation needs to be performed in a foreign language. Again, not necessarily. Many of the clients are USCs who were born and raised in the United States and speak English as their primary or only language, or else they might be LPRs who immigrated and have resided for decades in the United States and who are now more proficient in English than their native language. Additionally, you will have many clients who spoke

English in their country of origin or have made great efforts to learn English through rigorous study. However, if the evaluation needs to be conducted in a foreign language, there is no need to fret. Just as immigration court proceedings, immigration interviews at USCIS, and US State Department visa interviews are conducted through a wide array of interpretive services, you too can utilize these services, and you will quickly discover the use of interpreters can be of great benefit. We delve into this topic in Chapter 9.

The Adjudicator

Just as criminal and civil courts are separate from one another, with their own procedural rules and standards of proof, immigration court is a separate court in and of itself (as is, to cite another common example, bankruptcy court), but under the control of the Executive Branch's US Department of Justice. Unlike other federal courts, the Attorney General can handpick immigration cases and make decisions consistent with the Administration. In recent years, this has resulted in the weaponization of the immigration courts by whichever political party controls the White House. Making the forum even more dependent on the political whims of the day, immigration courts do not use juries (i.e., judges decide matters of both fact and law) and do not follow uniform federal or state rules of evidence or procedure. The policies and procedures change with each administration, within the jurisdiction of each federal district and circuit, and even locally.

Who will be adjudicating the case as a finder of fact is a paramount consideration when preparing a report. Immigration court proceedings are presided over by the black-robe wearing, behind-the-bench sitting, honorable IJ, a US Department of Justice employee formerly known as a "special inquiry officer." IJs have considerably less discretion than administrative law judges in what evidence is admitted or excluded, how the hearings are conducted, or even how they decide the outcome of a case. IJs will review reports by MHPs but rarely take their testimony in open court, so it is vital you prepare your report assuming you will not get the opportunity to explain or clarify anything in it once it is in the judge's hands.

To complicate things further, many immigration proceedings are not even handled in court in front of an IJ but are instead decided by USCIS's domestically stationed immigration officers at service centers or field offices or by US Department of State (USDOS) consular officials stationed abroad at embassies or consulates. In these types of adjudication officers might conduct a short in-person interview with the FN (who may or may not be the evaluee) or no interview at all. Where the adjudicator is an immigration officer solely reviewing paper records without speaking to the applicant or the applicant's attorney, you are never given the opportunity to clarify or explain any of your findings the adjudicator finds questionable or confusing unless they issue a Request for Evidence (RFE) or Notice of Intent to Deny (NOID), which will at least allow for supplementing the administrative record (more on these in Chapter 2).

This unfortunate and all-too-common scenario is precisely why you need to write a thorough—yet concise—report, keeping in mind who the reader will be. Chapter 7 thoroughly discusses report writing, but for now, it is important to understand that if your report is vague, confusing, or insufficient, you will not likely have the opportunity to answer any of the adjudicator's questions. Always be mindful of the reader, and attempt to be one step ahead of questions they might have. For example, if your report to substantiate a waiver application mentions the applicant's brother still living in their country of origin without explaining anything further about him, the adjudicator could interpret that as a community tie to their country of origin, thus mitigating the negative impact of a forced return to that country. On the other hand, if you explain briefly that the brother is an alcoholic who severed ties with the family years ago, then you will have clarified the situation to the adjudicator and avoided their placing undue mitigating value on the brother's presence when assessing the hardship.

Attorneys advocate for their clients, but MHPs, as independent evaluators, must stay focused on answering the psycholegal question at hand and to prioritize one's integrity over making an attorney happy. Even if your interest in doing this type of work stems from your personal values or life experiences, that should not get in the way of your ability to form an objective opinion. For example, stating on a report, "It would be unconscionable to separate this lovely young couple," or, "Deporting this honorable and devoted family man would be a huge mistake," will almost certainly diminish—if not altogether eradicate—the value and credibility of your report. Along these same lines, determining that the evaluee will "undoubtedly experience extreme hardship" if separated from their spouse is entering legal territory and, more specifically, making a legal conclusion you must always avoid. As we will discuss in the next chapter, *extreme hardship*, although common language, is also a legal concept in immigration law, and asserting such a legal conclusion is beyond the scope of your role as an expert witness. Whether an individual's hardship rises to the level of *extreme* is for the adjudicator to determine—not the evaluator. Your job is to present and describe the hardships and offer your opinion as to their psychological impact on the evaluee. The adjudicator will consider that along with many other pieces of evidence when making their final determination.

Ethical Considerations

Even though most clinicians receive some type of assessment training in graduate school, it likely did not cover the nuances inherent in immigration evaluations. Immigration law is one of the most complex patchwork of laws, policies, and procedures in the country, in large part because it is constantly changing and evolving. Naturally, MHPs are not expected to know everything about immigration law, but it is our ethical obligation to have a reasonable understanding of the rules, standards, and guidelines of the legal proceedings that guide the evaluation (American Psychological Association, 2013, 2017, 2020; Heilbrun et al., 2009).

There is, of course, great diversity among MHPs' education, training, and areas of practice, but most are able to perform psychological evaluations, provided that they are competent to do so. The American Psychological Association (2020) published the Guidelines for Psychological Assessment and Evaluation, which clearly state that "Psychologists who conduct psychological testing, assessment, and evaluation seek appropriate training and supervised experience in relevant aspects of testing, assessment, and psychological evaluation." In addition to training, they highlight the importance of skill development and collaboration with experts in the area of practice. According to the American Mental Health Counselors Association (AMHCA) Code of Ethics (2020), clinical mental health counselors are "expected to possess appropriate knowledge and competence" when conducting mental health assessments and to "objectively offer their findings without bias or investment in the ultimate outcome." Similarly, the National Association of Social Workers' Code of Ethics (2008) states that social workers who provide services in substantive areas that are new to them should engage in appropriate study, training, consultation, and supervision from people who are competent in those areas. It is clear that in order to undertake a psychological evaluation, any MHP must be qualified to do so, or else risk an ethical violation. Perhaps more importantly, though, practicing outside your scope of knowledge and experience also does a great disservice to those who seek your help.

As MHPs, we are indoctrinated to maintain confidentiality when working with our clients or patients, and the same holds true for immigration evaluations. Unless you are giving the report directly to the client, the client has to sign a release of information for you to submit the report to their attorney. It is extremely important, however, that the client understand the limits of confidentiality inherent in this type of work. When we conduct an interview, we ask some very personal questions that the client may not want their attorney or anyone else to know about. It is not unheard of for a client to disclose having been the victim of incest, for example. This is something extremely delicate and possibly not very relevant to the psycholegal question presented. Because maintaining confidentiality and respecting our clients' privacy is crucial, a good rule of thumb is to include only information that is absolutely relevant and necessary to answer the referral question—no more, no less. As per the Specialty Guidelines for Forensic Psychology (APA, 2013), MHPs are not to disclose information that is "irrelevant or does not provide a substantial basis of support for their opinions, except when required by law." There are many ways to convey information without delving into unnecessary details, and it can be as simple as stating something like, "When asked about childhood trauma, Mrs. Sanchez shared that she has had some very painful experiences that she would rather keep private."

Similarly, evaluators will need to mind the inclusion of probative, yet prejudicial, findings in reports because mentioning certain information could jeopardize a client's case. For example, if when conducting an interview for a U visa the client shares that, following the trauma he experienced, he started smoking marijuana to help him relax and get to sleep, you will probably want to avoid mentioning the fact that he was using what is a federally illicit substance. Instead, writing only that he struggled with insomnia might convey the information just as well without implicating him in criminal activity. As Otto et al. (2014) pointed out,

> When struggling to decide whether to include a particular piece of information, the [evaluator] should consider both the probative value of the information and the risk that the information is unfairly prejudicial. If the information is key to understanding the opinion, then it should be included, but if it is unfairly prejudicial regarding the person being examined, then it should be omitted unless it is absolutely key to the opinion.
>
> (p. 25)

Lastly, one situation that evaluators are often faced with is an attorney requesting a modification to the report. Sometimes these requests entail merely grammatical errors, erroneous dates, or incorrect spelling of names, which is perfectly acceptable. Other times, they might ask you to expand on an issue, such as how you arrived at the conclusion that the client was not being deceitful or to describe the criteria for a diagnosis. This is also appropriate. On the other hand, when the request involves omitting information that was relevant to your arriving at your conclusions, or to add factual information that the client did not share during the interview, even if it was in a provided affidavit or police report, the attorney is clearly crossing the line. An attorney has their client's best interest in mind and will naturally attempt to present information that substantiates their arguments, but as stated above, evaluators must preserve impartiality and—most importantly—honesty. It is tempting, especially as someone is building a steady source of referrals, to acquiesce to the referring attorney's requests. My advice is to resist that temptation. Would you rather build a reputation for a long-term professional practice as a "hired gun," or as a professional whose integrity is bulletproof?

Note

1 There are certain types of immigration evaluations, however, that can only be performed by licensed psychologists, such as competency to represent oneself in immigration court, violence or sexual offense risk, potential recidivism, and medical certifications for disability exceptions. This book focuses only on those that can be performed by any MHP. For guidance on conducting some of the aforementioned evaluations, refer to Evans and Hass (2018) and Meyers (2020).

Bibliography

American Mental Health Counselors Association. (2020). *AMHCA code of ethics.* Retrieved from www.amhca.org/viewdocument/2020-amhca-code-of-ethics.

American Psychological Association. (2013). Specialty guidelines for forensic psychology. *American Psychologist, 68* (1), 7–19.

American Psychological Association. (2017). *Ethical principles of psychologists and code of conduct* (2002, Amended June 1, 2010 and January 1, 2017). Retrieved from www.apa.org/ethics/code/index.aspx.

American Psychological Association, APA Task Force on Psychological Assessment and Evaluation Guidelines. (2020). *APA guidelines for psychological assessment and evaluation.* Retrieved from www.apa.org/about/policy/guidelines-psychological-assessment-evaluation.pdf.

Barber-Rioja, V., & Garcia-Mansilla, A. (2019). Special considerations when conducting forensic psychological evaluations for immigration court. *Journal of Clinical Psychology, 75*(11), 2049–2059. https://doi.org/10.1002/jclp.22863

Capps, R., Gelatt, J., Ruiz Soto, A. G., & Van Hook, J. (2020). *Unauthorized immigrants in the United States: Stable numbers, changing origins.* Migration Policy Institute.

Evans, F. B., & Hass, G. A. (2018). *Forensic psychological assessment in immigration court: A guidebook for evidence-based and ethical practice.* Routledge.

Flückiger, C., del Re, A. C., Wampold, B. E., & Horvath, A. O. (2018). The alliance in adult psychotherapy: A meta-analytic synthesis. *Psychotherapy, 55*(4), 316–340. https://doi.org/10.1037/pst0000172

Fontes, L. A. (2008). *Interviewing clients across cultures: A practitioner's guide.* The Guilford Press.

Frumkin, I. B., & Friedland, J. (1995). Forensic evaluations in immigration cases: Evolving issues. *Behavioral Sciences & the Law, 13*(4), 477–489. https://doi.org/10.1002/bsl.2370130404

Gordon, S. (2016). Crossing the line: Daubert, dual roles, and the admissibility of forensic mental health testimony. *Cardoso Law Review, 37* (4), 1345–1399.

Greenberg, S. A., & Shuman, D. W. (1997). Irreconcilable conflict between therapeutic and forensic roles. *Professional Psychology: Research and Practice, 28*(1), 50–57. https://doi.org/10.1037/0735-7028.28.1.50

Hake, B. A., & Banks, D. L. (2005). The hake hardship scale: A quantitative system for assessment of hardship in immigration cases based on a statistical analysis of AAO decisions. *Bender's Immigration Bulletin, 10,* 403–420.

Heilbrun, K., Grisso, T., & Goldstein, A. M. (2009). *Foundations of forensic mental health assessment.* Oxford University Press.

McLawsen, G., McLawsen, J., & Ruser, K. (2011). Demonstrating psychological hardship: A statistical study of psychological evaluations in hardship waivers of inadmissibility. *Bender's Immigration Bulletin, 16*(10).

Meyers, R. (2020). *Conducting psychological assessments for U.S.* immigration cases. Springer.

National Immigration Law Center (2014). *The affordable care act and mixed status families.* Retrieved from www.nilc.org/wp-content/uploads/2015/11/FAQ-ACA-and-mixed-status-families-2014-12-1.pdf.

Otto, R. K., DeMier, R. L., & Boccaccini, M. T. (2014). *Forensic reports and testimony.* Wiley & Sons.

Pew Research Center. (2020, August 20). *Facts on U.S. immigrants, 2018.* Retrieved from www.pewresearch.org/hispanic/2020/08/20/facts-on-u-s-immigrants/.

Workers, N. A. (2008). *NASW code of ethics (Guide to the everyday professional conduct of social workers).* NASW.

2 Assessing Hardship for Waivers of Inadmissibility

Mariela G. Shibley, Psy.D. and Matthew G. Holt, Esq.

Inadmissibility refers to someone being prohibited from entering the United States, just as *removability* refers to someone being prohibited from remaining in the United States. A person who is ineligible to receive either a nonimmigrant visa or lawful permanent residence based on prior immigration violations or criminal grounds, regardless of whether they have otherwise qualified for the benefit, is considered inadmissible. However, immigration waivers allow a noncitizen, or foreign national (FN), to have certain grounds of inadmissibility set aside in order to be admitted to the United States or obtain certain immigration benefits, removing obstacles on their path toward lawfully living in the United States.

Sections § 212 and § 237 of the Immigration and Nationality Act (INA) list the various reasons as to why an FN may be blocked from attaining a specific immigration benefit and the applicable exceptions or waivers. For example, an FN may need a waiver for unlawful presence (ULP), bringing their children into the United States without permission, lying on an immigration form or at a visa interview to get immigration benefits, and for certain theft crimes. Very often, a psychological evaluation, sometimes of the FN and other times of their family member, is instrumental in obtaining a waiver of inadmissibility arising from these offenses.

While there are a number of different waivers in immigration law, this book will include only those most commonly supported by a psychological evaluation and report. Below is a brief overview of those waivers, vignettes to show when and why a waiver would further an FN's immigration goals, how to ascertain the psycholegal question necessitating an evaluation, and how to prepare and present the evaluation's report. Note that although a moderate legal understanding is essential for any mental health professional (MHP) conducting immigration evaluations, a detailed exploration of immigration law is beyond the scope of this book and would likely only confuse you at this early stage—and possibly deter you from going any further. Just know that you will continue gaining greater expertise and insight as you do more of this work and that an attorney will always be your greatest resource for answers to your legal questions.

DOI: 10.4324/9781003139973-3

Waivers for Unlawful Presence

ULP and the waivers required to overcome it are among the most common reasons clients are referred to MHPs for an evaluation. When an FN has entered the United States without permission or a noncitizen who entered the country lawfully has remained in the United States beyond their authorized stay, they accrue ULP. Generally, less than six months of ULP triggers no punishment. However, as explained in INA § 212(a)(9) (B), ULP between 6 and 12 consecutive months levies a 3-year bar on returning to the United States, and ULP exceeding 12 consecutive months carries a 10-year inadmissibility punishment.[1] Multiple stints of ULP, as described in INA § 212(a)(9)(C), can cause long-term or even permanent inadmissibility. For example, if the FN accrues more than one year in the aggregate or is ordered removed and reenters (or attempts to reenter) the United States without authorization, the FN is permanently inadmissible, a law often referred to as the "permanent bar." The common term is a misnomer, though, because, as discussed below, the FN may become eligible to apply for a waiver of the permanent bar after having remained abroad continuously for ten years.

For cases involving a single stint of ULP after April 1997, when the law changed and began more harshly punishing ULP, there is a waiver listed in INA § 212(a)(9)(B)(v) for a qualifying FN who can show the FN's US citizen (USC) or lawful permanent resident (LPR), spouse or parent will suffer "extreme hardship" if the waiver is not approved. The waiver provides an exception so the FN will not be forced to endure the 3-year or 10-year bar to admissibility but can instead return to or remain living in the United States. This waiver utilizes one of two forms to be submitted by the FN:

- *Form I-601* is used to waive ULP, as well as other inadmissibility grounds, for FNs within the United States or abroad.
- *Form I-601A*, commonly known as the "provisional waiver," is used only to waive ULP and only for FNs currently in the United States. If the applicant is outside the country, or if they have other grounds of inadmissibility to cure apart from ULP, they must use *Form I-601*.

In either case, to waive ULP, the noncitizen must show *extreme hardship* to a USC or LPR spouse or parent. Let's consider an example of a client applying for a waiver of ULP:

Marco, a student from Brazil, came to California to study. In his final year of college, he began dating Amy, a USC. He decided to stay after graduation for nine more months because he was in love. He and Amy married, and four months later he found out his mom was sick, so he returned to Brazil. After his mom recovered, Marco wanted to come back to the United States to be with Amy. At his consular interview, the US government informed him he was inadmissible for ten years, which could potentially be waived by filing *Form I-601*. Amy's attorney referred Amy for an immigration evaluation to support Marco's waiver application.

Note that, if Marco had not left the United States, he could have used *Form I-601A* because he accrued ULP but had no other grounds that would make him inadmissible.

Waivers for Curing Certain Criminal Activity

FNs who are convicted of certain crimes face harsh immigration consequences. Fortunately, there is a waiver found in INA § 212(h) linked to various criminal offenses, including misdemeanors and felonies involving moral turpitude, a single offense for 30 grams or less of marijuana possession, prostitution, gambling, and some other criminal activities. Generally, an FN seeking such a waiver for crime must file *Form I-601* and show the existence of several positive factors. A meritorious waiver must show the FN falls within **one of the following four categories**:

1   The FN has a USC or LPR parent, spouse, son, or daughter who would suffer *extreme hardship* if the FN is removed.
2   The inadmissible incident(s) occurred at least 15 years ago, the FN is rehabilitated, and their admission is not contrary to national interests.
3   They are inadmissible only under the prostitution ground, they are rehabilitated, and their admission is not contrary to national interests.
4   They are a VAWA self-petitioner, and the waiver should be granted as a matter of discretion.

Lesley's case illustrates a typical situation of someone who would need this type of waiver, commonly referred to as a 212(h) waiver:

> Lesley came to the United States from Mexico as a tourist with her parents when she was 7 years old, and they never left. Lesley had a hard time fitting in during her teenage years and fell in with the wrong crowd. Between ages 17 and 19, she was caught five times for shoplifting, including three times after turning 18 years old. She married Sally, a USC, when she was 28 years old. Sally filed a visa petition for Lesley, and USCIS is now requesting a waiver for Lesley's criminal history.

In these cases, the FN is typically referred to an MHP to establish the FN's rehabilitation and remorse. In some situations, however, the MHP is asked to evaluate a family member as a means of showing why the FN should be able to stay with that family member. See Chapter 3 for more on remorse and rehabilitation.

Waivers for Fraud or Misrepresentation

Pursuant to INA § 212(a)(6)(A)(i), misstatements, lies, and omissions of material facts made to obtain immigration benefits may prevent an FN from becoming an LPR. Certain incidents of fraud and willful misrepresentation (except for false claims to US citizenship made on or after September 30, 1996) can be waived by INA § 212(i). Both offenses have specific elements. To find the FN inadmissible for willful misrepresentation, USCIS officers must find that the person made a knowingly false and material representation to a US government official while seeking to procure immigration benefits. The defined elements for fraud are much the same, except that they also include the FN making the misrepresentation with the intent of deceiving the official and the official acting upon the misrepresentation to grant benefits.[2]

Fraud and willful misrepresentation in the immigration context are probably more common than you would imagine. Particularly when FNs come from countries with lower standards of living, there is an assumption that many of them intend never to return to their own countries once they have entered the United States.[3] For this reason, they are required to apply for a visa, the approval of which depends on their proving substantial ties to their country (i.e., compelling reasons to return) and a lack of prior immigration violations. Getting a visa to visit the United States, whether to visit family, bring a child to Disneyland, or explore professional opportunities, is a big deal for many people, and so many FNs are willing to lie about having a family or a stable job to return to, or to omit important facts about violating the terms of their prior visa by overstaying or working unlawfully in the United States.

In border towns such as San Diego, many FNs with tourist visas live and work in the United States but frequently cross the border into Mexico to visit family or make purchases. At the border point of entry, they might tell the Border Patrol Officer that they are coming to shop or attend a birthday party, but they are in reality returning to their homes, jobs, and families in the United States. That is considered fraud. Still another common example of fraud is failing to disclose family relationships such as a USC spouse living in the United States.

The FN pursuing a waiver for fraud or misrepresentation is required to file *Form I-601* (regardless of whether they are in the United States or abroad) and carries the burden of proving denial of the waiver would result in *extreme hardship* to the USC or LPR parent or spouse. Let's look at Felipe as an example:

> Felipe always wanted to come to the United States from his native Cameroon. He started applying for tourist visas when he was 18 years old. The US government denied his visa application four times based on his lack of strong ties to Cameroon and, thus, the likelihood of his not departing the United States. For his fifth interview, he brought a fake wedding certificate, fake proof of ongoing college coursework, and fake

proof of recent home ownership. The immigration officer did not know the documents were fake and, finding that Felipe had sufficiently strong ties to his home country, approved his visa. Felipe entered the United States using the visa and three years later met Samantha, a USC. They eventually married, and she is now petitioning for Felipe's US residency. When Samantha applied for Felipe's adjustment of status, Felipe did not include information about any prior marriages. The US government requested an explanation from Felipe at the USCIS interview regarding the marriage certificate he had presented years earlier. He explained what he had done, and USCIS now requires a waiver for Felipe's prior misrepresentation.

While waivers for Marco and Lesley are to cure ULP and the commission of certain crimes, respectively, the waiver for Felipe is for fraud. However, all three will need to prove *extreme hardship* to a qualifying family member for their waivers to be approved.

What Is Extreme Hardship?

Extreme hardship, a common requirement in waiver practice, is one of two distinct legal standards relating to hardship, the other being *exceptional and unusual hardship*, which is discussed in Chapter 3. While both are considered for various forms of relief in immigration court, waivers only ever require the lower burden of *extreme hardship*. There is no statutory definition of extreme hardship; instead, the adjudicator will balance certain factors to determine the existence of extreme hardship to the FN's USC or LPR family member(s), commonly referred to as *qualifying relatives* (QRs). Finding extreme hardship is dependent on the facts and circumstances of each case. Generally, it requires an FN to show hardship beyond that which is commonly experienced when admission is denied.

According to USCIS, the US government recognizes that the following factors commonly occur but that their mere existence does not equate to the necessary hardship to the QRs:

- Family separation.
- Economic detriment.
- Difficulties of readjusting to life in the new country.
- The quality and availability of educational opportunities abroad.
- Inferior quality of medical services and facilities.
- Ability to pursue a chosen employment abroad.

While suffering the above factors would uproot and potentially devastate the FN's QRs, US immigration law requires more to merit a waiver's approval. Accordingly, the onus is on the FN to prove that the hardship is beyond these common consequences of inadmissibility. Fortunately, the hardship is considered cumulatively, including hardship to multiple relatives, and in totality, encompassing all factors. According to the USCIS Policy Manual (2021), the factors to be considered in assessing whether the hardship is extreme or common are the following: family ties and impact, social and cultural impact, economic impact, health conditions and care, and country conditions. Each of these is presented in Table 2.1 adapted from the USCIS Policy Manual (Vol. 9, Part B, Ch. 5, Sec. D), with some commentary and modifications for clarity and brevity.

Table 2.1 Factors and Considerations for Extreme Hardship

Factors	Considerations
Family ties	• Ties to family members living in the United States, including age, status, and length of residence of any children • Responsibility for the care of any family members in the United States • Ties, including family ties, to the country of relocation • Nature of relationship with the FN, including facts about the relationship that would either aggravate or lessen the hardship • Age of the QR • Length of residence in the United States • Length of prior residence in the country of relocation • Prior or current military service • Impact on the cognitive, social, or emotional well-being of a QR who is left to replace the noncitizen as caregiver for someone else, or impact on the QR (e.g., child or parent) for whom such care is required *[This factor is particularly important because while children, grandparents, and other extended family are not considered QRs, special factors relating to those family members as they relate to the QR may be considered if properly raised to the adjudicator.]*
Social and cultural impact	• The QR's loss of access to the US courts and the criminal justice system, including the loss of opportunity to participate in criminal investigations or prosecutions; proceedings to enforce labor, employment, or civil rights laws; family law proceedings, victim's compensation proceedings, or other civil proceedings; or the pursuit of court orders regarding protection, child support, maintenance, child custody, or visitation • Fear of persecution or societal discrimination to the FN or QR in the FN's country of birth • Prior grant of nonimmigrant status to the QR as the result of being victim to certain crimes • Existence of laws and social practices in the country of relocation that would punish the QR because he or she has been in the United States or is perceived to have Western values • The QR's access or lack of access to social institutions and structures (official and unofficial) for support, guidance, or protection. *[e.g., The QR has significant mental illness and will not have access to proper healthcare in the FN's country of birth; the QR is a US military veteran receiving care through the US Veterans' Affairs and will not be able to access that care abroad; or the QR's child receives state-provided support for a learning disability but would not get such support in the FN's country of birth.]*

Table 2.1 Cont

Factors	Considerations
	• Social ostracism or stigma against the QR based on characteristics such as gender, gender identity, sexual orientation, religion, race, national origin, ethnicity, citizenship, age, political opinion, marital status, or disability • The QR's community ties in the United States and in the country of relocation • Extent to which the QR has integrated into US culture, including language, skills, and acculturation • Extent to which the QR would have difficulty integrating into the country of relocation, including understanding and adopting social norms and established customs, including gender roles and ethical or moral codes • Difficulty and expense of travel/communication to maintain ties between QR and applicant if the QR does not relocate abroad with the FN • The QR's present inability to communicate in the language of the country of relocation, as well as the time and difficulty that learning that language would entail • Availability and quality of educational opportunities for the QR (and their children, if any) in the country of relocation • Availability and quality of job training, including technical or vocational opportunities, for the QR (and children, if any) in the country of relocation
Economic impact	• Economic impact of applicant's departure on the QR, including the applicant's or QR's ability to obtain employment in the country of relocation • Whether relocation would cause an economic impact resulting from the sale of a home, business, or other asset • How relocation may cause an economic impact resulting from the termination of a professional practice • Decline in the standard of living, including due to significant unemployment, underemployment, or other lack of economic opportunity in the country of relocation. • Ability to recoup losses or repay student loan debt • Cost of extraordinary needs, such as special education or training for children • Cost of care for family members, including children and elderly, sick, or disabled parents
Health conditions	• Health conditions and the availability and quality of any required medical treatment in the country to which the applicant would be returned, including length and cost of treatment • Psychological impact on the QR due to either separation from the applicant or departure from the United States, including separation from other family members living in the United States • Psychological impact on the QR due to the suffering of the applicant • Prior trauma suffered by the QR that may aggravate the psychological impact of separation or relocation, including trauma evidenced by prior grants of asylum, refugee status, or other forms of humanitarian protection

(continued)

Table 2.1 Cont.

Factors	Considerations
Conditions in the country of relocation	• Civil unrest or generalized levels of violence, current US military operations in the country, active US economic sanctions against the country, ability of country to address significant crime, environmental catastrophes like flooding or earthquakes, and other socioeconomic or political conditions that jeopardize safe repatriation or lead to reasonable fear of physical harm • Formal recognition by the US government of safety issues in the country of relocation, such as a Temporary Protected Status (TPS) designation, Danger Pay for US government workers stationed there, withdrawal of Peace Corps for security reasons, or US Department of State Travel Warnings or Alerts

Ideally, all attorneys would go through the above factors with their clients and their families and then craft detailed declarations discussing the applicable hardship, which are then made available for the MHP to review prior to the evaluation. Unfortunately, you will find that many attorneys instead rely on the MHP's report to draft such declarations afterward.

Waivers Based on Humanitarian Purposes, to Assure Family Unity, or Public Interest

There are several grounds of inadmissibility that require a waiver but do not require a showing of *extreme hardship* to a QR. Instead, the applicant must show that their being allowed to enter or remain in the United States is vital for humanitarian purposes, to assure family unity, or that it is otherwise in the public interest (many attorneys will bootstrap the hardship argument anyway, to bolster the waiver application). These waivers also require the filing of *Form I-601*, the same waiver application used to waive ULP, fraud and misrepresentation, and certain nonserious crimes based on extreme hardship to a QR.

Alien Smuggling

Whether convicted or not, alien smuggling makes an FN inadmissible under INA section 212(a)(6)(E)(i) and removable under INA section 237(a)(1)(E)(i). A finding of alien smuggling requires showing that the FN knew they were engaging in the smuggling and that they took affirmative steps such as following prearranged plans or sending money to the smugglee or smuggler. In some cases, an applicant is referred to an MHP to help demonstrate that the applicant was not aware they were engaging in this type of unlawful conduct due to mental illness. Most often, however, an MHP will be tasked with assisting an FN to prove their relative's extreme hardship, their rehabilitation or remorse, or one of the three factors mentioned above.

There are two basic requirements for this discretionary waiver: the person applying for the waiver must be (1) either an LPR who temporarily traveled abroad voluntarily and is otherwise admissible or is a person applying for a green card based on a family-based petition, and (2) the person must have smuggled only their spouse, parent, son, or daughter (and no other individual). For example, a father who brought his child into the United States without status 15 years ago and now seeks to adjust status would need a waiver for alien smuggling, as would a mother who left her children in the care of her own parents, came to the United States seeking better work, and eventually paid a smuggler to bring her children to join her in the United States. In recent years, the plight of the so-called Dreamers, the youngsters and young adults who were brought to the United States, has made international news. It has also highlighted the large number of parents who played a role in bringing those Dreamers here. Those parents almost assuredly will need waivers for alien smuggling if they are to adjust their status.

Refugees and Asylees

An FN-afforded refugee or asylee status in the United States is still subject to inadmissibility grounds when they apply for permanent residence. Through the filing of a uniquely broad and substantial waiver under INA § 209(c), such applicants might be able to cure their inadmissibility by showing that they should remain in the United States for humanitarian purposes, to assure family unity, or because it is otherwise in the public interest. This might be, for example, an FN who immigrated to the United States as a refugee and later engaged in unlawful conduct, was arrested by Homeland Security, was in turn referred to Immigration Court, and is now at risk of losing his refugee status.

Waivers Based on Positive Factors

FNs who were convicted of serious crimes or who are subject to a permanent bar can apply for certain waivers by demonstrating that the positive factors for being allowed to remain lawfully in the United States outweigh the reasons for their deportation.

Serious Crimes

One of the broadest waivers in immigration law, found in INA § 212(c), is now also one of the most narrowly applied because while it can waive anything in INA § 212(a) except security-related grounds, international child abduction, and certain aggravated felonies, it only applies to convictions that occurred before April 1, 1997. This waiver is commonly employed by a long-time permanent resident facing removal after either returning from a trip abroad, attempting to renew an expired permanent resident card, or after unsuccessfully applying for US citizenship. An example of this type of case is an FN who became an LPR in 1990 and was convicted of a crime in 1995. Even though he served his time in custody, completed parole, and has not reoffended, DHS can still place him in removal proceedings due to that old crime.[4]

For this type of waiver, USCIS balances the positive and negative factors in the case. An MHP may be asked to evaluate the FN for hardship to him or her, or to prove remorse and/or rehabilitation. Alternatively, an MHP may be sought out to evaluate and report on a family member as a way of proving why the FN applicant should be allowed to remain with that specific relative in the United States.

Permanent Bars and Prior Deportations

As mentioned early in this chapter, FNs who accrued at least one year of ULP and were ordered removed are subject to the permanent bar but can apply for a waiver to return to the United States after ten years. This waiver is actually a request for the US government to consent to an FN's opportunity to reapply for admission. The consent request is made by filing *Form I-212* with supporting evidence. According to USCIS, the government considers the following factors:

- Why the FN was deported.
- How recently the FN was deported.
- How long the FN lived in the United States.
- The FN's moral character.
- Whether the FN has shown respect for the law.
- The FN's family responsibilities.
- Whether the FN is inadmissible for other reasons.
- Hardship to the FN and to others (this waiver considers the FN, not just QRs).
- Whether the United States would benefit from the FN's return.

Note that hardship is again a delineated factor for consideration, but here the hardship could be to the FN (applicant), immediate family members, extended family members supported by the FN, and others of similar standing, even if not familial (e.g., if the FN is the legal guardian to nieces or nephews or to a disabled sibling). This is a good reminder that the MHP could be asked to evaluate a variety of people connected to an immigration process. Ultimately, however, it is for the referring attorney to determine which family member would be most instrumental in demonstrating the required hardship. It would be ideal for the referring attorney to provide the

MHP with context via a short summary of the positive and negative factors before the evaluation, and although that sometimes happens, be prepared to go ahead without it.

Requests for More Evidence and Notice of Intent to Deny

The assistance of an MHP is often requested when USCIS, the prosecutor, or the immigration judge does not consider the submitted evidence in support of a waiver to be sufficient to merit the waiver. Typically, USCIS will issue a Request for Evidence (RFE) or Notice of Intent to Deny (NOID) prior to denying a waiver. USCIS provides 87 days to respond to RFEs and 33 days to respond to NOIDs. The reasons for the RFE or NOID, ultimately determined for you by the referring attorney, could be related to many things, from the financial or educational aspects of the purported hardship to the QR's physical or mental health. In the case of the latter, for example, an MHP's evaluation would provide a vital expert finding of whether the QR's mental health will decompensate if the waiver is denied. Unlike the initial waiver application filing, which can be made any time after it becomes available, the clock is ticking for RFE or NOID responses, so the MHP and others involved in the response need to be mindful of the deadline.

How Do Reports and Evaluations Factor into a Waiver Analysis? Why Is the Evaluator's Role Essential?

Each of the waivers of inadmissibility discussed in this chapter requires one of the following:

- That a denial would result in extreme hardship to a QR.
- That an approval is warranted for humanitarian purposes, to assure family unity, or for some public interest.
- That the applicant, based on a weighing of the equities, is eligible and deserving of the waiver.

In many cases, a report by an MHP is instrumental in getting these waivers approved. Although the client coming in for the evaluation could be either the FN or one of their family members, the majority of those referred to my practice seek an evaluation to substantiate hardship to a QR. We will therefore focus on that type of evaluation. Evaluating rehabilitation and hardship to the FN applicant will be discussed in the following chapter.

The Evaluation

As mentioned in Chapter 1, the referral question is what guides the interview and what the report aims to answer. In cases where the applicant needs to demonstrate extreme hardship to their QR, the referral question can be broken down into two prongs:

- How would (or does) a **separation** or a **relocation** to the foreign national's country of citizenship affect the **QR**?
- Would (or are) the hardships experienced by the QR **beyond what is typically expected** following the separation from a loved one?

Notice that the first prong applies to two distinct scenarios: one where the QR would be separated from the FN, and another where the QR would leave the United States with the FN to establish residence in the FN's country of citizenship (or any other country). Even if the FN is not in the United States, the report still must address both, discussing the hardships the QR is experiencing as a result of a separation, how a prolonged separation would affect them, and either why they have deemed a relocation unviable or the hardships a relocation would create. Sometimes one of the scenarios is not an option, such as when the QR is an LPR who will lose their status if they reside outside of the United States. Nonetheless, the report must demonstrate that both scenarios were considered.

In cases where the QR already relocated to maintain physical closeness with the FN, you will evaluate the hardships they are experiencing because of the relocation, as well as why they chose that over a prolonged separation. However, if the applicant is still in the United States, you would instead be assessing how a prolonged separation from or a relocation with the applicant would affect the QR if the applicant were forced to leave. This can be a little bit trickier because the hardships might not be occurring currently but are likely to occur in the future. To further complicate things, sometimes the person being evaluated has not given much thought to the matter, either out of denial (i.e., not wanting to accept the agonizing reality of their situation) or because they have a stoic mentality and a profound need to convince themselves that "everything's going to be okay." Therefore, the MHP's job is to explore all the factors relevant to the psycholegal question and prompt the client to speculate on the hardships they might endure. The evaluator must then attempt to predict, based on the client's personality characteristics, the quality of their relationship with the FN, their past traumas and relevant background history, and how they would be affected.

One way to approach this is to use a cracked egg as an analogy. Imagine someone is going to throw an egg to you and you have to catch it. Presuming you are a good catcher, the egg will land in your hands, and as long as you don't squeeze it too hard, it will remain intact. But what if the egg has a crack? No matter how gently you catch it, the egg will most likely break because it is not strong enough to sustain the impact of landing in your hand. The task of the MHP is to assess the client's cracks—the vulnerabilities that will make him or her more susceptible to a psychological decompensation. This goes to the heart of that second prong, showing that the hardship is beyond what is typically expected following the separation from a loved one. Immigration officials are aware that any unwanted separation from a loved one results in hardship, but they will only waive the inadmissibility determination if, based on all the evidence submitted, the hardship rises to the level of *extreme*.

Setting the Frame

The interview should start by making sure you and the client are on the same page in terms of what you will be doing and the purpose for the evaluation. Clients often only contact you because their attorney told them to, and all they know is that "this will help with my immigration case." First, the client must be aware that this is an evaluation—not therapy—and that you will be asking some personal questions and probably delving into some uncomfortable topics. Next, clarifying the limits of confidentiality is crucial. Even though they are probably aware that the evaluation will yield a report, they need to know that anything they share with you could go on that report, which will be made available—per their request[5]—to their attorney and anyone their attorney chooses to share it with. Should they request that something not be included in the report, respect their privacy but discuss alternative ways to handle it. Finally, the client should be comfortable. It is not uncommon for clients to feel apprehensive and nervous when they come in, not knowing what to expect from what is often their first encounter with a mental health professional. Many a client has asserted right up front, "I'm not crazy, doctor!" Some people have particularly strong biases, often cultural, regarding mental illness and what it even means to set foot in your office; therefore, it is helpful to assure the client they are in a safe place.

Gathering Background Information

To better understand the person sitting across from you and form an adequate impression of their hardships, you must have a clear picture of their context, and therefore starting the evaluation interview with a thorough background history is essential. Much of what follows overlaps with other types of immigration evaluations that are covered in subsequent chapters. Focusing for now on the question of hardship, here are some key background areas to explore.

Family and Upbringing

You can start by asking them where they were born, where they grew up, and who raised them. Did they grow up in an intact family, or were the parents separated? Did a grandparent raise them? If one or both parents worked in the United States while the children resided in their native country, which is not uncommon for Central Americans, what was that experience like for them? Overall, how would they describe their childhood? These questions give you a good picture of not only the dynamics of their family of origin but also what family means to them, which will be relevant later to how a separation from their current family members would affect them. You would also want to know where their parents or siblings currently reside, how often they see each other, and the present quality of their relationships. Are they still a close-knit family? Do they rely on one another for support? How is their parents' health? Do they help care for them or any other loved one— either practically or financially? Having a thorough understanding of their family values and relationship dynamics is key in this type of evaluations.

Trauma History

It is also important to ask about any history of trauma or abuse throughout their upbringing. This entails physical, sexual, or psychological abuse; any painful losses in their lives; major illnesses or accidents; having been the victim of a crime, etc. Research has shown that adverse childhood experiences, specifically abuse and emotional trauma, affect neuroregulatory systems, which can have profound and enduring effects on physical and psychiatric health (Felitti & Anda, 2010). Such adverse childhood experiences are particularly more damaging if they occur in the context of an inadequate caregiving system (Luecken & Lemery, 2004). Although delving into the intricate details of the trauma may not be called for, it is definitely important to explore how they coped.

Immigration History

Many QRs are themselves first generation immigrants, so it is worth inquiring how they got from their native country to where they are now. Many fled their country of origin, which might be the same country where their loved one was born and might have to return to, which would likely result in some serious hardships if they no longer have any ties there. This is a factor that USCIS always considers.

In addition, it might be worth asking about their current immigration process. Whereas in many cases this is the beginning of their process, many have been struggling with a lengthy and cumbersome ordeal. It is sad but not unusual for individuals to have been the victims of fraud by former immigration attorneys or—as is more often the case—people who practice law without a license, such as *notarios,* or "immigration consultants." This naturally adds stress and suspicion to the process, doubt as to the outcome to their plight, and a sense of helplessness and fear which typically manifests in their current symptoms.

Relationship History

A relationship history, particularly if the QR is the applicant's spouse, is another key area to explore. If the client has been married before, briefly ask about their prior relationships. This can be more or less relevant depending on the case. For example, having experienced a painful loss or separation from a partner in the past can become a central focus of the assessment.

Children from previous relationships are particularly important to ask about, as they present potential difficulties for the client who wants to maintain contact with them but chooses to move abroad with the applicant. Choosing to stay, however, presents its own challenges when they only have so much available time for visits to their loved one abroad. This is typical for families who live in border towns, such as San Diego and Tijuana. A former client lamented that he had to work 50 hours a week to pay his bills and support his wife in Tijuana. Having only one day off from work put him in a tough position, as he had to choose whether to drive down to Tijuana to be with his wife and their 1-year-old son or to visit his daughters who lived with their mother in Central San Diego. This can get complicated when there is animosity between the client and their former spouse, who can make it even more difficult for the client to spend quality time with their children.

This brings us to a very important distinction to make: no given circumstance denotes hardship per se; the issue, rather, is the psychological impact the circumstance has on the individual. Two people in comparable situations could be affected very differently. For example, a person with a history of abandonment issues is likely to suffer much more hardship from a separation than someone who has always been confidently independent. This is what we are after when we interview our clients—their distinctive, exceptional circumstances that make them particularly vulnerable to such suffering (i.e., their "cracks").

Quality of Relationship to Applicant

In evaluations for waivers based on hardship the quality of the relationship between the applicant and the QR is a central focus. That is, the stronger the relationship, the greater likelihood of hardship if they are separated. Be on the lookout, however, for statements that portray a perfect relationship, which could raise questions about the veracity of the assessment. Candid statements such as "We have our ups and downs, like most couples" or "He has his quirks, and we sometimes argue, but I couldn't live without him" denote a realistic description of a relationship. To your chagrin, a client might confess, "Well, we barely see each other, and we've actually discussed the possibility of getting a divorce…" While on the surface such a comment might seem to negate any claim of hardship, there could still be other issues at play if the spouse had to leave the country, such as children, finances, and other significant factors.

The length of time they have known each other is also important. Sometimes a client's current spouse is their first and only significant relationship, or they have been together since they were very young, which is not uncommon. A client might say something like, "I've been with this person for more than half my life" (or even more than that in some cases) to explain how painful it would be to have to separate from their partner. "It would be like ripping off my right arm," one client told me. "I don't know how to function without him."

In discussing the evaluee's relationship history, focus should be on their general approach to relationships and ways of relating with their partner. Families differ in their views of marital happiness, gender roles, communication styles, and family-of-origin involvement. A relationship built on a strong foundation of trust, mutual support, and open communication is different from one that values independence, self-sufficiency, and clearly defined family roles. Such roles are also very important to explore. Does one partner stay home caring for the children while the other works full-time? Do they alternate schedules to be home with their young children? Are their marital roles so culturally delineated that either would be at a loss if they had to take over the duties of the other? In fact, look for any cultural factors that might be relevant to the family dynamics. Lastly, asking about any history of traumatic experiences as a couple is helpful, as overcoming difficult adversities together often strengthens the quality of a relationship.

Children

Even though children cannot be considered a QR for many waivers, their well-being is of utmost importance to a parent, and a child's suffering inevitably affects the parent. The government will typically take into consideration the QR's distress related to their children's welfare. Consequently, it is important to ask about their children's health, if they have any special needs, medical or psychiatric treatment, learning disabilities or academic difficulties, and their general well-being. All of these factors can be significantly impacted by stress in the environment, as when there is a disruption in the family unit.

Family dynamics are important to understand. How close are the children to each parent? Do they have established roles, where one parent is in charge of daily tasks like driving them to school while the other parent mainly spends time with them on the weekends? What do they do together as a family? Whenever possible, ask for specific examples rather than settle for broad statements such as "We're very close."

Medical History

Even though most MHPs do not have a medical background, we understand the relationship between mind and body and how one impacts the other. Stress is known to both result in and exacerbate physical ailments. There is no need to get into the details of a medical condition (the client will most likely have medical records to submit along with their waiver application anyway), but there should be a brief exploration of the ailments reported by the client, specific treatment, presumed prognosis and, most importantly, how emotional distress contributes (or might contribute) to a worsening of the medical picture.

Psychiatric History

A summary of any mental health issues, including therapy and hospitalizations, should be noted. Even if the client has not received specific mental health treatment, it is possible they have been encouraged to do so by a medical provider. As readers of this book are likely aware, mental illness is often stigmatized, for many reasons, and complaining about headaches, gastrointestinal issues, or physical pain is generally more culturally acceptable than sharing one's feelings of sadness or anxiety (Hulme, 1996). Most health care providers can often see through these complaints and either suggest mental health treatment or prescribe psychotropic medication. It is, therefore, also important to ask if they are taking any medication, if they have been prescribed medication for anxiety or depression in the past, and, if so, whether and how long they took it. Their not following through with recommendations is not as important as the fact that they were told they would benefit from such treatment, which clearly indicates that there is, in fact, a history of psychiatric complaints. Alternative healing methods are not uncommon among first- and second-generation immigrants and are often more internally acceptable than western medicine, particularly when it comes to emotional suffering (Abe-Kim et al., 2007; Ahn et al., 2006; Ortiz et al., 2007), so include whether they take any supplements, teas, or tinctures to "calm the nerves."

A history of psychiatric ailments is a strong predictor of future mental health problems. If they succumbed to depression in the past, stressful life events are most likely going to result in a second occurrence (Roca et al., 2013), and if it happened more than once, they are much more likely to go through another depressive bout in the future (Solomon et al., 2004).

If the client received or is receiving mental health treatment, ask about the frequency, quality, and helpfulness of the treatment. Any available treatment records would be a valuable complement to the evaluation, particularly those that mention prognosis or recommendations for future care. Regardless of whether the client is in treatment, you should ask about their preferred ways for coping with emotional distress. What do they do when they feel sad, worried, anxious, or angry? Do they lean on someone for emotional support? Are there other support systems in place, such as a church, support group, etc.?

The more robust their support system, the better their prognosis. Conversely, lack of adequate support or healthy coping skills is a very strong predictor of psychological deterioration (Rolf et al., 1990). It is also not unusual for people to hide their pain from their loved ones so as not to worry them or upset them, so you will likely hear statements such as, "I don't want to tell my husband how I'm feeling because I don't want to worry him more. He's already struggling with this situation, and I don't want to add to it."

Substance Abuse History

The abuse of substances, although an undeniable problem, is itself an unhealthy solution to a deeper problem. Looking at it from that perspective, we can avoid divulging information that might seriously jeopardize a client's case. When a person discloses that they went through a phase where they succumbed to alcohol or other substances, several relevant questions arise. Was it the result of peer pressure? Was it a means to cope with low self-esteem? To avoid emotional pain? How long did it go on? If the substance use was a short phase earlier in the client's life, there is no real concern for relapse, and the applicant was not involved in their recovery, then it is probably not relevant to the referral question and thus not worthy of further exploration. If, however, there is a strong likelihood for relapse—especially if under duress—or if the client's sobriety is dependent on the applicant's continuous support, this would be an area of concern. It would also indicate that the client lacks healthy ways of coping, which is important when considering the negative impact of a separation from a loved one or a country relocation.

Employment/Academic History

Unless for some reason the client's employment or educational background is specifically relevant to the question at hand, it would likely not warrant detailed inquiry. This is not to say that you ignore it completely but rather that there is no need to take inventory of every job the client has held throughout their life. Be careful not to overextend the interview unnecessarily and waste time that could be spent on more important areas.

> ### Quick Tip
>
> It is helpful to end the interview by asking something like: "Is there anything I haven't asked you that you think would be important for me to know?" This opens the door to the sharing of potentially relevant information that you failed to ask about, or that wouldn't have thought of if they didn't bring it up. Encourage the client to think about it for a minute and not just respond "no" immediately. Our lives are complex, so chances are something was left out that might be worth sharing.

Assessing Hardships

After gathering a thorough historical background, we want to home in on the referral issue. I might say something like, "Now that I have a pretty clear picture of where you come from and your past experiences, let's focus on what brought you in: your spouse/son/daughter/parent's immigration process." In addition to how much they know about the process and how they feel about it, the central question should be how a separation from their loved one might affect them (if they are still residing together in the United States) or is affecting them, and issues that emerge when considering relocating abroad to avoid a separation.

Have them focus on one scenario at a time, such as: "How do you imagine you would feel if your spouse/son/daughter/parent had to leave the country for an extended length of time?" Or, if they are already separated, "How is not being able to reside in the United States with your loved one affecting you?" Clients' concerns tend to center around a handful of themes: finances, health conditions, children's welfare, family ties (in the United States and abroad), employment, difficulty with travel, safety concerns, etc. If they do not mention one of these areas of concern, you might want to ask about it. Avoid leading questions, however, to make sure the concerns they describe are genuine and well-founded rather than just answers they feel expected to give. You might want to ask follow-up questions, such as, "How so? What exactly worries you? Where is that concern rooted?"

Once you have covered the scenario of a separation, shift to the other possibility, that of relocating abroad to maintain physical closeness to the FN. The areas of concern tend to be similar to those of a separation, which happen to be very much in line with the factors USCIS considers when evaluating the degree of hardship (family separation, economic detriment, difficulties of readjusting to life in the new country, quality and availability of educational opportunities abroad, inferior quality of medical services and facilities, and ability to pursue a chosen career or employment abroad). Again, it is important to go beyond general areas of concerns and to focus on specific examples. Remember that the government already considers these factors as potential hardships any person would experience under similar circumstances. The goal for the applicant is to demonstrate that the QR's suffering would be "beyond what is typically expected," based on the uniqueness of their personal experience and the degree of distress.

In addition to current and potential hardships, we need to understand the emotional impact of dealing with or having to contemplate such circumstances. "How are you feeling as you think about these different prospects for your family's future?" Remember that denial is a powerful defense. It keeps us from sinking and succumbing to hopelessness and helplessness, but when confronted with reality head on, the reaction could be that of a deer in the headlights. I have seen that expression in my clients' faces all too often, so be prepared for such reactions and to show empathy and sensitivity. The same holds for those who immediately burst into tears when faced with that question. The benefit of such emotional expressions is that they offer you a more direct and accurate impression of their current status.

Assessment Measures

The use of psychological tests helps to further assess the client's psychological symptoms. A standard instrument is the Structured Clinical Interview for DSM-5 Disorders – Clinician Version (SCID-5-CV; First et al., 2016). The SCID-5-CV is a semi-structured guide designed to evaluate a broad range of psychological problems and symptoms of psychopathology according to the diagnostic criteria established by the Diagnostic and Statistical Manual of Mental Disorders – Fifth Edition (DSM-5; American Psychiatric Association, 2013a). Instead of going through the entire guide in a mechanical fashion, you might just want to read through it a few times to familiarize yourself with some standard lines of questioning. Basically, it is a series of flow charts to identify psychiatric symptoms and arrive at diagnoses.

There are myriad other tests for evaluating psychiatric symptoms, such as the Beck inventories (Beck et al., 1988; Beck et al., 1996), Symptom Checklist-90- Revised (Derogatis, 1977), Patient Health Questionnaires (PHQ-9; Kroenke et al., 1999), Hopkins Symptom Checklist (Derogatis et al., 1974), and others. The Recent Life Changes Stress Test (RLCST; Miller & Rahe, 1997) is the newer version of the classic Social Readjustment Rating Scale (SRRS; Holmes & Rahe, 1967). Despite numerous criticisms regarding its reliability and validity (Dohrenwend, 2006), it is still one of the most used scales for assessing stress levels and its impact on a person's health.

Which measures to use as part of the evaluation is ultimately a matter of preference, but the main point is that they all rely almost exclusively on self-report, which is based on self-awareness and mitigated by level of comfort with personal disclosure. In other words, a client who does not want you to know they are depressed will undoubtedly generate a low score on a depression inventory. This does not mean that they are not depressed. Conversely, someone who wants to make sure you know how depressed they are will rate items on a test yielding a score that is off the charts (and likely questionable). Because of this, it is advisable to prioritize your own clinical judgment based on your knowledge, training, and experience, as that will most likely be more accurate than a self-report measure.

Some tests have less face validity and are more thorough in assessing symptomatology and personality characteristics, such as the different versions of the Minnesota Multiphasic Personality Inventory (MMPI-2-RF; Block et al., 2014; MMPI-3; Ben-Porath & Tellegen, 2020), the Millon Clinical Multiaxial Inventory (MCMI; Craig, 2006), or the Personality Assessment Inventory (PAI; Morey, 1991), among others. Be mindful, however, of each test's psychometric properties (e.g., standardization, reliability, and validity) and normative data.

Even though these forced and multiple-choice measures are not complex to administer (in comparison to the Weschler Intelligence Scales, for example), mental health professionals who choose to incorporate them in their evaluation must have foundational knowledge regarding test selection, administration, and scoring (American Educational Research Association et al., 2014; American Psychological Association, 2013, 2020). You can acquire such knowledge in a number of ways: by attending workshops or classes covering specific tests or measures; reading the test publisher's manual and familiarizing yourself with the test items and administration protocols; consulting with other mental health professionals who have vast experience administering that test; practicing administering the test with a colleague; or joining online forums or listservs where professionals have intellectual discussions about assessment and testing.

Since the characteristics of the client's relationship with the FN are central in this type of evaluations, assessing the quality of their attachment is vital. Measures such as the Experiences in Close Relationships – Relationship Structures (ECR-RS; Fraley et al., 2011) can be useful in identifying their attitudes about relationships with loved ones along dimensions of anxiety and avoidance. Similar to the symptom inventories, however, there are limitations to the use of these self-report measures. One way to circumvent such limitations is to go over the client's responses and ask follow-up questions to gain a clearer understanding of the quality of their bond to their loved ones.

Psychological testing is a useful approach to gathering information within the larger framework of evaluating an individual; however, you should not rely on any one measure or assessment method. Tests and questionnaires are useful in the aggregate, as they provide specific information that will assist you in forming your overall clinical impressions of the client. It is important to employ several sources of relevant and reliable information, as relying on any one test is not only useless, but likely unethical (American Educational Research Association, et al., 2014; American Psychological Association, 2013, 2020).

The Report

In the sample reports included in the Appendices, you will see how you can organize all the information gathered during the interview and test administration. Using simple, clear language, the goal of the report is to explain to the adjudicator how, in your professional judgment, a separation from the applicant—or moving to another country to reside together with them— would affect the client. Chapter 7 covers the report writing process in much more detail.

The report should not be a regurgitation of the client's concerns about the hardships they might experience or are experiencing but, rather, your expert opinion based on the client's personal experiences, personality characteristics, current concerns, and reported symptoms. USCIS has made it clear that the burden is on the applicant to demonstrate that their QR's suffering from a separation or relocation will be beyond what is commonly expected. Merely repeating the client's subjective concerns does not present clear and convincing evidence that the applicant's departure from the United States would result in anything other than ordinary consequences. It is for that reason that the report has to highlight the client's individual vulnerabilities that predispose them to a psychological decompensation. In my report, I concluded:

> Given [Mrs. Juarez's] current clinical diagnosis of *generalized anxiety disorder with panic attacks,* along with her trauma history, her personality characteristics, and her strong dependency on her husband, Mr. Juarez's departure from the United States will likely affect Mrs. Juarez **beyond what is considered to be a normal response to a separation from a loved one**. [emphasis added]

That is a key phrase that should be included when you determine it accurately represents the client's plight. Of course, that is ultimately for the adjudicator to determine, as they will be considering many other pieces of evidence to substantiate the client's claim, but if you deem that to be the case, include it.

Sometimes the client will not meet criteria for a psychiatric diagnosis, but this does not diminish the value of the report. As a matter of fact, McLawsen et al. (2011) analyzed hundreds of decisions from USCIS's Administrative Appeals Office (AAO) on whether waiver denial would result in hardship to the applicant's QR and found that an applicant's success in being granted a waiver was not dependent on their QR having been diagnosed with a mental disorder. Especially in cases where the applicant and their QR are still residing together in the United States, assessing potential hardships relies on speculation based on the presenting factors. Even though the client might not have symptoms severe enough to warrant a DSM-5 diagnosis, they are likely to have personality characteristics or unique experiences that make them more susceptible to significant emotional distress if separated from their loved one.

Many MHPs like to include research on country conditions but doing so is uncalled for and probably outside your scope of practice. Naturally, some attorneys will welcome it—or even request it—because you would be doing their job for them, but there are many experts on country conditions and numerous ways to demonstrate that to the adjudicator without making it your responsibility. Unless you have the adequate training, knowledge, and experience to discuss international sociopolitical factors, refrain from traversing into foreign territory (pun intended).

In the sample report I included in the Appendices I did, however, cite a study on the relationship between adverse childhood experiences (ACE) and a person's propensity for medical and psychiatric disorders to support my conclusions regarding Mrs. Juarez's prognosis. This is clearly within my area of expertise. If you choose to include references in your report, make sure to integrate the findings into your conclusions in a way that relates directly to the client being evaluated. Do not go overboard with the number of papers you cite (two is plenty), be very concise, and, as with the rest of the report, avoid psychological jargon.

Responding to a Request for More Evidence (RFE) or a Notice of Intent to Deny (NOID)

Sometimes applicants receive an RFE or a NOID that specifically mentions their QR's psychological hardship and the lack of convincing evidence. If this is a new client, I would conduct the evaluation as I would for anyone else applying for a waiver. If this is a client whom I have already evaluated, however, the process is a bit different. In general, I would interview the client and have them discuss any meaningful life events that transpired since the last time I saw them. Typically, receiving the RFE is itself a deeply disturbing experience. I would also have them complete some of the psychological measures again—namely, those that focus on symptoms that fluctuate with time, such as the SCID-5-CV and the RLCST. You would never re-administer a PAI or the ECR-RS, since the results are unlikely to be different from the first administration.

Instead of a full report of a psychological evaluation, I write an affidavit explaining why the client returned, the assessment process, the assessment results, and my conclusions. This is generally a three- to four-page document, and the client is charged half of the amount they paid when they came in for their initial evaluation. The same applies when the applicant receives a NOID or is altogether denied the waiver.

I recently saw a former client for a follow-up evaluation because his wife was denied a waiver. In the denial letter from USCIS, the officer specifically stated:

> The report [of the psychological evaluation] does not credibly describe any effects of your potential deportation beyond that which would normally be expected of others in similar situations. Nothing in the report differentiates your spouse from other US citizens facing deportation. Notably absent from the report is that the negative psychological effects would not be typical or expected.

Unfortunately, the officer was right. This was a case of a young man who had been married for two years and had no children. He had no history of trauma or losses, did not meet criteria for any diagnoses in the DSM-5, and had a resilient and optimistic personality evidenced by his ability to quickly adapt to a new line of work after losing his job due to the coronavirus disease 2019 (COVID-19) pandemic. After a thorough probing for all possible frailties and unique shortcomings, I came up empty handed. Even though he spoke very little Spanish, had no ties to Mexico (his wife's native country), and was concerned about his wife's safety in Mexico—all valid and acceptable factors that can result in significant adversities to a USC—his potential hardships were by no means extreme. Consequently, I did not include anything in the report that disingenuously portrayed his situation as anything other than what I objectively found it to be.

These cases, though few and far between in my experience, could sometimes be avoided by educating the referral sources about the benefits and limitations of a psychological evaluation. Hake and Banks (2005) developed "The Hake hardship scale" by analyzing 140 AAO appeal decisions to discern the factors that are most likely to get a waiver approved. The authors of the scale, both immigration attorneys, relied on their professional experience filing J-1 waivers for physicians (not covered in this book, but for which the hardship standards are the same). The purpose of this scale is to assist immigration attorneys in deciding whether to pursue a waiver application based on how likely it is to be successful.

I, too, came up with a questionnaire, called the Psychological Hardship Screening Questionnaire (Copyright 2013 by Mariela G. Shibley), to screen hardship waiver applicants for psychological factors that would warrant a referral for an evaluation by an MHP. This is a 36-item self-report questionnaire that asks a potential client to mark the items that apply to them. My intention was to avoid clients being referred for an evaluation when they are unlikely to benefit from it, but this attorney clearly did not have his client complete the questionnaire, or else he ignored the results. Many attorneys understandably argue that an MHP can unearth aspects of a client's personality or idiosyncratic issues in a client's history that a client might be reluctant to share with an attorney. I agree with that. Ultimately, it is the client's prerogative whether to choose to seek a psychological evaluation or not.

In other instances, the immigration officer's opinion regarding the insufficiency of the QR's claimed hardships seems unreasonable. Nonetheless, the clients need more evidence to demonstrate their suffering and are thus back for a follow-up evaluation. Often, the client's symptoms have noticeably increased and they warrant a more serious diagnosis (such as major depressive disorder) or they now meet criteria for a psychiatric diagnosis that they previously did not. Refer to the Appendices for a sample of this type of document.

It is very helpful to read the RFE or NOID if available, as it typically describes in detail the reason for the application's insufficiencies. This allows for a more tailored assessment and write-up (e.g., sometimes the issue being raised is why the QR is not receiving mental health treatment if they were diagnosed with a psychiatric disorder.)

Notes

1   The 3- and 10-year bars only apply since April 1, 1997; therefore, prior violations do not trigger punishments. There are also exceptions to counting unlawful presence relating to the FN based on their age, whether there is a pending asylum application, whether they are victims of trafficking, whether they are a beneficiary

of certain temporary status such as Deferred Action for Childhood Arrivals (DACA), and whether they are victims of domestic violence.

2 For greater detail and specific wording of these elements, see Chapter 2 of the USCIS policy manual (2021).

3 The Visa Waiver Program allows for citizens of certain countries with higher standards of living to enter the United States for tourism or business without a visa and stay for up to 90 days.

4 Even though nowadays after an LPR serves their time in prison they are immediately picked up by DHS and placed in removal proceedings, such was not the case prior to 1997, which is why DHS is coming after them now.

5 Most clients prefer to have the report sent directly to their attorney. However, some request that it be handed to them directly.

Bibliography

Abe-Kim, J., Takeuchi, D. T., Hong, S., Zane, N., Sue, S., Spencer, M. S., Appel, H., Nicdao, E., & Alegría, M. (2007). Use of mental health–related services among immigrant and US-born Asian Americans: Results from the national Latino and Asian American study. *American Journal of Public Health, 97*(1), 91–98. https://doi.org/10.2105/ajph.2006.098541

Ahn, A. C., Ngo-Metzger, Q., Legedza, A. T., Massagli, M. P., Clarridge, B. R., & Phillips, R. S. (2006). Complementary and alternative medical therapy use among Chinese and Vietnamese Americans: Prevalence, associated factors, and effects of patient–clinician communication. *American Journal of Public Health, 96*(4), 647–653. https://doi.org/10.2105/ajph.2004.048496

American Educational Research Association, American Psychological Association, National Council on Measurement in Education. (2014). *Standards for educational and psychological testing.* American Educational Research Association.

American Psychiatric Association. (2013a). *Diagnostic and statistical manual of mental disorders* (5th ed.). American Psychiatric Press.

American Psychological Association. (2013b). Specialty guidelines for forensic psychology. *American Psychologist, 68*(1), 7–19.

American Psychological Association, APA Task Force on Psychological Assessment and Evaluation Guidelines. (2020). *APA guidelines for psychological assessment and evaluation.* Retrieved from www.apa.org/about/policy/guidelines-psychological-assessment-evaluation.pdf

Beck, A. T., Epstein, N., Brown, G., & Steer, R. (1988). *Beck anxiety inventory.* PsycTESTS.

Beck, A. T., Steer, R. A., & Brown, G. (1996). *Beck depression inventory–II.* PsycTESTS.

Ben-Porath, Y. S., & Tellegen, A. (2020). *Minnesota multiphasic personality inventory-3 (MMPI-3): Manual for administration, scoring, and interpretation.* University of Minnesota Press.

Block, A. R., Marek, R. J., Ben-Porath, Y. S., & Ohnmeiss, D. D. (2014). *The Minnesota multiphasic personality inventory-2-restructured form (MMPI-2-RF): Manual for administration, scoring, and interpretation.* University of Minnesota Press.

Craig, R. J. (2006). The Millon Clinical Multiaxial Inventory-III. In R. P. Archer (Ed.), *Forensic uses of clinical assessment instruments* (pp. 121–145). Lawrence Erlbaum Associates Publishers.

Derogatis, L. R., Lipman, R. S., Rickels, K., Uhlenhuth, E. H., & Covi, L. (1974). *Hopkins Symptom checklist.* PsycTESTS.

Derogatis, L. R. (1977). *Symptom checklist-90–Revised.* PsycTESTS.

Dohrenwend, B. P. (2006). Inventorying stressful life events as risk factors for psychopathology: Toward resolution of the problem of intracategory variability. *Psychological Bulletin, 132*(3), 477–495. https://doi.org/10.1037/0033-2909.132.3.477

Felitti, V. J., & Anda, R. F. (2010). The relationship of adverse childhood experiences to adult medical disease, psychiatric disorders and sexual behavior: Implications for healthcare. In R. A. Lanius, E. Vermetten, & C. Pain (Eds.), *The impact of early life trauma on health and disease: The hidden epidemic* (pp. 77–87). Cambridge University Press.

First, M. B., Williams, J. B. W., Karg, R. S., & Spitzer, R. L. (2016). *Structured clinical interview for DSM-5 disorders, clinician version (SCID-5-CV)*. American Psychiatric Association.

Fraley, R. C., Heffernan, M. E., Vicary, A. M., & Brumbaugh, C. C. (2011). *Experiences in close relationships—Relationship structures questionnaire*. PsycTESTS.

Hake, B. A., & Banks, D. L. (2005). The hake hardship scale: A quantitative system for assessment of hardship in immigration cases based on a statistical analysis of AAO decisions. *Bender's Immigration Bulletin, 10*, 403–420.

Holmes, T. H., & Rahe, R. H. (1967). The social readjustment rating scale. *Journal of Psychosomatic Research, 11*(2), 213–218. https://doi.org/10.1016/0022-3999(67)90010-4

Hulme, P. A. (1996). Somatization in Hispanics. *Journal of Psychosocial Nursing and Mental Health Services, 34*(3), 33–37. https://doi.org/10.3928/0279-3695-19960301-17

Kroenke, K., Spitzer, R. L., & Williams, J. B. W. (1999). *Patient health questionnaire-9*. PsycTESTS.

Luecken, L. J. & Lemery K. S. (2004). Early caregiving and physiological stress responses. *Clinical Psychology Review 24*(2), 171–191. https://doi.org/10.1016/j.cpr.2004.01.003

McLawsen, G., McLawsen, J., & Ruser, K. (2011). Demonstrating psychological hardship: A statistical study of psychological evaluations in hardship waivers of inadmissibility. *Bender's Immigration Bulletin, 16*(10).

Miller, M. A., & Rahe, R. H. (1997). Life changes scaling for the 1990s. *Journal of Psychosomatic Research, 43*(3), 279–292. https://doi.org/10.1016/s0022-3999(97)00118-9

Morey, L. C. (1991). *Personality assessment inventory*. PsycTESTS.

Ortiz, B. I., Shields, K. M., Clauson, K. A., & Clay, P. G. (2007). Complementary and alternative medicine use among Hispanics in the United States. *The Annals of Pharmacotherapy, 41*(6), 994–1004. https://doi.org/10.1345/aph.1h600

Roca, M., Gili, M., Garcia-Campayo, J., Armengol, S., Bauza, N., & García-Toro, M. (2013). Stressful life events severity in patients with first and recurrent depressive episodes. *Social Psychiatry and Psychiatric Epidemiology, 48*(12), 1963–1969. https://doi.org/10.1007/s00127-013-0691-1

Rolf, J., Masten A. S., Cicchetti, D., Nuechterlein, K. H., & Weintraub, S. (1990). *Risk and protective factors in the development of psychopathology*. Cambridge University Press.

Solomon, D., Leon, A., Endicott, J., Mueller, T., Coryell, W., Shea, M. T., & Keller, M. (2004). Psychosocial impairment and recurrence of major depression. *Comprehensive Psychiatry, 45*(6), 423–430. https://doi.org/10.1016/j.comppsych.2004.07.002

United States Citizenship and Immigration Services. (2021). *USCIS policy manual*. Volume 9, Part B, Chapter 5. US Citizenship and Immigration Services.

3 The Appraisal of Exceptional and Extremely Unusual Hardship for Cancellation of Removal

Mariela G. Shibley, Psy.D. and Matthew G. Holt, Esq.

Foreign nationals (FNs) who violate certain immigration statutes or commit certain crimes can be charged as inadmissible or removable. To avoid deportation or a permanent ban from entering the United States, they can pursue cancellation of removal under INA §§ 240(a)(b)(1) & (2), a provision that allows certain FNs to have the removability or inadmissibility grounds levied against them to be cancelled. If they are successful with their application, they receive permanent resident status. If not, they are ordered removed or granted voluntary departure and have the right to appeal to the Board of Immigration Appeals (BIA). By contrast, only certain permanent residents are eligible to apply for cancellation of removal under INA § 240A(a). If the permanent resident is successful in that endeavor, they retain their permanent residency. If not, they are stripped of their permanent resident status and ordered removed but, similarly, allowed to appeal the immigration judge's (IJ) decision. Each of the above forms of relief requires the filing of a specific application (either *Form EOIR-42A* or *EOIR-42B*), the paying of a filing fee (unless the fee is waived), and the processing of biometrics for necessary background checks. Each form of relief has statutory requirements, and the respondent must prove that they are eligible and deserving of the relief sought. Additionally, certain respondents may apply for waivers of inadmissibility or removability (the same waivers discussed in Chapter 2) in order to receive or retain residency.

In immigration court (IC), FNs are called "respondents," as they are responding to charges brought by the US Department of Homeland Security. Both permanent and nonpermanent residents may appear in court. FNs can be charged as inadmissible or removable depending on their immigration or criminal violations. The most common reasons for being ordered to appear in IC are for being present in the United States without lawful status after entry without inspection, for violating nonimmigrant status such as overstaying a tourist visa, or for crimes that make one removable, such as theft crimes or controlled substance violations. In this chapter, we discuss some of the most common forms of relief in IC, the requirements for each relief, and how mental health professionals (MHPs) can play a vital role.

DOI: 10.4324/9781003139973-4

Cancellation of Removal for Certain Nonpermanent Residents

To apply for cancellation of removal for certain nonpermanent residents under INA § 240A(b)(1) the respondent must prove that they meet the following statutory eligibility requirements:

1 They have been physically present in the United States continuously for at least 10 years.
2 They have had good moral character for 10 years.
3 They have not been convicted of certain offenses (crimes listed in INA §§ 212(a)(2), 237(a)(2), or 237(a)(3)).
4 Their removal would cause *exceptional and extremely unusual hardship* to their legal permanent resident or US citizen spouse, child, or parent.

The most difficult element to prove is often the hardship requirement. When this form of relief was first developed by Congress in 1996, the legislative history, since quoted by the 2001 BIA's decision in Matter of Monreal, stated that *exceptional and extremely unusual hardship* means that a person undergoing removal proceedings must provide evidence of hardship to his qualifying spouse, parent, or child, where the hardship is "substantially different from, or beyond that which would be normally expected from the deportation of an alien with close family members [in the United States]."

When assessing *exceptional and extremely unusual hardship*, the IJ looks at the age, health, and circumstances of qualifying (LPR and US citizen (USC) relatives, considering all factors in the aggregate. For example, a respondent who has elderly parents in this country who are solely dependent upon him for support might well have a strong case. Another respondent will have a persuasive case because they have a USC child with very serious health issues or compelling special needs in school. While it may be typical that the country of removal has a lower standard of living or other adverse country conditions, the IJ will only consider these factors to the extent they affect a qualifying relative, but they generally will not be sufficient in themselves to support a finding of *exceptional and extremely unusual hardship*.

Special Rule Cancellation of Removal

Victims of domestic violence facing removal proceedings may seek relief under INA § 240A(b)(2) wherein they must satisfy lesser but still rigorous legal requirements than those found in INA § 240A(b)(1). Special Rule (also known as VAWA cancellation of removal) was crafted to stop removal proceedings for victims of abuse by a USC or LPR spouse or parent. In Chapter 5, we will discuss VAWA-related forms of immigration benefits in greater detail and focus on the victimization and relief outside the IC; here, we will focus on the requirements that domestic violence victims must meet to win their cases in front of an IJ. To qualify, the victim respondent must prove:

1 They, male or female, child or adult, have been battered or subject to extreme cruelty by their USC or LPR spouse or their parent, or they are a co-parent of a child who was battered or subject to *extreme cruelty* by the other co-parent, who is a USC or LPR.
2 They have been continuously physically present in the United States for at least three years preceding the date of the application for cancellation of removal.
3 They have been a person of good moral character for the required period of continuous physical presence.
4 They are not inadmissible or deportable under certain provisions of the INA and have not been convicted of an aggravated felony.
5 The removal would result in *extreme hardship* to the FN, the FN's child, or the FN's parent.

As you may have noticed, unlike cancellation of removal for certain nonpermanent residents—which requires that a USC or LPR spouse, parent, or child suffer *exceptional and extremely unusual hardship*—Special Rule cancellation more simply requires that the respondent's removal would cause *extreme hardship*, a lower bar and thus a lesser burden to be proven. Moreover, Special Rule cancellation considers hardship to the victim respondent, not just their USC or LPR parent(s), spouse, or child(ren). Nevertheless, the application is subject to scrutiny and difficult to win. The immigration judges also look at the following factors in determining the application's merit:

• The nature and extent of the physical or psychological consequences of abuse.
• The impact of loss of access to the United States courts and criminal justice system (including, but not limited to, the ability to obtain and enforce orders of protection, criminal investigations and prosecutions, and family law proceedings or court orders regarding child support, maintenance, child custody, and visitation).
• The likelihood that the perpetrator's family, friends, or others acting on behalf of the perpetrator in the home country would physically or psychologically harm the applicant or the applicant's child(ren).
• The needs of the applicant and/or their child(ren) for social, medical, mental health, or other supportive services for victims of domestic violence that are unavailable or not reasonably accessible in the home country.
• The existence of laws and social practices in the home country that punish the applicant or the applicant's child(ren) because they have been victims of domestic violence or have taken steps to leave an abusive household.

- The abuser's ability to travel to the home country and the ability and willingness of authorities in the home country to protect the applicant and/or their children from future abuse.

VAWA or Special Rule cancellation of removal is sadly a common form of relief in ICs. Typically, these cases result from an abusive spouse calling immigration officers or an arrest of both parties during a domestic disturbance. While there are immigration benefits for victims of domestic violence that are available outside of the IC, they have their limits, so a victim respondent's best form of relief, or only permanent form of relief, is often through the IC. The most compelling cases can be the most difficult to unravel and share, and they are typically best supported and developed with the assistance of an MHP.

Cancellation of Removal for Certain Permanent Residents

The last form of cancellation of removal we will address is seldom used but the easiest to obtain, at least for those FNs who are fortunate enough to qualify. The laxed requirements make sense when one considers this relief is only available to people who have already been granted permanent residency and lived continuously in the United States for several years but find themselves in trouble and threatened with termination of residency. For cancellation of removal for permanent residents under INA section 240A(a), the respondent's burden is less than that required under INA section 240(b) but is still onerous. They have to demonstrate to the satisfaction of the IJ the following:

1 They have been an LPR for at least five years.
2 They have continuously resided in the United States for at least seven years.
3 They have not been convicted of an aggravated felony.

Typically, LPRs face removal because they had a controlled substance violation, committed domestic assault, or were convicted of significant welfare fraud, all of which make them independently removable. The IJ determines whether to grant discretionary relief by balancing an array of positive and negative factors:

- The **positive factors** include family ties within the United States, residence of long duration in this country (particularly when the inception of residence occurred at a young age), evidence of hardship to the respondent and his family if deportation occurs, service in this country's armed forces, a history of employment, the existence of property or business ties, evidence of value and service to the community, proof of genuine rehabilitation if a criminal record exists, and other evidence attesting to a respondent's good character.

- The **negative factors** include the nature and underlying circumstances of the grounds of exclusion or deportation (now removal) that are at issue; the presence of additional significant violations of this country's immigration laws; the existence of a criminal record and, if so, its nature, recency, and seriousness; and the presence of other evidence indicative of a respondent's bad character or undesirability as a permanent resident of this country.

For cancellation of removal for certain permanent residents, the hardship considered is hardship to the respondent and their family. LPRs are not required to prove *exceptional and extremely unusual hardship* as required for cancellation of removal for nonpermanent residents or even *extreme hardship* as required for Special Rule cancellation of removal, but LPRs do have to focus on presenting evidence of *remorse and rehabilitation,* as those are the primary issues before the IC.

The Psychological Evaluation

Assessing Hardship to a Qualifying Relative (Cancellation of Removal for non-LPR)

Even though the hardship standards differ depending on the type of cancellation of removal case, the referral question is the same and one you are already familiar with:

- How would a **separation** or a **relocation** to the FN's country of citizenship affect the **qualifying relative** (or in some cases the applicant)?
- Would the hardships experienced by the qualifying relative (or applicant) be **beyond what is typically expected** following a separation from a loved one?

We will now home in on the hardship standard for each type of cancellation of removal discussed above, using hypothetical scenarios as examples.

Example #1: Rosa

Rosa was born in a small village in Michoacán, Mexico. When she got pregnant at the age of 15, she decided to come to the United States in search of work. Leaving her son, David, with a cousin in Tijuana, she found a job in California as a housekeeper. Years later, Rosa fell in love and married William, a US citizen. Upon being granted lawful permanent residency through her spouse, she began to visit David on a regular basis. In 2009, William was diagnosed with terminal cancer and died a few months later. Devastated, Rosa's health quickly deteriorated. David, who was 24 years old by then, came to live with her and support her through her grieving process. He started working at a carwash and, over the following 10 years, became his mother's only source of financial and practical support. On his way to work one morning, David was pulled over and arrested. DHS placed him in removal proceedings, and he retained the help of an attorney. Rosa scheduled an evaluation to support her son's cancellation of removal application.

Aside from any potential relief he may seek outside of the court, David has an excellent path to lawful permanent residency. He does not appear to have disqualifying criminal history, and he has lived in the United States for more than 10 years. The issue, then, will be hardship. More specifically, to be granted cancellation of removal as a nonpermanent resident, David must provide evidence that his forced removal from the United States would result in *exceptional and extremely unusual hardship* to his QR, Rosa. To place Rosa's potential hardships in context, we need to know a little bit about her upbringing, subsequent life experiences, and ways she has coped with adversities. You learn the following.

We know that Rosa experienced two major separations before she was even old enough to drive: a separation from her parents when she was forced out of her home and a separation from her infant son when she immigrated to the United States. Rosa's way of coping with her emotional distress was to focus on work and provide for her son, with whom she maintained regular contact.

She later fell in love with William, and they married, which subsequently allowed her to travel to Mexico to see her son. Even though she dreamt of the day when she and David could live under the same roof, she respected his decision to stay in Tijuana with his aunt and his school friends. Rosa shared how despite trying for years to get pregnant, she and William were unable to conceive. "All we had was each other," Rosa tearfully recalled. This comment was particularly touching, as she went on to describe how devastated she felt when she learned William had terminal cancer. After over 20 years of marriage, William passed away. This was Rosa's third significant loss and probably the hardest one thus far. "After he was gone, I had nothing," she said. Being that he and his mother had maintained a close relationship throughout the years, David was compelled to support his mother through such a painful tragedy, and he relocated to California in 2010 to live with her. Despite David's unwavering support, Rosa's depression evolved into physical ailments. She stopped working and became fully dependent on her son for financial and emotional support. As she was beginning to emerge from her profound grief, David's arrest and the potential for his forced removal from the United States knocked Rosa back into a state of utter hopelessness and helplessness.

Rosa's numerous adversities and losses, her unresolved grief over her husband's death, her complete dependence on David since his arrival in the United States, and her crippling depression are all unique (*exceptional*) and extraordinary (*unusual*) factors that make her particularly vulnerable to a separation from David. Although still generally young, at 51 years of age Rosa's prognosis is poor. She has been struggling with depression for over a decade, has not worked in several years, and has developed physical pain that impairs her mobility. Aside from her only son, David, Rosa does not have any other family on whom she could rely for practical or emotional support.

Now that we know Rosa's "cracks," (i.e., her individual vulnerabilities), we can place them in context with the potential hardships she would experience if she were to be separated from David and the hardships she might endure if she had to return to Mexico in order to stay physically close to him.

> When contemplating the effects of a separation from her son, Rosa mentions how she fully depends on him financially. Uncertain of David's ability to find gainful employment in Mexico, she worries that she would have to rely on governmental assistance to pay her bills. She also says she would worry about David's welfare in Mexico due to the indiscriminate crime in the area where he would reside, and she breaks down in tears as she imagines being apart from the person on whom she relies for emotional, practical, and financial support. A relocation to Mexico, a country she has not lived in since her adolescence, would be equally difficult, according to Rosa, as it would entail having to leave her familiar environment, her church, and—most importantly—her medical providers.

If we were to focus only on Rosa's possible hardships—namely, her financial concerns, fear for her son's safety due to country conditions, need for continued medical care, and lack of meaningful ties with Mexico—they do not appear to rise to the level of *exceptional and extremely unusual*. When we add Rosa's individual vulnerabilities to the mix, we have a very different picture. Let's go back to that analogy from Chapter 2, where we discussed that a cracked egg will not withstand the force it otherwise would have if it had been whole. In Rosa's situation, she has some significant cracks which would predispose her to objective and plausible suffering.

The focus of this type of evaluation should not be so much about the hardships, but more so about the client's vulnerabilities.

Let's contemplate a different scenario. What if instead of presenting with crippling depression Rosa comes across as a stoic, resilient woman whose motto is "*No hay mal que por bien no venga*" (i.e., every cloud has a silver lining)? Even though that is a positive outlook to take in life, and one that promotes personal strength, we must consider the possibility that such a front conceals deep suffering. One of the most common defense mechanisms humans employ to protect their minds from serious distress is denial (i.e., unconsciously refusing to accept reality or facts because doing so would be intolerably painful). By definition, this is something outside of a person's awareness. Sensitive probing and the administration of personality assessments such as the Personality Assessment Inventory (PAI; Morey, 1991) will help the MHP determine that distinction.

It is also important to take culture into consideration. Idioms of distress, that is, those particular ways in which individuals express their suffering, vary across cultures (Hinton & Lewis-Fernandez, 2010), as do their preferred resources and strategies for coping (Wilson, 2007). Frequently, individuals will deny any emotional concerns but will openly complain about their physical ailments, a tendency that is especially common among Hispanics (Hulme, 1996). Even though it is highly unlikely that the client will attribute their physical symptoms to emotional distress, asking about their onset and the quality of the symptoms' progression can shed light into their causal factors. "You mentioned you've been suffering from gastrointestinal issues and migraines. Do you remember when you started experiencing these symptoms?" is a good probe. While they still may not make the connection to an actual event, you can determine the onset based on time frames (i.e., "Two years ago," which happens to be around the time of a major life event, for example). All this is to say that we need to look beyond the surface and rely on our own clinical judgment as opposed to solely trusting the client's self-report.

What if the client is truly that resilient and optimistic? If you cannot identify any individual liabilities that make the client more susceptible to suffering than the average person, then your only option is to center the report on their claimed potential hardships. As discussed in Chapter 2, a client's subjective concerns will not carry as much weight as objective, demonstrable, and relevant factors. But since the hardship standard is determined by considering a number of elements and not just one, the psychological report may be one small piece of evidence that the attorney will use to support their client's case. As I previously mentioned, I do my best to try to avoid such cases by helping attorneys determine which of their clients are most likely to benefit from a psychological evaluation and which probably will not.

Example #2: Claudio

Claudio, now 45 years old, came to the United States from Ecuador at age 17. He traveled through Mexico, and a smuggler brought him by boat into the United States. He and his wife, who also does not have legal status in the United States, built a prosperous landscaping company with several employees. With his earnings, he has fully supported his six children. When one of his competitors called DHS to report him, DHS came to Claudio's home and arrested him in front of his children. He was detained for four weeks before an immigration judge set bond and released him. Claudio's 12-year-old son, Luiz, struggles from severe depression and recently expressed suicidal ideations after seeing his father get arrested. Facing a strong likelihood of being deported back to Ecuador, a country he has not visited since he came to the United States almost 30 years ago, Claudio and his family are going through the most stressful experience in their lives.

Claudio calls your office to request an evaluation for his family to help fight his deportation orders. When you hear "family," you should immediately begin discerning which family members should come in to see you, as evaluating all eight of them would be not only prohibitively expensive for them, but also likely unnecessary. If the attorney making the referral is experienced in these cases and has worked with MHPs in the past, they will most likely determine who should be evaluated. As with Claudio, however, this is not always the case. For a cancellation of removal, we know that the QR can be either a USC or LPR parent, spouse, or child. Claudio's wife is also undocumented, so she clearly does not qualify. Demonstrating hardship to Claudio is of no use, as he is the FN and hardship to the FN in this case does not count. That leaves us with the children, but there are six of them. Your first questions might be,

> Are any of your children receiving mental health treatment? Do any of them have a medical condition? Academic difficulties? Has anyone been noticeably sad, angry, or wanting to isolate? Are you concerned about any one of your children in particular?

Basically, you want to narrow it down to the child or children who are most likely to meet the standard of *exceptional and extremely unusual hardship*. Claudio tells you that all of the children have been affected, as they are a very close-knit family, but he mentions that his son Luiz, his second to youngest, was recently overheard telling a classmate he "would rather die" than see his father deported. This being the most striking information you uncover among all the children, 12-year-old Luiz is therefore the one you will be evaluating.

As explained earlier in the chapter, sons and daughters under the age of 21 are considered qualifying relatives in cancellation of removal cases. The goal of evaluating a minor child is to gather enough information so that you can present your professional opinion about how a parent's deportation would affect the child. You will base that opinion on what you learned about the child's biopsychosocial history, quality of relationship with the parent, and presenting concerns. As with adults, the focus of the evaluation is to uncover the child's specific vulnerabilities that would place them at risk of psychological decompensation.

Luiz is brought in by Claudio and his wife. Since Luiz is only 12, you will want to interview the parents to obtain his developmental history: his birth, developmental milestones, health concerns, academic difficulties, behavioral problems, history of trauma, etc. You will also want to obtain the parents' account of Claudio's immigration history and what resulted in his being placed in removal proceedings. Whenever there is a traumatic incident, such as Claudio being arrested in front of the children, it is important to ask the parents about any behavioral or mood changes they noticed in the child following the trauma. For example, it is not uncommon for children to experience nightmares, insist on sleeping with the parents, regress to an earlier developmental stage, display odd or ritualistic behaviors, act out, or suffer great distress when separating from a parent or caregiver (Chaudry et al., 2010; Lovato et al., 2018). Children are also prone to developing troublesome eating habits (such as refusing food or overeating), being moody and irritable, engaging in self-harm, or to being unusually worried or easily frightened. These are all behaviors that children may not be able to share directly, as their self-awareness is more limited the younger they are. Therefore, you have to ask the parents about these behavioral changes.

Open-ended questions such as "Have you noticed anything different in your child's behavior?" are a good place to start, but they may not be specific enough to elicit sufficient information. A typical conversation might go something like this:

MHP: Have you noticed any unusual behaviors in your child lately?
PARENT: No. He's been fine.
MHP: Anything that concerned you about his emotional state?
PARENT: Not really.
MHP: How about any changes in his eating habits, or reactions to separating from mom or dad, like when going to school?
PARENT: Well, he has been refusing to go to school lately. He says his stomach hurts, or he has a headache.
MHP: Is he generally prone to stomach aches or headaches?
PARENT: Now that I think about it, he's been complaining about that more recently.
MHP: Recently?
PARENT: For the past couple of months, I guess.
MHP: When was your husband detained by DHS?
PARENT: Two months ago.

After obtaining a thorough developmental history from the parents, you can either invite the child to join you or you ask the parents to wait outside while you meet with the child alone. Much of that depends on the age of the child; older children feel more comfortable when interviewed separately. Observing the interactions between the child and the parents (and siblings, if present) can be very informative, regardless of the child's age. Sometimes you are able to do that by bringing the family into the room and asking them to engage in an activity together, and other times you might want to employ the help of your office staff to report back to you the family's behavior in the waiting room. I have trained my staff to pay attention to such nuances, so I might get the following account:

> The mother was focused on the little daughter, pulling her onto her lap and trying to distract her with her cell phone while the boy sat in a chair next to his dad. When the dad got up to get something out of the car, the boy insisted on going with him. He then showed his dad a video he pulled up on his phone and both laughed.

Naturally, you cannot generalize based on a single observation in one specific setting, but it is helpful to gather as much information as possible.

> While interviewing Claudio and his wife, you learn that Luiz has struggled with separation anxiety since he was very young. The parents attributed this to the fact that when Luiz was a toddler, an intruder broke into the home at night and was attacked by their dog. Despite moving residences and no one having been hurt, Luiz refused to sleep in his room for a long time and cried every time he had to get on the school bus. Claudio started working very early in the morning, which resulted in his being gone by the time Luiz woke up. His father's absence was upsetting for Luiz, who often threw tantrums during breakfast. His mother described him as a quiet, shy child with few friends, adding, "He looks up to his dad and wants to go to work with him when he is off from school."

Are you starting to see Luiz's cracks? The most notable are probably a history of trauma, separation anxiety, and timid personality.

Whereas when interviewing an adult you would be interested in their concerns about a potential separation from their loved one or a relocation outside the United States, asking a child to envision such scenarios may not be as fruitful. It is easier, therefore, to inquire about events in the past and how they impacted the child.

> When you ask Luiz to share with you what it was like for him when his father was arrested by DHS, his eyes immediately fill with tears, and he lowers his gaze. "I don't like to talk about it," he says. It is pretty evident that this is something very painful for him.

You would definitely want to inquire about Luiz's alleged suicidal ideation, which could warrant a referral to a therapist if he is not already being helped by a counselor at his school. If he is receiving some form of mental health treatment, you might want to obtain a release from the parents so you can contact the counselor or therapist, corroborate the facts, and ask about her clinical observations, goals for treatment, and prognosis. You would include all that information in the report.

Evaluating children entails numerous variables to consider, and it is particularly complex because working with a 4-year-old is very different from working with a 12-year-old or with a 17-year-old. The way children manifest their emotional distress spans a wide gamut across developmental stages. Consequently, assessment modalities will differ depending on the child's age and maturity level. For the sake of brevity and simplicity, we will not be delving into such intricacies in this book. If child assessment is beyond your scope of expertise, we encourage you to seek training prior to taking on such a case.

In addition to the interviews, it is helpful to administer some objective and projective tests to further assess the child's personality, attachment style, psychological symptoms, and any other prominent features relevant to the referral question. These will vary depending on the child's age. For example, kinetic drawings are useful with younger children, as they shed light on their inner world. Wimmer's (2014) book, *The Complete Guide to Children's Drawings* is a wonderful resource for understanding and interpreting children's artistic expressions. The Child Attachment Interview (CAI; Shmueli-Goetz et al., 2008) is an excellent semi-structured interview that assesses children's internal working models of attachment and relationships with primary caregivers. Children aged 7–12 are asked open-ended questions to describe their current attachment relationships and explore their self-concept, interpersonal conflicts, distress, illness, hurt, separation, and loss.

With older children, both the adolescent and pre-adolescent versions of the Millon Inventories (Millon & Davis, 1993) are extremely helpful. The Pediatric Symptom Checklist-35 (Jellinek et al., 1988) is a questionnaire parents complete that detects psychological and behavioral problems in children. Other symptom screeners for children include the Children's Depression Inventory (Kovacs, 1978) and the Hopelessness Scale for Children (Kazdin et al., 1986), among others.

As with other cases that involve the showing of hardship, it is important to mention the difficulties the child is likely to encounter if they have to relocate to their parent's country of citizenship. One could argue that children are resilient and malleable and that they would naturally adjust quickly to a major change such as a relocation to a foreign country, but that is not always true. In most cases, the children have never even visited that country. If they happen to understand the language spoken there, they are frequently not fluent enough to be able to attend school. This would not only hinder their education but it could also compromise their socialization with peers. If the child already has a learning disability or is benefitting from an individualized education program (IEP), their prognosis is not good.

Furthermore, tweens and teenagers are particularly vulnerable to a forced separation from their peers. As children approach this developmental stage, they tend to look to their friends as they consolidate their identity (Meersand & Gilmore, 2013). Consequently, tearing them away from their social group can have devastating consequences. It is important to ask about their peer group, any extracurricular activities they are engaged in, and their involvement in organized sports in and outside of school. Much like with adults, the more ties children have to the United States, the more difficult emigrating to another country is likely to be.

People are becoming increasingly more aware of the suffering mixed status families experience when faced with a loved one's impending removal from the United States. Numerous studies have shown that a parent's immigration status and potential for deportation affects children's emotional well-being in significant ways (Brabeck & Qingwen, 2010; Cavazos-Rehg et al., 2007; Chaudry et al., 2010; Lovato et al., 2018). The pervasive fear of being found out keeps most undocumented individuals from talking about their experiences, and their children, unbeknownst to the parents, often bear the heavy load of the family secret.

> Just like assessing hardship in adults, your focus when evaluating a minor child should be on the child's individual vulnerabilities that would qualify their suffering as **beyond what is typically expected in a similar situation**.

Assessing Hardship to Self (Special Rule or VAWA Cancellation of Removal)

As we discussed earlier in the chapter, special rule or VAWA cancellation of removal applies in situations where an FN is the victim of abuse perpetrated by a USC or LPR spouse or parent. In addition to providing proof of the abuse or extreme cruelty (which we will explore in Chapter 5), the FN must show hardship to a USC or LPR child or parent (the QR) or to themselves. Discussed below are two hypothetical cases where the FN does not have any QRs to show hardship and, therefore, must show how they themselves would suffer *extreme hardship* if not allowed to remain in the United States. In these situations, we would be looking for the FN's vulnerabilities in relation to a forced return to their country of origin. In many cases, these individuals have made drastic changes in their lives in order to relocate from their homeland to the United States to live with their USC or LPR spouse.

Example #1: Natalia

Natalia, a citizen of Moldova, came to the United States after meeting Jerry through an online dating website. She came as a visitor on two separate trips. Jerry also flew out to Moldova and met her parents. On her third trip to the United States as a visitor, they eloped. For the next four years, Jerry promised he would "fix her papers" but instead used Natalia's status to manipulate her into doing things for him she did not want to do. As she began to resist him, he became violent. The police were called multiple times by neighbors, and Jerry was arrested twice for domestic violence. The third time the police came to the house, Natalia had a bloody nose and fat lip, but Jerry also had blood pouring from scratch marks to his face and neck. The police arrested them both, and DHS placed Natalia in removal proceedings for overstaying her tourist visa. Natalia's attorney, who is handling her criminal case and immigration case, has reached out for an evaluation.

Natalia shares with you that leaving her family and home country to marry Jerry was not easy. Natalia, the only daughter among six children born to her parents, described herself as her father's "jewel." She recalled how over-protective her parents always were, not just controlling whom she spent time with but insisting that one of her brothers act as a chaperone any time she left the house.

When she met Jerry online, she kept it a secret for several months before confiding in her mother, who immediately advised her to end the relationship because her father would never approve of her marrying an American citizen. Nonetheless, Natalia was smitten. She convinced her parents to let her come to the United States for an international conference on biotech trends, her field of study, and that is when she finally met Jerry in person. She was able to visit him one other time under the premise of a potential job opportunity, and upon her return she confronted her parents and told them she had met Jerry and wanted to marry him. Despite Jerry flying to Moldova to meet Natalia's parents, her father never approved their union. Natalia, at 25 years of age, decided to follow her heart and start a new life with Jerry in Indiana. Despite maintaining regular contact with her family back home, her relationship with her father was damaged beyond repair. Fast forward to the present circumstances: Natalia is separated from Jerry and is struggling to rebuild her life with the solid support of two dear friends she met at church in Indiana. She has been offered a job at a small pharmaceutical company as soon as she can get authorization to work in this country. She has told her parents neither about the abuse she endured at the hands of her estranged husband, nor that she was filing for divorce. She is convinced beyond a doubt that she will not be allowed back in her family home and that her parents will shun her if she returns home after the failed marriage. In addition, she is now 30 years old, which, according to her, would make finding gainful employment in Moldova exceptionally difficult.

Are you able to see the cracks in Natalia's shell? On top of everything else, you learn that her mother has a history of bipolar disorder. Being well aware of the interaction between genetic predisposition and environmental influences, you anticipate the likelihood that Natalia will herself succumb to a mood disorder if under significant environmental stress. These are the unique circumstances, life experiences, and personality characteristics you will want to focus on when evaluating someone involved in this type of immigration proceeding.

Example #2: Marcos

> Marcos is a 27-year-old El Salvadoran who came to the United States at age 22. A smuggler brought him through a tunnel. After entering the United States, he has not departed. He met his wife, Sarah, a US citizen, four years ago, and they married two years later. Sarah suffers from various conditions, including bipolar disorder. She abuses drugs and has repeatedly been unfaithful and occasionally violent. He has pursued counseling separately and as a couple. He also tried a family intervention to help Sarah with her drug addiction, Sarah only got angry, destroyed his immigration records, took all the money out of their joint bank account, and fled with her drug dealer, but not without first calling DHS to "anonymously report" Marcos's presence in the United States. DHS arrested Marcos and placed him in removal proceedings. He is unrepresented (pro se) and has called to ask for "a letter" to help his immigration case.

Marcos's case is similar to Natalia's in terms of the legal context but very different when it comes to his potential hardships and what the focus of the evaluation should be.

> One year after his father's sudden death, Marcos decided to move to the United States in search of profitable employment with which to support his mother and two younger sisters back home in El Salvador. When his relationship with his wife deteriorated beyond repair, Marcos promised himself that he would do anything in his power to remain in the United States. "I don't care what I have to do or what happens to me, but I just know for a fact that I cannot return to El Salvador empty handed," he said. Despite his painful experiences, Marcos carries himself with a questionable air of buoyancy. You initially chalk that up to cultural factors, believing the notion that Latino men are indoctrinated to be tough, masculine, and resilient (which they often are not, by the way [Falicov, 2010]). As you delve into Marcos's historical background, you learn that he was raised in a loving home environment that placed great value on *familismo* (a strong sense of dedication, commitment, and loyalty with nuclear and extended family common in Latino cultures). Marcos's determination permeates through all aspects of his life, and this was evident in his numerous attempts to improve his relationship with his estranged wife and get her to accept the help she needed. In exploring his views on life and family values, Marcos tears up and shares with you that his father's last wish was for Marcos to "stay strong and

look after mom and the girls." You also learn that Marcos has been volunteering at a food bank and that he helps his elderly neighbors with their weekly grocery shopping. Marcos loves to help others, but being on the receiving end is not a familiar position for him. Thus, the reason he did not retain an attorney. "What would happen if you're not allowed to stay in the United States?," you ask. Marcos stares at you like a deer in the headlights. "That is not an option," he shoots back. As Marcos starts to explain all the reasons why he cannot, will not, and would not return to El Salvador, you notice a drastic change in his affect. He gets anxious, his speech gets louder and pressured, and he starts to fidget in his seat.

Marcos does not seem to meet criteria for a psychiatric diagnosis. Nonetheless, we now know quite a bit about his personality characteristics, his strengths, and his weaknesses, and that is precisely what you want to focus on throughout the interview. It would be a shame if the interview only centered on his relationship with his estranged wife because you would likely miss all the other information that allowed you to form a more holistic impression of Marcos. In the majority of cases, a client's upbringing and their personality shed light into their choices for romantic partners and how they ended up being the victim of cruelty. A focus on the hardships he would experience if he were forced to return to his country of citizenship is, of course, important to explore and discuss in the report.

Assessing Remorse and Rehabilitation (Cancellation of Removal for LPR)

FNs who have been granted LPR status in the United States and are later placed in removal proceedings due to unlawful conduct can also fight deportation orders by proving hardship to themselves or their family. However, the primary issues the IC will consider relate to evidence of *remorse and rehabilitation*. Let's take two examples.

Example #1: Pablo

Pablo, a citizen of Chile and permanent resident for eight years, recently got arrested for possession of a small amount of cocaine for personal use. Police discovered the cocaine during a routine traffic stop when the bag fell out of his glove box while grabbing his car registration for the officer. The police turned Pablo over to DHS, who placed him in removal proceedings. His USC girlfriend, a single mother with three young kids, has reached out to you asking you to help her boyfriend because the couple plans to marry if he does not get removed.

In cases such as this, where an FN who has been residing lawfully in the United States for several years is now involved in removal proceedings for having been charged with minor offenses, the referral question might be to show evidence of rehabilitation, hardship to the respondent if removed, or hardship to their USC or LPR immediate relatives. One approach you can take, if you have the adequate training and experience to do so, is to focus on the rehabilitation. (And sometimes that is indeed the angle from which the referring attorney would like you to assess their client.) To do that, you will want to not only explore their unlawful behaviors but more so their personality characteristics, what drove them to engage in such behaviors, and how likely they are to engage in that behavior in the future.

Pablo, who is 26 years old, is in a relationship with Amanda, a 36-year-old single mother of three whose parents are also from Chile. Pablo met Amanda through friends, and they began dating right away. Even though their 10-year difference did not deter them from becoming romantically involved, it became more noticeable as soon as Pablo moved in with Amanda and her daughters. Pablo tells you that he was a junior in college when he and Amanda met and that despite feeling comfortable with Amanda being a mother of three young children, the situation felt weightier when they started living together and he took on the role of "man of the house." Whereas he had been used to going out with his friends to the bars on the nights that he was not with Amanda, such instances grew less and less frequent as their relationship got more serious and he became a father figure to the girls. After almost nine months living under the same roof, Pablo had a "young life crisis." He felt torn between being a young college guy and a family man with three young girls to help raise. This resulted in tension between the couple, and Pablo decided to take a weekend off and go to Las Vegas with his friends. He and his friends rented a car, and since Pablo was the driver, he was the one charged with possession of a controlled substance when the officer pulled them over for speeding and found a small bag of cocaine in the glove compartment. According to Pablo, he had only experimented with cocaine once before in his life and was not—by any stretch of the imagination—a regular user, nor did he abuse any other substances. This incident and the ensuing consequences made Pablo realize that he truly loves Amanda and wants nothing more than to marry her and be the father figure her young daughters need. Even though returning to Chile would be "rough," according to Pablo, both his and Amanda's parents live in Chile and they have traveled to Chile together to meet each other's families. Pablo shares that he and Amanda have even discussed the possibility of moving back to Chile together once her daughters are old enough to live on their own. Given that there does not seem to be much there to substantiate hardship if he were not allowed to remain in the United States, the focus of your evaluation should center on evaluating his *rehabilitation*, which in Pablo's case is showing that he never had a problem with substance use in the first place.

Even though it seems pretty clear that Pablo does not meet the criteria for a substance use disorder, it would still be useful to have him complete some objective measures to rule out such a diagnosis. The Substance Abuse Subtle Screening Inventories (SASSI) (Lazowski & Geary, 2019) is a good choice, as it measures both overt and subtle behaviors and symptoms. The MMPI (either 2-RF or 3) (Tellegen & Ben-Porath, 2011) or the PAI (Morey, 1991) can shed light into some other personality characteristics that might help you understand the client's involvement with substances.

Example #2: Achara

> Achara, a citizen of Thailand and permanent resident of the United States since 2005, got hooked on painkillers after a car accident where she, her husband, and two children were hit by a drunk driver and she and her son both had to have surgery for multiple broken bones. Her addiction led her to repeated shoplifting to pay for drugs. After her sixth conviction for misdemeanor shoplifting, DHS placed her in removal proceedings. She was detained by ICE for nine months and was just recently released from custody. Achara is in therapy and seems to be benefiting from the treatment. She is also committed to maintaining sobriety, as she has acknowledged how her addiction has affected her loved ones. Her family is supportive and understanding and, despite having endured a series of challenges due to Achara's addiction, are committed to standing by her and maintaining the family unit. Her son in particular has suffered significantly from his mother's erratic behaviors.

In Achara's case, you could approach the evaluation from three angles: assessing hardship to Achara, hardship to her immediate family members, or her own remorse and rehabilitation. Ultimately, however, the focus of the assessment is the attorney's decision.

If you were to evaluate hardship to self, an important area of focus would be Achara's mental health status, current treatment, and prognosis, particularly if removal from the United States would force her to discontinue her treatment. There is no need to research the availability of mental health in Thailand, as that is not within your scope of practice, but you should discuss the potential hardships to Achara if she were not able to continue her therapy.

Assessing hardship to her husband or children is another option. Since the son was also severely injured in the accident and appears to have struggled the most as a result of Achara's conduct, he might be the one to evaluate. The focus would be on his mental health status, his physical well-being, and how a separation from his mother or having to relocate to Thailand would affect him.

Lastly, focusing on Achara's remorse and rehabilitation is another adequate approach. You would explore her substance use history, her efforts towards rehabilitation, and her propensity for relapse. Collateral information from her treating therapist and evidence of completion of substance abuse programs are key.

As I hope the above examples make clear, knowing the statutory requirements for the different forms of relief from deportation is extremely important, as it would inform your evaluation process and ultimately guide what you include on the written report.

The Report

Writing up the assessment results for a cancellation of removal case is very similar to any other hardship evaluation. However, unlike reports provided to USCIS, these reports will go to an IC, where it will be scrutinized by the IJ and potentially challenged by the DHS prosecutor assigned to the case. Always try to substantiate your opinions with objective evidence, such as test results, records reviewed, and any collateral information you were able to access.

As with other reports, you will want to detail the client's biopsychosocial history, what resulted in their being placed in removal proceedings, and any information relevant to the referral question. Some attorneys might contact you ahead of time and tell you what they specifically want the report to address. For example, the attorney for Pablo might be well aware that the hardships of losing his green card are not beyond what the average person would experience and instead instruct you to focus on his involvement with substances and assess his rehabilitation. More often, though, an attorney gives you no other instruction than, "It's for a cancellation of removal," and leaves the rest to you. As you are conducting the interview you will identify the areas that call for detailed consideration and select what information is relevant to include in the written report. Refer to the Appendices for a sample of this type of report.

Bibliography

Brabeck, K., & Qingwen, X. (2010). The impact of detention and deportation on Latino immigrant children and families: A quantitative exploration. *Hispanic Journal of Behavioral Sciences, 32*(3), 341–361. https://doi.org/10.1177/0739986310374053

Cavazos-Rehg, P. A., Zayas, L. H., & Spitznagel, E. L. (2007). Legal status, emotional well-being and subjective health status of Latino immigrants. *Journal of the National Medical Association, 99*(10), 1126–1131.

Chaudry, A., Capps, R., Pedroza, J., Castaneda, R. M., Santos, R., & Scott, M. M. (2010). Facing our future: Children in the aftermath of immigration enforcement. *Facing our Future: Children in the Aftermath of Immigration Enforcement, 96.*

Falicov, C. J. (2010). Changing constructions of machismo for Latino men in therapy: "The devil never sleeps." *Family Process, 49*(3), 309–329. https://doi.org/10.1111/j.1545-5300.2010.01325.x

Hinton, D. E., & Lewis-Fernández, R. (2010). Idioms of distress among trauma survivors: Subtypes and clinical utility. *Culture, Medicine, and Psychiatry, 34*(2), 209–218. https://doi.org/10.1007/s11013-010-9175-x

Hulme, P.A. (1996). Somatization in Hispanics. *Journal of Psychosocial Nursing and Mental Health Services, 34*(3), 33–37. https://doi.org/10.3928/0279-3695-19960301-17

Jellinek, M. S., Murphy, J. M., Robinson, J., Feins, A., Lamb, S., & Fenton, T. (1988). Pediatric symptom checklist: Screening school-age children for psychosocial dysfunction. *The Journal of Pediatrics, 112*(2), 201–209. https://doi.org/10.1016/s0022-3476(88)80056-8

Kazdin, A. E., Rodgers, A., & Colbus, D. (1986). The hopelessness scale for children: Psychometric characteristics and concurrent validity. *Journal of Consulting and Clinical Psychology, 54*(2), 241–245.

Kovacs, M. (1978). *Children's depression inventory.* PsycTESTS.

Lazowski, L. E., & Geary, B. B. (2019). Validation of the adult substance abuse subtle screening inventory-4 (SASSI-4). *European Journal of Psychological Assessment, 35*(1), 86–97.

Lovato, K., Lopez, C., Karimli, L., & Abrams, L. S. (2018). The impact of deportation-related family separations on the well-being of Latinx children and youth: A review of the literature. *Children and Youth Services Review, 95*, 109–116. https://doi.org/10.1016/j.childyouth.2018.10.011

Meersand, P., & Gilmore, K. J. (2013). *Normal child and adolescent development: A psychodynamic primer.* American Psychiatric Publishing.

Millon, T., & Davis, R. D. (1993). The Millon adolescent personality inventory and the Millon adolescent clinical inventory. *Journal of Counseling and Development, 71*(5), 570–574.

Morey, L. C. (1991). *Personality assessment inventory.* PsycTESTS.

Shmueli-Goetz, Y., Target, M., Fonagy, P., & Datta, A. (2008). *Child attachment interview.* PsycTESTS.

Tellegen, A., & Ben-Porath, Y. S. (2011). *Minnesota multiphasic personality inventory–2 restructured form (MMPI-2-RF): Technical manual.* Pearson.

Wilson, J.P. (2007). The lens of culture: Theoretical and conceptual perspectives in the assessment of psychological trauma and PTSD. In Wilson J.P., & Tang C.S. (Eds.), *Cross-cultural assessment of psychological trauma and PTSD.* International and Cultural Psychology Series. Springer.

Wimmer, M. (2014). *The complete guide to children's drawings: Accessing children's emotional world through their artwork.* Ibidem Press.

4 Evaluating Factors Concerning Protection-Related Relief

Asylum/Withholding of Removal/ Convention Against Torture (CAT)

Mariela G. Shibley, Psy.D. and Matthew G. Holt, Esq.

Millions of people all over the world are forced to flee their homes, communities, jobs, and schools in search of a safer life. According to the United Nations High Commissioner for Refugees (2018), in 2018 there were 20.4 million refugees globally. Eligibility for refugee or asylum status in the United States requires the principal applicant meet the definition of a refugee set forth in INA § 101(a)(42), which states, in part:

> A refugee is a person who is unable or unwilling to return to their country of nationality because of persecution or a well-founded fear of persecution on account of race, religion, nationality, membership in a particular social group, or political opinion.

Those applying for refugee status do so overseas and often wait years in camps and elsewhere while their applications are pending. Upon approval of their application, they enter the United States as refugees and can apply for permanent residency one year later. The US government sets a "ceiling," or limit, on refugee admission each year,[1] and such ceilings vary by country of origin.

In contrast, foreign nationals (FNs) seeking asylum apply from within the United States or when they arrive at a US port of entry or other locations along the international border. They are then taken into custody by the US Department of Homeland Security (DHS). Applicants may have to wait months in civil detention for a hearing at an immigration court (IC) before an immigration judge (IJ) or even years for an interview with a USCIS asylum officer or hearing with an IJ outside a detention facility. Asylees are recorded by their country of origin, and the success rates per country vary widely.[2]

DOI: 10.4324/9781003139973-5

Eligibility for asylum requires the foreign national to show they <u>have suffered past persecution</u> in the country where they were born or had residency or that they <u>fear future persecution</u> if returned to that country. An asylum seeker may apply for asylum from more than one country if the person has a legal right to live in but suffered, or fears they will suffer, persecution in multiple countries. Such persecution must be:

- Perpetrated by the government or individuals that the government is unwilling or unable to control.
- On account of the person's race, religion, nationality, membership in a particular social group, or political opinion.

Given that the refugee process occurs overseas, the focus of this chapter will be on issues relating to asylees and asylum applicants. Applicants for asylum can apply either "affirmatively" with USCIS or "defensively" in proceedings before an IJ in IC.

Affirmative Asylum

A person can *affirmatively* apply for asylum if they are already in the United States but not in removal proceedings in the IC. Affirmative filing is common for people who enter the United States as tourists or students and determine they will not be safe returning to their country because of their sexual orientation, their political involvement or imputed political opinion, or their conversion to a religion that could place them at risk in their country of origin. It is also common for applicants who entered the United States without permission and wish to remain.

The applicant must complete *Form I-589, Application for Asylum and Withholding of Removal* and send it to the proper USCIS office within one year of entering the United States, supporting the application with corroborative evidence provided at the time the application is filed or at any time up to and during the asylum interview. After USCIS receives the *Form I-589*, the applicant will be placed in a queue to await the interview. During that time, USCIS will fingerprint the applicant, who may request employment authorization and permission for international travel under advance parole. This process is handled administratively and privately, outside of the court system.

If the applicant failed to submit their asylum application within one year of entering the United States, they must prove that they were unable to do so because of *exceptional or extraordinary circumstances. Exceptional circumstances* may include changed conditions in the applicant's home country, applicable changes in US law, or recent changes in the applicant's personal contexts such as political activism, conversion to a new religion, coming out as homosexual, etc. *Extraordinary circumstances* may include the applicant's health (physical or mental), death or serious illness in the family, delays related to abuse or crime, or incompetent legal representation, among others.

If an asylum seeker is not successful in the affirmative setting, they will be referred to the IC, where they can attempt to clarify any inconsistencies, present additional corroborative evidence and witness testimony, and testify in an adversarial setting. This now becomes a "defensive asylum" application.

Defensive Asylum

An FN can file an asylum application with the IC and have a trial before an IJ if and when the US government places the FN in removal proceedings. This is called a "defensive" application, as it is employed as a defense to being removed (i.e., deported). Typically, a defensive asylum application is filed by someone whom DHS discovers is staying unlawfully in the United States and puts in removal proceedings, or someone who comes to the US border and requests asylum and is placed in proceedings following a *credible fear* or *reasonable fear* interview with an asylum officer.

DHS provides a *credible fear interview* to any FN who has not been previously removed, is detained within 14 days or 100 miles of the international border, and claims a fear of return to their country of citizenship. For an FN to pass the interview, pursuant to INA § 208, DHS must find the FN has a "reasonable likelihood" (i.e., a 10% chance) of persecution or torture if removed.[3] If so, the FN is referred to an IJ to file their asylum application and seek any other relief for which they are eligible. If the FN fails the interview, they are either removed or may request review by an IJ. If an IJ then upholds DHS's finding that the FN has failed their credible fear interview, there is no appeal, even in cases where such failure was due to a misunderstanding, poor interpretation, or inadvertently neglecting to share pertinent information. Sometimes the failure to share or recall information is related to the psychological impact of trauma, which will be addressed later in the chapter.

If the FN has been previously ordered removed and caught by DHS officers within the United States, the FN is subject to reinstatement of the prior removal order. Basically, DHS can deport the FN without them seeing an IJ, seeking relief, or even saying good-bye to their loved ones. However, if that same FN claims fear of return, DHS must afford them a *reasonable fear interview*. Like in a *credible fear interview*, a *reasonable fear interview* is pass/fail. To pass, however, the FN must convince DHS of a stricter standard: that there is a "clear probability" (i.e., a 51% chance) that the applicant will be persecuted or tortured if removed.[4] If the FN passes this more difficult standard, they are able to pursue "withholding of removal" or protection under article III of the Convention Against Torture. If DHS finds the FN did not meet their burden in the *reasonable fear interview*, the FN may seek review of the decision before an IJ. Given the stricter standard, successfully overcoming DHS's denial of reasonable fear in front of an IJ is extremely challenging.

The Asylum Application

The applicant has the burden to support their asylum application by providing testimony and reasonably available corroborative evidence. As a trier of fact, the IJ makes the threshold determination on credibility, pursuant to INA § 208, by considering the totality of the circumstances and all relevant factors, such as the demeanor, candor, or responsiveness of the applicant or other witnesses, the inherent plausibility of the sworn account, the consistency between the applicant's or witness's written and oral statements, the internal consistency of each such statement, the consistency of such statements with other evidence of record (including the reports of the Department of State on country conditions), and any inaccuracies or falsehoods in their statements.

INA § 208 specifically requires the trier of fact, whether the USCIS asylum officer or IJ, to weigh the testimony and evidence. If successful, asylum applicants are permitted to remain in the United States and are entitled to certain resettlement aid, employment authorization, and social security benefits. They are also allowed to travel internationally.[5] Moreover, their family members who are in the United States and were included in the original asylum application are granted relief and may petition to bring their eligible family members to the United States. Those granted asylum relief may go on to apply for lawful permanent residence and citizenship.

Related Forms of Protection for the Persecuted

Many people who fear returning to their home country will not qualify for asylum for a variety of reasons. If they do not have a qualified excuse for untimely filing for asylum, for example, their asylum application will be denied. Likewise, having been convicted of or admitted to committing certain crimes will preclude them from receiving asylum. There are, however, alternative types of relief the applicant may pursue that, unlike asylum, are not discretionary. In other words, if the FN qualifies for one of the next two forms of relief, the US government must provide the relief.

Withholding of Removal

Some applicants who fear persecution but for some reason do not qualify for asylum may instead be eligible for withholding of removal under INA § 241(b)(3). Unlike having to prove a 10% chance of persecution to be granted asylum, an applicant for withholding of removal must prove they will "more likely than not" (i.e., a 51% chance) suffer persecution if removed. Also unlike asylum, which can be granted either administratively or by an IJ, withholding of removal can be granted only after presenting the application to an IJ. An applicant who is granted withholding of removal is protected from being returned to his or her home country and receives the right to remain in the United States and work legally. In an odd display of procedural acrobatics (odd to those of us who are not lawyers or judges, that is), an IJ does in fact enter a removal order but then tells the government they cannot execute that order. In other words, the "removal" to a person's home country is "withheld." However, the government may still deport that person to a different country if that country agrees to accept them.

A recipient of withholding of removal can apply for work authorization, but they cannot seek permanent residence or citizenship and cannot petition to bring family members to the United States. Nevertheless, for someone fearing persecution or even death, withholding of removal is a welcome remedy. Should the person ever leave the United States, they are considered to have abandoned their application for withholding of removal, and the removal order is executed (or, no longer withheld). The government can also revoke withholding of removal if conditions improve in the person's home country, even years after they are granted protection.

Protection under Article III of the Convention Against Torture

Individuals who are not eligible for asylum or withholding of removal because they were convicted of "particularly serious crimes" or who fear torture by their government can qualify for another type of relief under Article III of the Convention Against Torture (CAT) known as "deferral of removal," a protection that is harder to win than withholding of removal and that offers even fewer benefits. Under this treaty provision, the United States agrees not to "expel, return, or extradite" FNs to another country where they would be tortured.

Relief under CAT requires an applicant to establish it is *more likely than not* they would be tortured if removed to a specific country. Title 8 of the Code of Federal Regulations (CFR) (Aliens and Nationality, 1999) defines torture, which is essentially the intentional infliction of "severe pain or suffering, whether physical or mental," by a government official for the purpose of punishment, intimidation, or obtaining a confession. Although torture can be similar to persecution, and the two often overlap, they are distinct. Also, torture need not be associated with one of the five protected grounds required by asylum and withholding (race, religion, nationality, membership in a particular social group, or political opinion). Whereas the grant of asylum is discretionary, meaning that an adjudicator weighs rehabilitation and remorse in determining whether to grant asylum, the granting of protection under CAT is not discretionary, so rehabilitation and remorse are not considered. However, whether an applicant poses a danger to society if released from detention is considered (and yet, almost paradoxically, CAT relief may be granted to criminals, terrorists, and persecutors, as they cannot be returned to a country where they would face torture).

A CAT recipient may be detained indefinitely and may be removed to a third country where they would not be tortured. If allowed to remain in the United States, CAT recipients are eligible to apply for work authorization, but they cannot seek residency status or petition any family members to the United States.

The Mental Health Provider's Role in Asylum Cases

When one speaks of asylum, the MHP's first thought might be to evaluate trauma. The role of the MHP in asylum cases, however, can be much more than that. As we discussed, the applicant must prove that their fear of persecution is reasonable, and based on the applicant's testimony and corroborative evidence, the courts and immigration officers will analyze the asylum claim and determine whether the applicant is credible. A report written by an MHP can be a valuable addition to the applicant's evidence to substantiate their claim of fear. MHPs are also often requested to assess credibility or, in certain cases where the applicant did not file for asylum in a timely fashion, mental health status. Lastly, if the applicant has a criminal history, an evaluation by an MHP can help the applicant demonstrate that they do not pose a danger to society.

The Evaluation

As with any other immigration evaluation, the referral question will determine how you conduct the assessment. Most asylum applicants seeking your services will likely have an immigration attorney, and it is the attorney who recommends that the applicant undergo a psychological evaluation, so it is with the attorney that you must clarify the reason for the referral. Will you be evaluating how the trauma the applicant experienced impacted their mental health status, or are you being asked to assess their credibility? Is the evaluation meant to help explain the applicant's failure to apply for asylum in a timely manner? Do they want an MHP to determine whether the applicant poses a threat to society based on prior criminal conduct? Or something else? You can see how, depending on the reason for referral, the evaluation can go in very different directions.

Assessing the Psychological Impact of Torture or Persecution

Unlike U visa cases (discussed in Chapter 6), these protection-related forms of immigration relief do not require the applicant to demonstrate the physical or psychological harm they suffered as a result of the torture or persecution but, rather, the fact that they were victim of such conduct. Naturally, any victim of such cruel treatment will suffer some degree of harm, but in general, the goal of evaluating a victim of torture or persecution is to assess the degree of consistency between the individual's account of the crime and the psychological findings observed during the evaluation.

The UN Office of the High Commissioner for Human Rights (OHCHR, 2004) published the Manual on the Effective Investigation and Documentation of Torture and Other Cruel, Inhuman or Degrading Treatment or Punishment (commonly known as the "Istanbul Protocol"). This manual, which is considered the gold standard in assessing and documenting the impact of torture (Saadi et al., 2021), is a wonderful resource and a must-read for those interested and unfamiliar with these assessments.

In addition to a detailed account of the torture or persecution the client faced, obtaining a thorough personal history that includes any other traumatic experiences in the client's lifetime—both prior to and following the alleged crimes—is important. Being able to discern the causes of psychological distress is key, both in the report and if called to testify as a witness in IC. For example, an adjudicator might question an applicant's fear of returning to their native country if they learn that the applicant, prior to being brutally attacked for being transgender, was a victim of burglary and witnessed their mother being pistol-whipped. Especially when documenting the results of a trauma measure such as the Trauma Symptom Inventory (TSI-2; Briere, 2010) or the Clinician Administered PTSD Scale for DSM-5 (CAPS-5; Weathers et al., 2018), you need to clarify what the "specific traumatic event" was that the client's responses refer to.

As we will discuss further in Chapter 9, being aware of culture-specific syndromes and idioms of distress through which symptoms are communicated is of utmost importance for conducting the interview and formulating clinical impressions and conclusions. Likewise, the language spoken by the client during the evaluation must be considered, as the content of their testimony and their affective expressions can vary depending on whether they retell their story in their native or second, less proficient, language (Aragno & Schlachet, 1996; Bloom & Beckwith, 1989; Bond & Lai, 1986; Buxbaum, 1949; Marcos, 1976; Rozensky & Gomez, 1983; Waisman, 2005).

In addition to a semi-structured interview that covers the client's biopsychosocial history and the event or events that prompted them to flee their country of origin, a thorough assessment of posttraumatic symptomatology via objective instruments is vital. In many cases, a great deal of time has passed since the client endured the traumatic experiences, so their current presentation may not be an accurate representation of the degree of harm they suffered, and you need to explain that. Even if they are unlikely to generate elevated scores for posttraumatic stress disorder (PTSD) on the Posttraumatic Symptom Checklist (PCL-5; Blevins et al., 2015) or the Clinician Administered PTSD Scale for DSM-5 (CAPS-5; Weathers et al., 2018), the Trauma Symptom Inventory (TSI-2; Briere, 2010) is a valuable instrument because it assesses not just current symptoms but also coping strategies and long-term sequelae from trauma and has been found particularly useful in evaluations for IC (Filone & DeMatteo, 2017).

Assessing Credibility

Looking at what an IJ considers when determining an applicant's credibility, there are a number of factors that can put the applicant's trustworthiness into question. The MHP's role is to help the adjudicator understand why there are inconsistencies in their testimony, why the applicant has trouble remembering certain details from the past, or why the applicant's demeanor is inconsistent with what would be expected from a victim of trauma or torture. The following is a common example of how the psychological impact of trauma may affect the credibility finding:

> Irina, a citizen and native of Moldova, came out to her parents as a lesbian when she was 13 years old. Her father refused to accept her and repeatedly beat her. Throughout her life and into adulthood, she tried to keep her sexual orientation to herself for fear of how she would be treated. However, some male coworkers at the factory where she worked learned her secret and, because of that, sexually abused her on multiple occasions. During the abuse, she blacked out multiple times. The coworkers threatened to make her sexual orientation public if she reported them. Even if she were to report them, she knew the authorities would not get involved and might even find her culpable. Irina fled to the United States at age 23 to request asylum. Her attorney has requested she be evaluated because Irina has trouble recalling chronology and details of the abuse she endured.

In Irina's case, her credibility is questionable because she cannot remember certain details of the sexual trauma she experienced in Moldova. Her current mental health status is not as important in this case as what is interfering with her ability to recall specific aspects of her traumatic experiences and to maintain consistency in her testimony. In this case (which we will return to in a moment), as well as with all other asylum cases, it is helpful to have access to as many records as possible, such as the applicant's written declaration, the completed *Form I-589*, police reports or news articles pertaining to the traumatic incident in question, and any other medical or psychiatric records available to you. In some cases, you might have access to a transcript of the applicant's *credible fear* or *reasonable fear* interview, which would be especially valuable when exploring credibility issues.

Go through the records before meeting with the client so that you can identify any inconsistencies or omissions, and address them during the interview. Some factors that might help explain such discrepancies are language barriers (e.g., when a *credible fear* or *reasonable fear* interview was conducted with the assistance of an interpreter some details can get lost in translation, or if the interviewer spoke the applicant's language, but not fluently, leading to miscommunication), the mental state of the client at the time of the USCIS interview or court hearing (e.g., some asylum seekers are kept in uncomfortable detention facilities where sleep is disrupted and they are not adequately fed, which can significantly impair their cognitive functioning), or cognitive impairments such as faulty memory.

To evaluate the client's cognitive functioning, adequate testing is necessary. If you have not had formal training and experience administering certain tests, you might want to employ the help of someone who does or to refer the client to a different provider. Because most asylum cases are handled in IC, there is a high probability that you will have to testify. Therefore, you will have to demonstrate that you have the required training and experience to administer and interpret these measures. The Weschler Adult Intelligence Scale or the Weschler Abbreviated Scale of Intelligence (WAIS-IV, WASI-II; Drozdick et al., 2012), the Kaufman Brief Intelligence Test (KBIT 2; Kaufman et al., 2004), and the Woodcock–Johnson (Canivez & Madle, 2017) are well-researched measures of cognitive abilities. Tests such as the Delis–Kaplan Executive Function System (D-KEFs; Delis et al., 2001), the Behavior Rating Inventory of Executive Function—Adult (BRIEF-A; Dean & Green, 2007), and the classic Wisconsin Card Sorting Test (Grant & Berg, 1948) are great for assessing executive functioning. Cognitive functioning can also be assessed via the Trail Making Test (Armitage, 1946), the Rey Complex Figure Test (Meyers & Meyers, 1995), the Montreal Cognitive Assessment (MoCA; Nasreddine et al., 2005), which is available in several languages, or the Test of Non-Verbal Intelligence (TONI; Evans-McCleon & Maddux, 2014), which, as the title states, does not require the use of language. If you and your client speak Spanish, the Neuropsi Atencion y Memoria (Ostrosky-Solís et al., 1999) is a useful instrument for evaluating a broad range of cognitive functions in Spanish-speaking populations.

If the issue has to do with the client's difficulty remembering details or events, you will want to assess their retention and recall. You could do that via a variety of instruments, including some of the aforementioned, as well as the Weschler Memory Scale (WMS-IV; Wechsler, 1997), the Wide Range Assessment of Memory and Learning (WRAML; Dunn & Haynes, 2005), or the Benton Visual Retention Test (BVRT; Benton Sivan, 1991), among others. In these cases, it is extremely important to assess for malingering. Tests such as the Test of Memory Malingering (TOMM; Vitelli, 2001) and Validity Indicator Profile (VIP; Frederick, 1997) are useful because they do not require verbal communication. The Structured Inventory of Malingered Symptomatology (SIMS; Smith & Burger, 1997) is also a good measure for assessing symptom validity, as are any tests that have validity scales, such as the MMPI-2-RF/3 (Block et al., 2014; Ben-Porath, & Tellegen, 2020), the PAI (Morey, 1991), the MCMI-III (Craig, 2006), and the TSI-2 (Briere, 2010), to name a few.

In Irina's example above, it does not seem that she has any cognitive deficits, since her only struggle is recalling details from the trauma she experienced. After evaluating her memory skills and ruling out any cognitive impairments, you will likely want to explain to the adjudicator the interplay between memory and trauma. Research has shown that asylum seekers suffering from PTSD and depression have difficulty recalling specific memories (Saadi et al., 2021; Graham et al., 2014). When a person experiences a traumatic event, the increased secretion of norepinephrine disrupts the functioning of the hippocampus and prefrontal cortex, thus interfering with the normal consolidation of memory (Boulanger, 2002). The result is that certain parts of the traumatic experience (and sometimes its entirety) are never encoded and thus cannot be recalled. This appears to be the case with Irina, who herself admitted to having "blacked out" during the sexual abuse.

This blacking out is also referred to as dissociative amnesia, which is typically experienced by survivors of trauma (Cohen, 2001).

Memories are also vulnerable to outside influences. Every time we retrieve a memory, false information can weave itself into that memory, consequently distorting the memory of what was originally perceived (Cohen, 2001; Genova, 2021). For example, two people might be recalling the same incident but one says there were three assailants and the other one corrects him: "No, there were four." That first person will then incorporate that correction and from then on continue to "recall" that there were four assailants, when in reality, there were only three. Another susceptibility is when a person is questioned in a stressful environment. We have come across many asylum applicants who have provided details that they did not actually remember because they wanted to comply with the officer's probing. Their statements later came back to haunt them when in a more relaxed environment they admitted they were not sure about the answer. This leads the trier of fact to ask the dreaded question, "Were you lying then, or are you lying now?" Even though studies have shown that questioning an asylum seeker's credibility based on inconsistency of recall is problematic (Herlihy et al., 2002), most immigration officials are not aware of this, so you must understand and if necessary, be able to explain to the adjudicator, the root of a discrepancy.

Assessing Exceptional Circumstances

When the past persecution or trauma affected the timeliness of the application or may affect the applicant's ability to recall information accurately and consistently, an evaluation and report by an MHP can be vital for inclusion in the administrative record.

Research has unequivocally demonstrated the interplay between trauma and cognition (Hayes et al., 2012). Some of the hallmark symptoms of PTSD involve alterations to cognitive processes such as memory, attention, planning, and problem-solving. It is not unusual for individuals who have suffered trauma to become forgetful or distracted and to have difficulty following through with complex tasks. Those who suffer from severe depression will complain about a "foggy brain," difficulty focusing and retaining information, and profound anhedonia. Imagine a time when you felt down and unmotivated, simple tasks required too much effort. Now imagine that multiplied by ten. That approximates the typical mental state of a refugee: a person who is in a foreign land, hearing a foreign language, eating foreign food, and coping with not only trauma, but also a deep sense of loss. Consider the following example:

> Alphonse, a citizen of the Democratic Republic of Congo, was politically active in his home country until his family was murdered by the opposition in a car-bombing meant to target him. Because the opposition party took control of the government, the crime was not investigated and the perpetrators were never brought to justice. Fearing

for his life, Alphonse fled to the United States to live with his cousin in New Jersey using his brother's passport. For the next three years, he took on his brother's identity while living in the United States as a means to cope with his loss. He was recently detained by immigration officers on a routine warrant and arrested for overstaying his visa. His attorney has referred Alphonse for an evaluation regarding why he failed to apply for asylum during his first year in the United States.

Even though years have passed since the trauma Alphonse experienced in his native country, it is evident that he suffered posttraumatic symptoms for quite some time. In addition to intrusive memories, nightmares, and hyperarousal, he reported having been profoundly depressed as he grieved his brother's death. When asked why he used his brother's documents instead of his own, Alphonse broke down and stated, "Because he should not be dead. I was the one who should have died." Taking on his brother's identity, therefore, was a way for Alphonse to cope with his brother's tragic demise. Alphonse's mental state while adjusting to a new life in the United States was significantly compromised, and his depression resulted in impairments in his cognitive functioning. He recalled that he was "sleeping all the time" and that it took months for him to gather the strength to look for a job. His intention was to apply for asylum, but he was unable to follow through with filing the required paperwork. He said, "I started filling out the form, and when it asked to describe what had happened to my family… I just couldn't write it. I couldn't go back there [in my mind]. I just couldn't." This is a credible explanation for Alphonse not being able to fulfill the requirements for an asylum application in a timely manner.

For individuals seeking refuge from objective danger, it is possible if not probable that filing asylum paperwork is the last thing on their mind—if on their mind at all. Upon arriving in a new country in search of safety and stability, a person's priorities are those that guarantee their survival (Bernardes et al., 2010; Liebling et al., 2014). I have heard asylum seekers say things such as, "All I wanted, all I cared about, was finding a place where I felt safe." When I was interviewing an asylum seeker in an immigration detention center, she shared, "I much prefer being in jail here than back in Honduras. I feel safer here, and I am finally able to close my eyes and sleep through the night." Consequently, filing paperwork in a foreign language and initiating a process they may not fully understand is unlikely to take precedence while they are adjusting to a new environment and still coping with trauma.

Some individuals say they were not aware that they could apply for this type of immigration relief. This, however, is not an acceptable justification. Case law specifically states that "Ignorance of legal requirements does not excuse noncompliance.[6]" Hopefully, your referral source will have already weeded out such individuals, but if someone claims this to be the case, you can still explore whether their not knowing about it was at all related to their mental state at the time.

Assessing Danger to Society

Applicants seeking immigration relief under Article III of the CAT sometimes have to demonstrate to the trier of fact that, despite their criminal background, they do not pose a danger to society. If they are unable, the IJ orders the applicant to remain in detention to protect the public. Jorge's case is a good illustration:

> Jorge, a citizen of El Salvador, was convicted for drug smuggling when he was 18 years old. Desperate for a better quality of life, he had agreed to engage in such unlawful conduct in order to come to the United States, where he planned on settling down and finding a job with which to help his family back home. In exchange for a more lenient sentence, Jorge testified against the other smugglers. Once released from prison, he was immediately detained by DHS and placed in removal proceedings. There is clear evidence that, if Jorge returns to El Salvador, he will be tortured and killed by the leaders of the drug smuggling ring for having "snitched." Making matters worse, there are widespread reports that the drug smuggling ring has several local politicians and law enforcement on its payroll. Jorge's attorney referred him for an evaluation to determine whether he poses a danger if allowed to remain in this country.

Can you think of how you would approach this evaluation? What tests would you administer? The Hare Psychopathy Checklist—Revised (PCL-R; Hare, 1991), the Rorschach, and the MMPI-2-RF are three measures which, when administered together, provide excellent convergent and discriminant data for assessing psychopathy (Meloy & Gacono, 2016). The PCL-R is a 20-item inventory of personality traits and observed behaviors that is intended to be completed as part of a semi-structured interview along with a review of collateral information, such as official records. Although considerable research supports its utility in predicting violence and unlawful behavior under certain circumstances and with certain populations, Edens (2001) and others (Serin et al., 2016) warn about the potential misuse of this popular test, particularly by MHPs who are not adequately trained to administer it and interpret the results. Evans and Hass (2018) devote a chapter to the use of the Rorschach in immigration evaluations. Unless you have sufficient training and experience assessing psychopathy, however, you are advised to refer to an MHP who does.

The Report

Asylum seekers fill out *Form I-589*, where they are instructed to describe in detail their experiences of persecution. They also have to submit a written declaration where they explain their reason for seeking refuge in the United States. Because inconsistencies are often the main reason asylum applications are denied, avoid opportunities for discrepancies in your report by leaving out unnecessary details of the applicant's traumatic experiences and sticking to the referral question. This does not mean you do not inquire about such experiences, obviously, but the objective is to write a report that is concise and to the point. Expand on the areas that the adjudicator will be most interested in—namely, your findings and professional opinion regarding the issue at hand (i.e., the applicant's mental health, their cognitive functioning, risk concerns, etc.).

As with other immigration reports, you will want to avoid jargon and explain your findings in words the reader is likely to understand. Provide diagnostic criteria for the mental disorder, and clearly describe the symptoms that warrant your diagnosis. In particular, the section on behavioral observations should be carefully written, especially when the referral question has to do with the client's credibility.

Sometimes IJs question the asylum seeker's credibility because their demeanor and emotional expressions do not match the content they are describing. The client might present as stoic, with restricted facial expressions and somewhat monotone voice, when the IJ expects them to be emotionally fraught. There are people, however, whose presentation does not waver when they are honestly and sincerely recounting a traumatic incident. This is because when a person recalls traumatic incidents, they often dissociate from the affective component of the trauma while still retaining knowledge of the traumatic experience itself (Hegeman & Wohl, 2000). The result is a monotone, robot-like presentation. Describing in detail how the client presented to you is important. This is essential when the issue is lack of consistency in their accounts. If the client has difficulty recalling specific dates or events from the past, you will want to mention that. If they had trouble accessing their memory in a calm and supportive environment, it is hardly likely that they will find it any easier when testifying in front of an IJ.

I once evaluated an asylum seeker who neglected to tell me that he had been kidnapped on his way to the US border. It was not until the very end of the interview that he suddenly recalled such a traumatic experience. Clearly, this was not because it was insignificant or a confabulation. Repression (i.e., "forgetting"), much like dissociation, is another common defense mechanism for coping with trauma (Boulanger, 2002; United Nations, 2004). The human brain works in intricate ways to defend against intolerable feelings!

To explain such variabilities in a client's presentation, a report of an asylum evaluation might call for citing research. As highlighted in previous chapters, you are not expected to investigate the conditions in the applicant's home country, but exploring dangers the client anticipates being subjected to if they are denied asylum is often warranted. Similarly, the inclusion of relevant research to educate the adjudicator can be useful to back up your claims. For example, you might cite studies that demonstrate the impact of trauma on memory consolidation, or, as we covered earlier in this chapter, explain how common it is for refugees to prioritize safety over filing legal paperwork. However, do so sparingly; the objective of the report is to conceptualize the applicant's experiences, not to produce a literature review.

> When citing information from external sources, explain it in your own words. You can add the reference as a footnote, as opposed to within the text as we do in APA style.

Demonstrating to the trier of fact you employed critical and objective judgment, including exploring alternative causes for symptoms and ruling out malingering or exaggeration, is key. Make sure to address both inconsistencies in the client's statements during the interview (as when stories or dates do not add up) as well as discrepancies between what they disclose in the interview and what they wrote in their application or said in their testimony. To safeguard against inaccuracies, it helps to pause the interview every so often and repeat back to the client what they shared so far. This also often leads to more details from the client (Gudjonnsen, 1992).

Notes

1 The Trump Administration significantly reduced the ceiling during 2016–2020. For example, the ceiling was 110,000 in 2017 but only 30,000 in 2019 (Baugh, 2020).
2 In recent years, Guatemala, El Salvador, and Honduras, with Mexico not far behind, have led among countries from where most people sought asylum, but applicants from those countries also had among the very highest rates of denial. For example, the US government denied asylum to more than 87% of applicants from Honduras and 85% of applicants from Mexico. By contrast, the US government denied asylum to less than 25% of applicants from China and 38% of applicants from India (Transactional Records Access Clearinghouse, 2020).
3 See *INS v. Cardoza-Fonseca, 480 U.S. 421, 440 (1987)*. See also *Tilija v. Att'y Gen., 930 F.3d 165, 171 (3rd Cir. 2019)*.
4 As explained at INA § 241(b)(3).
5 Needless to say, traveling to the country from which they sought asylum could seriously jeopardize their asylee status.
6 See, for example, *Federal Crop Ins. Corp. v. Merrill, 332 U.S. 380, 384–385 (1947); Antonio-Martinez v. INS, 317 F.3d 1089, 1093 (9th Cir. 2003) (applying the general rule that "ignorance of the law is no excuse" to the asylum context); Kay v. Ashcroft, 387 F.3d 664, 671 (7th Cir. 2004) (other circumstances, ignorance of the law did not establish exceptional circumstances).*

Bibliography

Aliens and Nationality. 8 C.F.R. § 1208.18 (1999).
Aragno, A., & Schlachet, P. J. (1996). Accessibility of early experience through the language of origin: A theoretical integration. *Psychoanalytic Psychology, 13*(1), 23–34. https://doi.org/10.1037/h0079636
Armitage, S. G. (1946). *Trail making test*. PsycTESTS.
Baugh, R. (2020). Refugees and asylees: 2019. *Annual flow report*. www.dhs.gov/sites/default/files/publications/immigration-statistics/yearbook/2019/refugee_and_asylee_2019.pdf.

Ben-Porath, Y. S., & Tellegen, A. (2020). *Minnesota Multiphasic Personality Inventory-3 (MMPI-3): Manual for administration, scoring, and interpretation*. Minneapolis, MN: University of Minnesota Press.

Benton Sivan, A. (1991). *Benton visual retention test – Fifth edition*. PsycTESTS.

Bernardes, D., Wright, J., Edwards, C., Tomkins, H., Dlfoz, D., & Livingstone, A. (2010). Asylum seekers' perspectives on their mental health and views on health and social services: Contributions for service provision using a mixed-methods approach. *International Journal of Migration, Health and Social Care, 6*(4), 3–19. https://doi.org/10.5042/ijmhsc.2011.0150

Blevins, C. A., Weathers, F. W., Davis, M. T., Witte, T. K., & Domino, J. L. (2015). The posttraumatic stress disorder checklist for DSM-5 (PCL-5): Development and initial psychometric evaluation. *Journal of Traumatic Stress, 28*(6), 489–498. https://doi.org/10.1002/jts.22059

Block, A. R., Marek, R. J., Ben-Porath, Y. S., & Ohnmeiss, D. D. (2014). *The Minnesota Multiphasic Personality Inventory-2-Restructured Form (MMPI-2-RF): Manual for administration, scoring, and interpretation*. University of Minnesota Press.

Bloom, L., & Beckwith, R. (1989). Talking with feeling: Integrating affective and linguistic expression in early language development. *Cognition and Emotion, 3*(4), 313–342. https://doi.org/10.1080/02699938908412711

Bond, M. H., & Lai, T. (1986). Embarrassment and code-switching into a second language. *Journal of Social Psychology, 126*(2), 179–186.

Boulanger, G. (2002). The cost of survival: Psychoanalysis and adult onset trauma. *Contemporary Psychoanalysis, 38*(1), 17–44. https://doi.org/10.1080/00107530.2002.10745805

Briere, J. (2010). *Trauma symptom inventory: Second edition (TSI-2)*. Psychological Assessment Resources.

Buxbaum, E. (1949). The role of the second language in the formation of the ego and superego. *Psychoanalytic Quarterly, 18*, 279–289.

Canivez, G. L., & Madle, R. A. (2017). Review of the Woodcock-Johnson IV. In Carlson, J. F., Geisinger, K. F., Jonson, J. L. (Eds.), *The twentieth mental measurements yearbook* (pp. 875-882). Buros Center for Testing.

Cohen, J. (2001). Questions of credibility: Omissions, discrepancies and errors of recall in the testimony of asylum seekers. *International Journal of Refugee Law, 13*(3).

Craig, R. J. (2006). The Millon clinical multiaxial inventory-III. In R. P. Archer (Ed.), *Forensic uses of clinical assessment instruments* (pp. 121–145). Lawrence Erlbaum Associates Publishers.

Dean, G. J., & Green, K. E. (2007). Behavior rating inventory of executive function—Adult version. In K. F. Geisinger, R. A. Spies, J. F. Carlson, & B. S. Plake (Eds.), *The seventeenth mental measurements yearbook [Electronic version]*. Retrieved from the Buros Institute's Test Reviews Online website: www.unl.edu/buros

Delis, D. C., Kaplan, E., & Kramer, J. H. (2001). Delis-Kaplan executive function system. PsycTESTS.

Drozdick, L. W., Wahlstrom, D., Zhu, J., & Weiss, L. G. (2012). The Wechsler Adult Intelligence Scale—Fourth Edition and the Wechsler Memory Scale—Fourth Edition. In D. P. Flanagan & P. L. Harrison (Eds.), *Contemporary intellectual assessment: Theories, tests, and issues* (pp. 197–223). The Guilford Press.

Dunn, T. M., & Haynes, S. D. (2005). Test review of the Wide Range Assessment of Memory and Learning, Second Edition. *The sixteenth mental measurements yearbook [Electronic version]*. Retrieved from the Buros Institute's Test Reviews Online website: www.unl.edu/buros

Evans-McCleon, T. N., & Maddux, C. D. (2014). Test of nonverbal intelligence, Fourth edition. In J. F. Carlson, K. F. Geisinger, & J. L. Jonson (Eds.) *The nineteenth mental measurements yearbook* [Electronic version]. Retrieved from the Buros Institute's Test Reviews Online website: www.unl.edu/buros

Evans-McCleon, T. N., & Maddux, C. D. (2014). Test of nonverbal intelligence, Fourth edition. *The nineteenth mental measurements yearbook.*

Filone, S., & DeMatteo, D. (2017). Assessing "credible fear": A psychometric examination of the Trauma Symptom Inventory-2 in the context of immigration court evaluations. *Psychological Assessment, 29*(6), 701–709.

Frederick, R. I. (1997). *Validity indicator profile.* PsycTESTS.

Genova, L. (2021). *Remember.* Harmony Books.

Graham, B., Herlihy, J., & Brewin, C. R. (2014). Overgeneral memory in asylum seekers and refugees. *Journal of Behavior Therapy and Experimental Psychiatry, 45*(3), 375–380. https://doi.org/10.1016/j.jbtep.2014.03.001

Grant, D. A., & Berg, E. A. (1948). *Wisconsin card sorting test.* PsycTESTS.

Gudjonnsen, G. (1992). *The psychology of interrogations, confessions and testimony.* John Wiley & Son.

Hare, R. D. (1991). *Psychopathy checklist—Revised.* PsycTESTS. https://doi.org/10.1037/t01167-000

Hayes, J., VanElzakker, M., & Shin, L. (2012). Emotion and cognition interactions in PTSD: A review of neurocognitive and neuroimaging studies. *Frontiers in Integrative Neuroscience, 6.* https://doi.org/10.3389/fnint.2012.00089

Hegeman, E., & Wohl, A. (2000). Management of trauma-related affect, defenses, and dissociative states. In R. H. Klein & V. L. Schermer (Eds.), *Group Psychotherapy for Psychological Trauma,* (pp. 64–88). Guilford Press.

Herlihy, J., Scragg, P., & Turner, S. (2002). Discrepancies in autobiographical memories: Implications for the assessment of asylum seekers: Repeated interviews study. *British Medical Journal, 324*(7333), 324–327. https://doi.org/10.1136/bmj.324.7333.324

Kaufman, A. S., Kaufman, N. L., Pearson Education, Inc. (Firm), & PsychCorp (Firm). (2004). KBIT2: Kaufman brief intelligence test. Pearson/PsychCorp.

Liebling, H., Burke, S., Goodman, S., & Zasada, D. (2014). Understanding the experiences of asylum seekers. *International Journal of Migration, Health & Social Care, 10*(4), 207–219. https://doi.org/10.1108/ijmhsc-06-2013-0016

Marcos, L. R. (1976). Bilinguals in psychotherapy: Language as an emotional barrier. *American Journal of Psychotherapy, 30*(4), 552–560. https://doi.org/10.1176/appi.psychotherapy.1976.30.4.552

Meloy, J. R., & Gacono, C. B. (2016). Assessing psychopathy: Psychological testing and report writing. In C. B. Gacono (Ed.), *The clinical and forensic assessment of psychopathy: A practitioner's guide* (2nd ed., pp. 276–292). Routledge/Taylor & Francis Group.

Meyers, J. E., & Meyers, K. R. (1995). Rey complex figure test under four different administration procedures. *Clinical Neuropsychologist, 9*(1), 63–67.

Morey, L. C. (1991). *Personality assessment inventory.* PsycTESTS.

Nasreddine, Z. S., Phillips, N. A., Bédirian, V., Charbonneau, S., Whitehead, V., Collin, I., Cummings, J. L., & Chertkow, H. (2005). *Montreal cognitive assessment.* PsycTESTS.

Ostrosky-Solís, F., Ardila, A., & Rosselli, M. (1999). NEUROPSI: A brief neuropsychological test battery in Spanish with norms by age and educational level.

Journal of the International Neuropsychological Society, 5(5), 413–433. https://doi.org/10.1017/s1355617799555045

Rozensky, R.H., & Gomez, M.Y. (1983). Language switching in psychotherapy with bilinguals: Two problems, two models, and case examples. *Psychotherapy: Theory, Research, and Practice, 20*(2), 152–160. https://doi.org/10.1037/h0088486

Saadi, A., Hampton, K., de Assis, M. V., Mishori, R., Habbach, H., & Haar, R. J. (2021). Associations between memory loss and trauma in US asylum seekers: A retrospective review of medico-legal affidavits. *Plos One, 16*(3), e0247033. https://doi.org/10.1371/journal.pone.0247033

Serin, R. C., Brown, S. L., & De Wolf, A. H. (2016). The clinical use of the Hare Psychopathy Checklist—Revised (PCL-R) in contemporary risk assessment. In C. B. Gacono (Ed.), *The clinical and forensic assessment of psychopathy: A practitioner's guide* (2nd ed., pp. 293–310). Routledge/Taylor & Francis Group.

Smith, G. P., & Burger, G. K. (1997). *Structured inventory of malingered symptomatology.* PsycTESTS.

Transactional Records Access Clearinghouse. (2020). *Asylum denial rates continue to climb.* https://trac.syr.edu/immigration/reports/630/.

United Nations. (2004). *Istanbul Protocol: Manual on the effective investigation and documentation of torture and other cruel, inhuman, or degrading treatment or punishment.* United Nations.

United Nations High Commissioner for Refugees. (2018). *Global trends: Forced displacement in 2018.* www.unhcr.org/globaltrends2018/.

United Nations High Commissioner for Refugees. (2021). *Inside the world's 10 largest refugee camps.* www.arcgis.com/apps/MapJournal/index.html?appid=8ff1d1534e8c41adb5c04ab435b7974b.

UN Office of the High Commissioner for Human Rights (OHCHR). (2004). Manual on the effective investigation and documentation of torture and other cruel, inhuman or degrading treatment or punishment ("Istanbul Protocol"), HR/P/PT/8/Rev.1. www.refworld.org/docid/4638aca62.html [accessed 5 January 2022].

Vitelli, R. (2001). Test of memory malingering. In B. S. Plake & J. C. Impara (Eds.), *The fourteenth mental measurements yearbook. [Electronic version].* Retrieved from the Buros Institute's Test Reviews Online website: www.unl.edu/buros

Waisman, P. A. (2005). *Emotional expression of Spanish-English bilinguals in traumatic narratives.* Alliant International University, California School of Professional Psychology, San Diego.

Weathers, F. W., Bovin, M. J., Lee, D. J., Sloan, D. M., Schnurr, P. P., Kaloupek, D. G., Keane, T. M., & Marx, B. P. (2018). The clinician-administered PTSD scale for DSM–5 (CAPS-5): Development and initial psychometric evaluation in military veterans. *Psychological Assessment, 30*(3), 383–395.

Wechsler, D. (1997). *WMS-III administration and scoring manual.* The Psychological Corporation.

5 Evaluations Related to the Violence Against Women Act (VAWA)

Mariela G. Shibley, Psy.D. and Matthew G. Holt, Esq.

US immigration law provides several benefits specifically to foreign nationals (FNs) who are subjected to domestic abuse by their US citizen (USC) or lawful permanent resident (LPR) family members. Many of these benefits are provided by the Violence Against Women Act (VAWA). These benefits enable victims of domestic abuse to receive deferred action (i.e., indefinitely delay deportation) and employment authorization, pursue or retain lawful resident status, request waivers for certain grounds of inadmissibility, seek cancellation of their removal in immigration court, and expeditiously apply for naturalization. Mental health professionals (MHPs) are often key to clients' pursuit of these benefits.

The Battered Spouse Waiver

Most people believe that when a USC marries an FN, the FN automatically receives legal status, but the reality is more complicated. A USC has to petition or sponsor their FN spouse, and their FN spouse needs to prove they are admissible. If they have been married less than two years, the FN's resident status is considered *conditional*, and it is valid for only two years. At the end of this conditional period, they must jointly file a petition to remove the conditions, making the FN's resident status *permanent*. While this rule is an effective way for the government to weed out fraudulent marriages entered into for the sole purpose of obtaining immigration benefits, the joint filing requirement can also create an unhealthy power dynamic where the USC may attempt to control and/or manipulate the FN, knowing the FN is reliant on the USC's assistance for the conditions to be removed.

The "battered spouse waiver," as defined in INA § 216(d)(4), is an exception to the joint filing requirement, allowing victims of domestic abuse to remove the condition of their status without their spouse's cooperation. Both FN adults and FN children may apply for the battered spouse waiver. Adult FNs must show by a "preponderance of the evidence" (a standard often referred to as "more likely than not") that they entered the marriage in good faith but have been battered or subject to extreme cruelty by their

DOI: 10.4324/9781003139973-6

petitioning spouse. Likewise, an FN child would show that their conditional resident parent entered the marriage in good faith but that the child FN has been battered or subject to extreme cruelty either by their parent's USC or LPR spouse or by their own conditional resident parent.

To be successful, the adult or child FN must file *Form I-751* along with supporting evidence, which may include copies of reports or official records issued by police, courts, medical personnel, school officials, clergy, social workers, and other social service agency personnel that corroborate the abuse. The evidence may also include legal documents relating to an order of protection against the abuser or relating to any legal steps the FN has taken to end the abuse. The FN may also submit proof that they sought safe haven in a shelter for the abused or similar refuge, as well as photographs evidencing their injuries. If their marriage was terminated by divorce on grounds of physical abuse or extreme cruelty, the FN should provide a copy of their divorce decree.

Self-Petitioning for LPR Status

FNs who are victims of domestic abuse pursuant to INA § 245(a) and 8 U.S.C. § 1255(a) may self-petition for deferred action and LPR status. The granting of deferred action by USCIS prevents an FN who receives it from being removed from the United States and enables them to receive a work permit. For some victims of domestic abuse, particularly those with prior immigration or criminal history, deferred action is as much of an immigration benefit as they can receive. Still for other FNs who are victims of domestic abuse by a USC or LPR abuser, the FN may be eligible not just for deferred action but also for LPR status.

VAWA self-petitions are available to several groups of victims:

- Spouses of abusive USC or LPRs.
- Divorced spouses when the termination of the marriage was related to the abuse and if the application is filed within two years of the termination of the marriage.
- Children of abusive USC or LPRs if they file before turning 25.
- A parent of an abused noncitizen child, even if the noncitizen parent is not herself abused.
- Noncitizen spouses whose children are abused by the child's other USC or LPR parent.
- Noncitizen parents of abusive USC children.

To be successful, the self-petitioning spouse, child, or parent must file *Form I-360* with corresponding supportive evidence, which includes confirmation of the abuser's USC or LPR status, legal documents verifying the relationship to the abuser, proof of cohabitation, evidence of abuse, substantiation of the noncitizen's good moral character, and proof that the marriage was entered into in good faith (if applicable). Ultimately, the FN has the burden to prove the abuse. An FN may submit any relevant credible evidence in place of what USCIS suggests, but the determination of what evidence is credible and the weight to be given that evidence is within the sole discretion of USCIS.

An FN may self-petition for LPR status if they satisfy the following several requirements:

1   The FN has a "qualifying relationship" with an abusive USC or LPR, meaning that they are now or were recently the victim of battery or extreme cruelty by a USC or LPR spouse, a USC or LPR parent, or a USC son or daughter who is at least 21 years of age when the FN files the petition.
2   The FN is residing with or has resided with the USC or LPR abuser.
3   The FN is a person of good moral character.
4   The FN, in cases where the FN is a spouse and not the child or parent, entered into the marriage to the USC or LPR abuser in good faith.

The FN may file a self-petition within two years of the date of the USC abuser's death, within two years of the USC or LPR abuser's loss of status as a result of an incident of domestic abuse, or within two years of the termination of the marriage to the USC or LPR abuser if there is a connection between the termination of the marriage and the battery or extreme cruelty. For self-petitioning spouses, the FN may remarry after USCIS approves their self-petition without affecting their eligibility to become an LPR or have grounds for revocation of the approved self-petition. Generally, an LPR must wait five years to become a USC. However, LPRs who were approved for lawful US residency under VAWA can, in some cases, apply for US citizenship after only three years.

The Role of the Mental Health Provider

The task of an MHP in VAWA immigration petitions is typically to substantiate the client's claim of domestic abuse. More specifically, the FN needs to show that they were the victim of battery or *extreme cruelty* perpetrated by a USC or LPR spouse, parent, or adult child.

Extreme Cruelty

Extreme cruelty includes a wide range of hostile, aggressive, or abusive acts that may affect the physical, emotional, or psychological well-being of the victim. Such conduct must be intentional or voluntary (as opposed to hitting someone by accident). Abusive behaviors come in many forms—physical, sexual, verbal, psychological, and financial—and there are myriad ways that these forms of abuse are carried out.

Physical Abuse

Physical abuse is any intentional act that results in injury or trauma to another person (or animal) by way of corporal contact. This includes slapping, pinching, shoving, kicking, punching, choking, scratching, or using objects to cause bodily harm. Threatening physical violence is also considered abuse, especially if done recurrently. We specifically mention animals because cruelty towards a pet is a powerful method of inflicting emotional pain on its owner. A client recently shared how affected she was by her husband's violent behavior towards their dog. She cried as she recalled when the dog peed inside the house and the husband kicked it and yelled, "If he does it one more time, I'm getting my gun." Another client was visibly anxious as she described her wife holding their little dog over the balcony and threatening to drop it.

Sexual Abuse

Any intentional touching of the genitals—directly or through clothing— against a person's will is abuse, as is the use of physical force to compel a person to engage in a sexual act (whether or not the act is completed) or the attempted or completed sex acts involving a person who is unable to understand the nature or condition of the act, to decline participation, or to communicate unwillingness. Sexual abuse also involves stalking or harassment with a sexual subtext.

Within the category of sexual abuse is marital rape, that is, nonconsensual sex in which the perpetrator is the victim's spouse. In the United States, prior to the mid-1970s marital rape was exempted from rape laws. Throughout the years laws have changed and evolved, but most states still treat marital rape differently from nonmarital rape. Some states have more narrow laws that require use or threat of force, penetration, or that the victim be mentally incapacitated, and other states have lesser penalties and/or shorter sentences. Internationally, marital rape is seen very differently among different cultures, with some countries not criminalizing it at all. In other countries, where marital rape has only recently been criminalized, people are much less likely to even consider it rape. It does not help that the abuser often coerces the victim into the sexual act by saying something like, "It's your duty because you're my wife/husband." Keeping this in mind helps us understand the client's perception of their experiences within a cultural context.

Psychological Abuse

The goal of psychological abuse is to weaken or frighten a person mentally and emotionally via a range of verbal and nonverbal actions, thus distorting their sense of trust, safety, self-worth, and autonomy. Psychological abuse includes stonewalling or emotionally withdrawing as punishment; arbitrary or unpredictable behavior; intimidation; enforcing adverse consequences for disobedience; monitoring and controlling the victim's behaviors; keeping the victim from contacting friends and family; shaming and humiliating; making demeaning insults and derogatory comments (i.e., verbal abuse); and ridiculing or spreading damaging gossip, including via text and social media (i.e., cyberbullying).

> The one constant component of this type of psychological abuse is one partner's consistent efforts to maintain power and control over the other via coercive behaviors.

Coercion results where there is inequality of the partners and oppression of one by the other because of the oppressor's sense of entitlement. Psychological aggression has been found to be the most reliable predictor of later physical aggression (Murphy & O'Leary, 1989). Even in cases where the aggression does not escalate to physical violence, the coercive control progresses, and the victim organizes his or her life around self-protection.

One very powerful form of psychological abuse is *gaslighting*. Gaslighting is a manipulation tactic that makes the victim question their own judgment and perceptions. For example, an abuser vehemently denies having said or done something, telling the victim something like, "It's all in your head" or accusing them of faulty memory. In this type of relationship, the abuser elicits constant insecurity and anxiety in their partner, thereby pulling the victim by the strings.

Financial or Economic Abuse

Financial abuse consists of limiting the victim's access to economic resources, thus forcing them to depend on the perpetrator financially. Some examples are spending the victim's money without their consent, incurring debt in the victim's name, confiscating the victim's salary, putting the victim on a strict "allowance," and withholding money or access to resources. Financial abuse also involves exploiting the victim for financial purposes without compensation or anything aimed at decreasing the victim's financial security. For example, a client's wife withdrew all of their money from their joint bank account when the client intended to separate and rent a room on his own, essentially leaving him penniless. Controlling the victim's present or future earning potential by preventing them from obtaining a job or education also constitutes economic abuse.

Immigration Status Abuse

Unique to FNs is their being subject to immigration abuse, that is, their partner taking advantage of their immigration status to control and manipulate them. Some examples are deliberately not following through on promises to petition for their lawful US residency, withdrawing their sponsorship for adjustment of status, or threatening to get them deported if they call the police to report the abuser's behaviors. When victims have children in the United States, these threats are particularly potent and have a significant traumatic impact.

I have repeatedly come across USC wives who threaten their noncitizen husbands with taking their children from them. They scare their husbands into inaction by telling them they will never be granted custody because they are undocumented, or that if they go to family court, they will get flagged and deported. A client recalled his wife telling him, "No judge would ever keep a child from their mother." Presuming they have no options, these men endure abusive relationships out of fear of losing their children. It is truly a heart-breaking scenario.

Other Forms of Abuse

In addition to the abusive behaviors described above, there are many other actions that are cruel and sadistic. Title 8 of the Code of Federal Regulations (§204.2(iv)) specifically mentions that other abusive actions which may not initially appear violent can, under certain circumstances, also be considered a part of an overall pattern of violence, such as actions that target the victim's values and beliefs, cultural background, or personal experiences and characteristics. When asked to recall the worst thing his wife did to him, a client could barely hold back his tears as he shared that she burned the only picture he had of his dead mother. "It hurt more than if she had stabbed me. It's a pain that will never go away," he lamented. Another client's intense resentment was palpable as she shared when her spouse drew caricatures of Mohammed on a notepad for her Muslim parents to see when they visited. She cried, "I know it was just a drawing, but he did it on purpose to hurt me and my parents."

The Evaluation

VAWA applicants tend to be the most vulnerable clients coming into our office. Not only have they been victims of abuse, but it was perpetrated by someone they once loved very much. It is not uncommon to encounter some ambivalence about disclosing their experiences, as many victims fear getting their spouse in trouble or, more specifically, causing harm to their children's other parent.

Because they have long since fallen into a state of helplessness, they do not often recognize the abusive quality of many behaviors (marital rape being a common example). For this reason, it is useful to have the clients complete a questionnaire that specifically asks about their spouse's behaviors and their experiences in the relationship. One such instrument is the Abusive Behavior Inventory (Shepard & Campbell, 1992), which I modified to include immigration abuse and other abusive acts that my clients have reported throughout the years. It is often the case that clients start crying as they complete this questionnaire, only at that moment realizing the degree of torment and cruelty they have gone through. I always have them complete the questionnaire prior to starting the clinical interview, as it might prompt them to share something they might not otherwise have thought of.

Even though the focus of the evaluation is to assess the degree to which they were affected by the abuse, it is still very important to start by gathering information about the client's upbringing. Often, they either witnessed domestic abuse growing up or were the victims of such violence. Research has shown a strong correlation between experiencing domestic abuse in childhood and intimate partner violence in adulthood (Bensley et al., 2003; Ernst et al., 2006; Whitfield et al., 2003). While these early experiences might prime the victim to quickly recognize abusive behaviors and set immediate boundaries, it is more often the case that their familiarity with such treatment has kept them from realizing that they are being victimized (Bensley et al., 2003). Being accustomed to suffering mistreatment does not make it any less painful, but it could lead them to stay in the relationship longer than they should (Dare et al., 2013).

Rarely is there just one single incident. Abusive behaviors tend to escalate gradually in frequency and severity. I always ask the client to describe the first, worst, and last incidents of abuse. This also helps streamline the interview.

Since most VAWA cases are adjudicated administratively, that is, an USCIS officer reviews the evidence submitted in support of the application rather than there being an in-person interview or hearing, it is useful to imagine what the officer's questions might be and address them preemptively. These questions typically have to do with why the applicant stayed in the relationship, what kept them from seeking help, or why they waited so long to seek immigration relief. What you will discover, if you are not already aware, is how powerful an abuser's threats can be and how prevalent it is for victims to experience an overwhelming sense of helplessness and guilt. When someone feels they lack control over a situation, a common psychological defense is to assume undue blame, as that restores some degree of agency (Baly, 2010; Stein, 2012).

A good rule of thumb is to ask the client about the <u>first, worst, and last</u> abusive occurrence.

Assessing the Psychological Impact of Domestic Abuse

Unlike applications for asylum or other nonimmigrant visas, where the trauma the FN experienced could have taken place years prior to the psychological evaluation, VAWA applications require that the evaluee's traumatic experiences be much more recent. Consequently, they are more likely to be presenting with current symptoms and to meet criteria for psychiatric diagnoses. To assess clients' current mental health status, psychometric instruments can be very helpful. Some of the most commonly used tests are the Structured Clinical Interview for DSM-5 Disorders – Clinician Version (SCID-5-CV; First et al., 2016), the Beck Inventories (Beck et al., 1988; Beck et al., 1996), Symptom Checklist-90-Revised (SCL-90-R; Derogatis, 1977), Patient Health Questionnaires (PHQ-9; Kroenke et al., 1999), Hopkins Symptom Checklist (Derogatis et al., 1974, and others. All of these instruments, as explained in Chapter 2, are self-report measures and thus have their limitations. Nonetheless, they provide valuable information about the client's current emotional state. As previously mentioned, however, do not base your diagnostic impressions on any one measure alone or forgo a thorough diagnostic interview; your clinical judgment should trump most test results.

Sometimes a client who has been the victim of domestic abuse does not endorse any symptoms on any of the tests administered, but they still could be experiencing emotional distress. There are countless explanations for such outcomes, including personality characteristics, lack of self-awareness, conscious or unconscious denial of symptoms, cultural factors, problematic features of the assessment instruments, and so forth. These should be looked into and addressed when writing the report (i.e., explain the incongruency between the client's presentation and the items endorsed on the tests).

Understanding the client's personality characteristics and ways of relating with others is of utmost importance in this type of evaluation. To that end, personality assessment instruments such as the Personality Assessment Inventory (PAI; Morey, 1991) or Millon Clinical Multiaxial Inventory (MCMI; Craig, 2006) can be useful when administered judiciously. The psychological impact of trauma can be determined with the aid of measures such as the Trauma Symptom Inventory-2 (TSI-2; Briere, 2010), the Posttraumatic Stress Disorder Checklist – Civilian Version (PCL-5; Blevins et al., 2015), and the Clinician Administered PTSD Scale for DSM-5 (CAPS-5; Weathers et al., 2018). When the victim is a child, tools such as the Millon Adolescent or Pre-Adolescent Clinical Inventory (MACI or M-PACI; Millon & Davis, 1993) are called for, as are projective tests such as kinetic figure drawings, the Thematic Apperception Test (TAT; Morgan & Murray, 1936), or Sentence Completion Tests (Wallon & Webb, 1957). At the risk of sounding repetitive, I again stress how important it is to not rely on test results alone when arriving at a clinical diagnostic impression.

Lastly, it is worth mentioning how valuable it is to review any relevant materials the client or their attorney provides, such as the detailed affidavit VAWA applicants have to write in support of their application. Reading these documents ahead of the interview will help you to address inconsistencies, to corroborate some of their claims, and to ask about certain areas they do not bring up themselves during the interview. When clients ask what documents or other materials they should bring along to the evaluation, my approach is to err on the side of too much. If need be, I can skim through whatever they bring and determine which materials are going to be more relevant than others.

The Importance of Neutrality

Although I have discussed the importance of being a neutral and objective evaluator, I want to highlight that again as it pertains to VAWA cases. Regardless of what the client tells us, we have to remind ourselves that we are only hearing one side of the story. The unique requisites of immigration petitions through VAWA prioritize the applicant's safety from their abuser, so the alleged abuser is never notified about the filing of the immigration petition and, hence, never get an opportunity to explain their version of the events.

Whenever someone reports, "He came home from work and started yelling at me, and I had to lock myself in the bathroom," a logical question should be, "What prompted him to do that?" Frequently, the answer is something along the lines of, "He was drunk and belligerent," or, "He was high on drugs and was convinced I had a lover hiding in the house," or "A coworker told him they saw me kissing another man, and he lost his mind." This is not to imply that there is any justification for domestic abuse, but the context is crucial to a thorough evaluation. We do not want to *justify* the abuse; we do want to *explain* it. A client once shared that her husband grabbed all of her expensive makeup and stomped on it to pieces. Horrified by such a malicious act, I asked, "Why would he do that?" to which the client responded, "I was mad because he had been playing videogames all day, so I smashed his X-box against the wall. So, he went to the bathroom and grabbed my make-up bag." Would you say this constitutes abuse? Remember, the one constant element of domestic abuse is one partner's consistent efforts to maintain power and control over the other. In this case, though, it was clearly retaliation. Another way to get a more holistic understanding of the marital dynamics is to ask the evaluee, "I have a clear picture of what he did to you. But if he were here, what would he say you did?" Again, this is not to put the victim's experience in question, but to form a more comprehensive image of the events.

> Look beyond specific incidents and pay attention to the relationship dynamics and patterns of power and control (Evans & Hass, 2018).
>
> • Is there a clear power differential in the relationship?
> • Who exerts control over whom?
> • Was the infliction of violence to maintain power and control, or for self-protection? Or out of retaliation? Or something else?

Proving the Bona Fides of the Marriage

Not all VAWA cases entail evaluating the psychological impact of abuse. Sometimes clients are referred for an evaluation to help demonstrate that their marriage to their USC or LPR spouse was entered into in good faith and that its dissolution was against their original intentions. There are plenty of Hollywood movies with storylines of friends who marry in order for one of them to get a green card, but they end up falling in love. Although these films do well at the box office and in our hearts, in the real world, fraudulent marital arrangements are no laughing matter for immigration officials. Proving that a marriage is legitimate is something all FNs need to do to obtain immigration benefits, and victims of domestic abuse are no exception. Let's consider Miguel's case:

> Miguel, a citizen of Spain, moved to the United States to marry Lara, a USC he had met when she was studying in Spain for a year. They got married, and Miguel received conditional resident status one year later. During their second year of marriage, Miguel found out that Lara had been unfaithful. She expressed her profound remorse and promised never to do it again. Upon returning from work one evening, Miguel realized that Lara had packed some of her belongings and left. When she finally returned his calls a few days later, she told him she was in Las Vegas but that she had made a mistake by leaving. She said she truly loved him, that she was pregnant with his baby, and she was coming home. Miguel showed up at the airport and watched in disbelief as everyone exited the gate while he stood alone with a bouquet of flowers and Lara nowhere in sight. He again did not hear from her for days until she suddenly came home in a bad mood, telling him she did not want to talk about what happened because she was struggling with morning sickness. Lara's mood fluctuated daily. One minute she was sweet and loving towards Miguel, making plans for their future, and the next she was cold and grumpy, criticizing Miguel for everything he did. During a particularly heated argument, she confessed that the baby she was carrying was not his but that of a lover whom she had followed to Las Vegas only for

him to dump her. Despite such utter betrayal, Miguel forgave her and vowed to raise the child as his own. Lara promised she would never lie to him again and that they would jointly file the *Form I-751* so they could live as a family in the United States. However, Miguel came home two months later to find that Lara had taken all of her belongings and disconnected her cell phone. He never heard from her again but eventually learned through a friend that she had moved to Las Vegas with her new boyfriend.

Being unfaithful does not itself constitute domestic abuse, but a person's behaviors connected to their infidelity can be excruciatingly cruel to their partner. Knowing full well that Miguel loved her dearly and wanted nothing more than to settle down and start a family with her, Lara mercilessly toyed with his feelings. Understanding Miguel's personality characteristics would be important for ruling out any credibility issues and to confirm that he married Lara with the genuine intention of making her his partner for life. Even if Lara was not abusive, we want to evaluate the degree to which her callous attitudes and behaviors affected Miguel emotionally and psychologically. We would pay attention to his demeanor as he shares his experiences. Did he cry or hold back tears, or did he seem disingenuous? Is his story coherent and plausible, or full of inconsistencies? In his own words, how does Miguel feel about his failed marriage? Has it impacted his view of himself, others, and the world in a negative way?

While deferred action or cancellation of removal require some showing that it is not in the applicant's interest to return to their country of citizenship, that is not so for those seeking to lift conditions of their resident status. As a matter of fact, one could argue that not wanting to go back to their home country only puts the legitimacy of their marriage further into question. Remember, since the abusive spouse does not have a chance to contribute, the burden of proof lies entirely on the FN, and their fate is in the hands of a USCIS officer or IJ. Anything that raises concerns about the FN's claimed intentions could, at best, delay their immigration process or, at worst, undermine their case altogether. When in doubt, consult with the referring attorney as to what exactly they want you to evaluate and what information they want included in the report.

The Report

There are a few things to keep in mind when writing a report in support of a VAWA application. Be sure to present a persuasive and detailed account of the abuse, being careful not to sound like you are trying to convince the adjudicator to approve the case. Objectivity is key. When appropriate, be conservative in the inclusion of potentially compromising information. Lastly, stick to what is pertinent, and avoid unnecessary minutiae. Let me expand on each of these.

Be Thorough

When VAWA applicants have a well substantiated claim of abuse, such as when medical records from the emergency room and police reports clearly demonstrate that the victim was abused, they usually have enough evidence and a psychological evaluation is not necessary. In general, attorneys refer their clients to MHPs when they lack corroborative proof that they were victimized by a USC or LPR spouse, parent, or adult child. For that reason, it is important to focus in detail on the quality, intensity, and frequency of the abusive behaviors. General statements such as "Her husband was emotionally abusive," "He often hit her and said insulting things," or "She manipulated him constantly" are not informative enough.

Strive for Objectivity and Impartiality

In absence of other corroborative evidence, it falls on the MHP to provide a detailed, objective account of the client's reported experience, yet we cannot take the client's statements as facts and present them as such. Instead, make it clear that the account given is based on the client's reporting, and not your own unqualified factual assertions, by using phrases such as "He stated that," "She reported that," and "According to Mr. Sanchez."

If you have worked with victims of violence or domestic abuse, you are already familiar with the countertransference their experiences evoke. While a sympathetic, supportive stance is warranted during the interview process, do not let that carry over too much into the report, making you come across as an advocate. One clinician at my practice had such compassion and empathy for his clients that I always joked one could wring out his reports and tears would drip from it. Thankfully, I got to edit his reports before they were finalized.

I always explain to my clients that although I will not compromise my integrity by writing something I know not to be true, I will not write a report when my findings are not in their best interest either. Aside from very few disgruntled clients, most are understanding when this happens, as it is usually (and very unfortunately) the case that their attorney was the one who suggested they undergo a psychological evaluation in the hopes that I would uncover some juicy information to help their claim. Binna's is a case in point:

> Binna's attorney referred her for an evaluation because she was allegedly being abused by her 22-year-old USC son, Jon. After detailing her upbringing, what brought her to immigrate to the United States, and the birth of her only son, the MHP suggested they delve into her relationship with Jon. She went on to complain about Jon sometimes leaving home for a few days at a time and not answering her calls, his protesting every time she asked him to run an errand for her, and, most

notable, his volatile temper, to which she added, "He tells me to shut up and slams the door to his room." Upon further inquiry, Binna said Jon never hit her, never did things to purposely hurt her feelings (other than slamming his door, which he knows bothers her), supports her financially by paying most of the rent, and never used her immigration status to control her. As a matter of fact, Jon was the one who sought an immigration attorney once he was old enough to petition for his mother. Puzzled, the MHP confirmed that Binna was indeed self-petitioning for LPR status under VAWA. "Well, I was involved in a big case of fraud, and I have some dings on my record, so the attorney said my best option would be to apply for VAWA," Binna replied. It was evident at that point that the attorney had referred Binna for an evaluation in hopes that the MHP would "uncover" evidence of abuse, but clearly, no abuse was taking place.

Be Mindful of Compromising Material

The story your report tells should be thorough with respect to the issue(s) you have been hired to assess but not at the risk of compromising the client's case. Always be mindful not to divulge information in the report that could bring the client's moral character into question or admit to conduct that precludes them from the relief they seek. Revealing the client's substance abuse history or that they engaged in some previously undisclosed criminal activity are best kept out of the report if they are not absolutely essential to your findings. When in doubt, consult with the attorney.

Preserve Relevance and Succinctness

As explained earlier in the chapter, there is ample research that prior trauma predisposes a person to experience trauma in the future and compromises their overall well-being. When describing prior trauma, it is important to tie it into the presenting concerns, and if it is completely unrelated and irrelevant, it might be best left out. For example, if a client shares that she was involved in a car crash when she was 12 where she sustained several broken bones and was unable to go to school for a year but that she eventually healed and did not have any lingering issues stemming from the accident, it is unlikely that such information is worth including in the report.

When there are other traumatic experiences in a client's history, do not let them overshadow or obfuscate the client's current suffering. A client once brought in a 15-page psychological report where the MHP described in explicit detail the abuse she had endured from her first husband but devoted no more than two paragraphs to her current husband's physically and psychologically abusive behaviors for which she was filing a *Form 751*. Even though her earlier experiences impacted her and likely predisposed her to subsequent suffering, what she needed to demonstrate most was how her current husband's cruel treatment was affecting her. Since she lacked any other corroborative evidence (though she did have clinical records from the counseling she received after divorcing her first husband!) a psychological report was key in substantiating her claim, and her attorney referred her to my office for a new evaluation.

It is acceptable to cite research findings on the psychological impact of trauma, how adversities in childhood compromise a person's well-being, and other relevant information as long as you do so with the explicit purpose of educating the trier of fact or supporting your findings. Do not bore the reader with statistics or unrelated data to make yourself sound smart. They will see right through that, and you will risk your credibility. A seven- or eight-page thorough and concise report is always better than a dissertation, and it makes everyone's life easier. For a sample of this type of report, refer to the Appendices.

Bibliography

Baly, A. R. (2010). Leaving abusive relationships: Constructions of self and situation by abused women. *Journal of Interpersonal Violence, 25*(12), 2297–2315. https://doi.org/10.1177/0886260509354885

Beck, A. T., Epstein, N., Brown, G., & Steer, R. (1988). *Beck anxiety inventory.* PsycTESTS.

Beck, A. T., Steer, R. A., & Brown, G. (1996). *Beck depression inventory–II.* PsycTESTS.

Bensley, L., van Eenwyk, J., & Wynkoop Simmons, K. (2003). Childhood family violence history and women's risk for intimate partner violence and poor health. *American Journal of Preventive Medicine, 25*(1), 38–44. https://doi.org/10.1016/s0749-3797(03)00094-1

Blevins, C. A., Weathers, F. W., Davis, M. T., Witte, T. K., & Domino, J. L. (2015). The posttraumatic stress disorder checklist for DSM-5 (PCL-5): Development and initial psychometric evaluation. *Journal of Traumatic Stress, 28*(6), 489–498. https://doi.org/10.1002/jts.22059

Briere, J. (2010). *Trauma symptom inventory: Second edition (TSI-2).* Psychological Assessment Resources.

Craig, R. J. (2006). The Millon clinical multiaxial inventory-III. In R. P. Archer (Ed.), *Forensic uses of clinical assessment instruments* (pp. 121–145). Lawrence Erlbaum Associates Publishers.

Dare, B., Guadagno, R. & Muscanell, N. (2013). Commitment: The key to women staying in abusive relationships. *Journal of Interpersonal Relations, Intergroup Relations and Identity, 6,* 58–64.

Derogatis, L. R., Lipman, R. S., Rickels, K., Uhlenhuth, E. H., & Covi, L. (1974). *Hopkins symptom checklist.* PsycTESTS.

Derogatis, L. R. (1977). *Symptom checklist-90–Revised.* PsycTESTS.

Ernst, A. A., Weiss, S. J., & Enright-Smith, S. (2006). Child witnesses and victims in homes with adult intimate partner violence. *Academic Emergency Medicine, 13*(6), 696–699. https://doi.org/10.1197/j.aem.2005.12.020

Evans, F. B., & Hass, G. A. (2018). *Forensic psychological assessment in immigration court: A guidebook for evidence-based and ethical practice.* Routledge.

First, M. B., Williams, J. B. W., Karg, R. S., & Spitzer, R. L. (2016). *Structured clinical interview for DSM-5 disorders, clinician version (SCID-5-CV).* American Psychiatric Association.

Kroenke, K., Spitzer, R. L., & Williams, J. B. W. (1999). *Patient health questionnaire-9*. PsycTESTS.

Marital Rape Laws by Country. (2021, May 10). *Wikipedia*. https://en.wikipedia.org/wiki/Marital_rape_laws_by_country

Millon, T., & Davis, R. D. (1993). The Millon adolescent personality inventory and the Millon adolescent clinical inventory. *Journal of Counseling and Development*, *71*(5), 570–574.

Morey, L. C. (1991). *Personality assessment inventory*. PsycTESTS.

Morgan, C., & Murray, H. (1936). *Thematic apperception test*. PsycTESTS.

Murphy, C. M., & O'Leary, K. D. (1989). Psychological aggression predicts physical aggression in early marriage. *Journal of Consulting and Clinical Psychology*, *57*(5), 579–582. https://doi.org/10.1037/0022-006x.57.5.579

Petitions for relatives, widows and widowers, and abused spouses and children. (1998). 8 C.F.R. §204.2(iv).

Shepard, M. F., & Campbell, J. A. (1992). The abusive behavior inventory. *Journal of Interpersonal Violence*, *7*(3), 291–305. https://doi.org/10.1177/088626092007003001

Stein, A. (2012). Engendered self-states: Dissociated affect, social discourse, and the forfeiture of agency in battered women. *Psychoanalytic Psychology*, *29*(1), 34–58. https://doi.org/10.1037/a0024880

Wallon, E. J., & Webb, W. B. (1957). *Sentence completion test*. PsycTESTS.

Weathers, F. W., Bovin, M. J., Lee, D. J., Sloan, D. M., Schnurr, P. P., Kaloupek, D. G., Keane, T. M., & Marx, B. P. (2018). The clinician-administered PTSD scale for DSM–5 (CAPS-5): Development and initial psychometric evaluation in military veterans. *Psychological Assessment*, *30*(3), 383–395.

Whitfield, C. L., Anda, R. F., Dube, S. R., & Felitti, V. J. (2003). Violent childhood experiences and the risk of intimate partner violence in adults. *Journal of Interpersonal Violence*, *18*(2), 166–185. https://doi.org/10.1177/0886260502238733

6 Assessing Psychological Impact of Trauma in Victims of Violent Crime or Human Trafficking

Mariela G. Shibley, Psy.D. and Matthew G. Holt, Esq.

Foreign nationals (FNs) who are victims of crime in the United States have several channels by which to apply for immigration benefits, aside from the Violence Against Women Act (VAWA) covered in Chapter 5. The Victims of Trafficking and Violence Protection Act of 2000 (TVPA) provides relief for victims of certain violent crimes ("U" visas) and victims of sex or labor trafficking ("T" visas). Both visas were created so that an FN would be more likely to cooperate with law enforcement investigating and prosecuting criminal activity. In this chapter we discuss the requirements and application process for each of these types of immigration relief, followed by how a mental health professional (MHP) should evaluate noncitizen victims and present their findings in a report.

The U Visa

The U nonimmigrant status (U visa) is for victims of certain crimes who have suffered mental and/or physical abuse so long as they are helpful to law enforcement or government officials in the investigation or prosecution of the criminal activity. Petitioners and recipients of U visas and their qualifying family members are temporarily shielded from removal, authorized for employment, and may be eligible to adjust status to permanent residency. Congress allows the United States Citizenship and Immigration Services (USCIS) to grant 10,000 such visas annually.

Eligibility

To be eligible for a U visa, the FN, considered the principal applicant, must satisfy specific criteria set forth by the USCIS. First, they must be the direct, indirect, or bystander victim of a qualifying crime which occurred in the United States or violated US law. Second, the crime must be one of the following (including the attempt, conspiracy, or solicitation to commit any of the following): abduction, abusive sexual contact, blackmail, domestic violence,[1] extortion, false imprisonment, female genital mutilation, felonious assault, fraud in foreign labor contracting, hostage, incest, involuntary

DOI: 10.4324/9781003139973-7

servitude, kidnapping, manslaughter, murder, obstruction of justice, peonage, perjury, prostitution, rape, sexual assault, sexual exploitation, slave trade, stalking, torture, trafficking, witness tampering, unlawful criminal restraint, and other related crimes, including any activity where the elements of the crime are substantially similar.

Next, the FN must have suffered direct and proximate harm on account of the criminal activity. The FN must also have been helpful, is being helpful, or is likely to be helpful to law enforcement in the investigation or prosecution of the crime in coordination with members of law enforcement such as social workers, judges, magistrates, police, sheriffs, and city or district attorneys.[2] Lastly, the FN must be admissible to the United States.

Who Might Be Eligible for a U Visa?

The survivor of a qualifying crime that occurred in the United States or violates US laws and who:

- Has suffered *substantial* mental or physical abuse as a result of those crimes.
- Has information about the criminal activity.
- Was helpful, is helpful, or is likely to be helpful to law enforcement in the investigation or prosecution of the crime.

Application Requirements

To apply (petition) for a U visa, the FN principal applicant must submit the requisite forms, filing fee or fee waiver, and supporting evidence. The forms include:

1   *Form I-918*, Petition for U Nonimmigrant Status.
2   *Form I-918*, Supplement B, U Nonimmigrant Status Certification.
3   *Form I-918*, Supplement A, Petition for Qualifying Family Member of U-1 Recipient (if applicable).
4   *Form I-192*, Application for Advance Permission to Enter as Nonimmigrant (if the FN is subject to any inadmissibility grounds).

Supporting evidence must include the FN applicant's personal statement describing the criminal activity along with evidence to establish each eligibility requirement.

To verify that the FN was a victim of qualifying criminal activity, a certifying official from the law enforcement agency that investigated or prosecuted the crime must sign *Form I-918, Supplement B,* certifying that the crime violated US law or occurred in US territory, that the FN possesses information concerning the qualifying criminal activity of which he or she has been a victim, and that the FN's prior, current, or future involvement in the investigation or prosecution of the case was helpful. The certifying law enforcement agency can be, for example, the local police or sheriff's department, the district attorney's office, the Federal Bureau of Investigation, or the US Department of Labor.

If the FN is subject to any inadmissibility grounds, they may apply for a waiver.[3] The U visa's inclusive nature allows the FN, as the principal applicant, to include certain family members for derivative benefits. A principal applicant who is under 21 years of age may include their spouse, children, parents, and unmarried siblings under age 18. If the principal applicant is 21 years of age or older, they may petition to include only their spouse and children.

Congress limits U visas to 10,000 per year although there is no cap for family members deriving status from the principal applicant. There is a substantial backlog of pending U visa petitions (over 290,000 at the time of this writing), and USCIS has created a waiting list for eligible principal and derivative petitioners awaiting a final decision and U visa. Petitioners placed on the waiting list are eligible to apply for work authorization and will be granted deferred action or parole (meaning they are allowed to remain in the United States) while waiting for additional U visas to become available. Fortunately, USCIS recently announced a change in policy which will enable U visa petitioners to be granted employment authorization within a matter of months after applying for a U visa instead of the current several-year delay. The delayed adjudication and granting of U visas have led to several different legislative proposals, including increasing the U visa cap from 10,000 to 18,000 or even 30,000 per year, or even removing the cap entirely. However, for now, FNs seeking U visas have a substantial delay between filing and receiving the full immigration benefits afforded through the U visa.

Benefits

After an FN receives a U visa as a principal or derivative beneficiary, they may be eligible to apply for an adjustment of status to become a legal permanent resident (LPR) if they have been physically present in the United States for a continuous period of at least three years while in U nonimmigrant status and if, since receiving the U visa, they have not unreasonably refused to provide assistance to law enforcement. Certain additional qualifying family members, such as an after-acquired spouse, who married the visa holder after they filed their application, may also be eligible to apply to become a lawful permanent resident (LPR).

The T Visa

Along with creating the U visa, Congress created T nonimmigrant status (commonly referred to as a T visa) in October 2000 as part of the Victims of

Trafficking and Violence Protection Act. The status was created not only to protect victims of trafficking but also to support law enforcement's efforts to curb and eradicate human trafficking. Also known as trafficking in persons, human trafficking is a form of modern-day slavery in which traffickers use force, fraud, or coercion to compel individuals to provide labor or services, including commercial sex. Traffickers often take advantage of vulnerable individuals, especially those lacking lawful immigration status. T visas offer protection to victims and strengthen the ability of law enforcement agencies to investigate and prosecute. The T visa is a temporary immigration benefit that enables certain victims of a severe form of human trafficking and their qualifying family members to remain in the United States for up to four years if they have assisted law enforcement in an investigation or prosecution of human trafficking. As with the U visa, T visa recipients are shielded from removal, receive work permits, and may be eligible to adjust status to permanent residency. Congress allows USCIS to grant 5,000 visas annually.

Eligibility

T visas are reserved for victims of severe trafficking who satisfy specific related eligibility requirements. Under federal law, a "severe form of trafficking" is either sex trafficking or labor trafficking. Sex trafficking is when someone recruits, harbors, transports, provides, solicits, patronizes, or obtains a person for the purpose of a commercial sex act, where either the commercial sex act is induced by force, fraud, or coercion, or the person being induced to perform the act is under 18 years of age. Labor trafficking is when someone recruits, harbors, transports, provides, or obtains a person for labor or services through the use of force, fraud, or coercion for the purpose of involuntary servitude, peonage, debt bondage, or slavery.

At the time of filing, the applicant must be in the United States, American Samoa, the Commonwealth of the Northern Mariana Islands, or at a port-of-entry due to the trafficking. They must comply with any reasonable request from a law enforcement agency for assistance in the investigation or prosecution of human trafficking unless the FN is under the age of 18 or unable to cooperate due to physical or psychological trauma. They also must demonstrate they would suffer extreme hardship involving unusual and severe harm if removed from the United States. Lastly, the FN must be admissible to the United States and may be eligible to apply for a waiver of certain grounds of inadmissibility.

Like with the U visa, certain qualifying family members are eligible for a T visa. Regardless of the FN principal applicant's age, the FN may apply for their parents, unmarried siblings under 18 years of age, and the children of any age or marital status of the qualifying family members if they are in present danger of retaliation as a result of the principal applicant's escape from trafficking or on account of their cooperation with law enforcement. If the principal applicant's family members are not in present danger of retaliation, they can still apply if they are under 21 years old for their spouse, unmarried children, parents, unmarried siblings who are under 18 years old, and if the principal applicant is 21 years old or older, they can still apply for their spouse and unmarried children who are under 21 years old.

Application Requirements

To apply for a T visa, the FN victim of trafficking must submit *Form I-914, Application for T Nonimmigrant Status;* a personal statement explaining in their own words how they were a victim of trafficking; evidence that they complied with reasonable requests from law enforcement; and, if applicable, *Form I-914, Supplement A, Application for Immediate Family Member of T-1 Recipient.* Further, they may submit *Form I-914, Supplement B, Declaration of Law Enforcement Officer for Victim of Trafficking in Persons* to demonstrate they are a victim of trafficking and they complied with any reasonable request to assist law enforcement.

They may also submit other evidence instead of or in addition to the *Form I-914, Supplement B,* such as trial transcripts, court documents, police reports, news articles, affidavits, or other relevant credible evidence. Lastly, they must submit evidence that they meet all other eligibility requirements and/or *Form I-192, Application for Advance Permission to Enter as a Nonimmigrant* to cure any real or potential inadmissibility grounds.

Benefits

T visas are generally granted for four years and may be extended in certain situations. Additionally, T visa recipients may be eligible to apply for lawful permanent residence after three years in T nonimmigrant status or once the investigation or prosecution of the trafficking is complete, whichever occurs earlier. Like the U visa, there is an annual cap on how many T visas may be granted annually. Unlike the U visa, the T visa cap of 5,000 is not reached on an annual basis and there is no backlog for obtaining one.

U Visa vs. VAWA vs. T Visa

Many U visa cases involve victims of domestic violence. You might wonder, then, why not apply for VAWA? As explained in Chapter 5, the requirements for VAWA applicants entail that the abuser be the victim's USC or LPR spouse, parent, or child, and that the victim must have cohabitated with the abuser. In addition, a VAWA petition does not require law enforcement's involvement to substantiate the abuse. If the abuser is also undocumented, or if the couple is not legally married and/or lacks a history of cohabitation, then the victim can qualify for a U visa instead (so long as law enforcement certifies the abuse occurred and the victim was helpful in the reporting, investigating, or prosecuting). The victim could also qualify for a U visa instead of relief under VAWA if more than two years have passed since the couple divorced, the abuser lost LPR status, or the abuser died. Lastly, whereas for a VAWA petition victims of domestic violence need to meet the *extreme cruelty* standard, victims of criminal activity applying for a U visa need to demonstrate *substantial physical or mental abuse*. Although similar in several ways, the two differ in who is being considered. For VAWA, the law focuses on the perpetrator and whether they acted with extreme cruelty; for the U visa, the focus is on how the victim suffered as a result of the abuse.

A U visa applicant must address how a return to their country of citizenship would affect them, but the focus is much more on the degree of harm they suffered as a result of the crime. Conversely, for a T visa, the impact of the criminal activity tends to take a backseat, and the purpose of the report is to document the harm they are likely to incur if they were forced to return to their home country. Since many applicants are unable to provide convincing evidence that returning to their country of citizenship would result in unusual or severe harm (a pretty difficult standard to meet), they will more often qualify for a U visa instead.

How Can a Mental Health Professional Be of Assistance?

For both U visas and T visas, the MHP would be evaluating the direct victim of the crime or, in some cases, the indirect or bystander victim of the crime. An indirect victim, for example, would be the parent of a child who was molested by another adult, or the adult son or daughter who witnessed their father being stabbed. Even though both U and T visa applicants have to have been the victims of criminal activity, the evidence they need to submit in support of their applications differs for each. A U visa applicant must show that, as a result of the crime they suffered, they have sustained substantial injury, harm, or impairment to their physical, emotional, or psychological health. On the other hand, to be granted a T visa, an applicant must demonstrate that a return to their country of citizenship would result in unusual or severe harm.

The Psycholegal Question

The purpose of the psychological evaluation is to help the adjudicator determine whether the applicant merits immigration relief. The scope of the evaluation is limited by the psycholegal construct it aims to address:

> - **U Visa:** To what degree has the crime of which the applicant was a victim affected them—emotionally and psychologically?
> - **T Visa:** How would a return to their country of citizenship result in unusual or severe harm to the applicant?

Note that the referral question is not whether the harm was *substantial*; that is not for the MHP to determine. MHPs are to evaluate the degree to which the victim suffered, and it is then up to the adjudicator to decide whether they deem the victim's suffering to be *substantial*. In fact, it is best to leave the word out of your report entirely. Similarly, the MHP is not to research country conditions when describing how a forced return would affect the T visa applicant. Our job is to evaluate the person in front of us and to anticipate—based on the client's experiences, personality characteristics, and plausible concerns—the potential negative impact of an involuntary return to their country of citizenship.

Evaluating U Visa Applicants

Much like VAWA applicants, undocumented victims of crime are some of the most vulnerable individuals in the country, as their pursuit of justice is often laden with fear. This is why many victims do not pursue immigration relief based on having been the victim of a crime until someone else convinces them to do so. Consequently, some of the crimes that qualify them to apply for a U visa took place years before the filing of their application. This not only impacts the client's presentation, but also opens the door to potentially problematic inconsistencies or lapses in memory.

Understandably, a person might omit important information pertaining to a traumatic event, either because they cannot remember or because they did not think it relevant. Questioning their veracity, however, will likely hinder your ability to establish rapport and to convey a sense of safety, which are essential for a client to open up about their painful (and sometimes humiliating) experiences. Instead, you will want to obtain a good understanding of inconsistencies or inaccuracies so as to be able to explain it to the adjudicator in your report.

What Constitutes Substantial *Harm?*

According to Title 8 of the Code of Federal Regulations (Alien Victims of Certain Qualifying Criminal Activity, 2021), whether harm rises to the level of *substantial* depends on a number of factors, including but not limited to:

1 The nature of the injury inflicted or suffered.
2 The severity of the perpetrator's conduct.
3 The severity of the harm suffered.
4 The duration of the infliction of the harm.
5 The extent to which there is permanent or serious harm to the appearance, health, or physical or mental soundness of the victim, including aggravation of pre-existing conditions.

Title 8 also specifies that no single factor is a prerequisite to establish that the abuse suffered was substantial, nor does the existence of one or more of the factors automatically create a presumption that the abuse suffered was substantial, but a series of acts taken together may be considered to constitute substantial physical or mental abuse even where no single act alone rises to that level.

Collateral Information

Without proper certification, an FN cannot pursue the filing for a U visa. This means that every person who is referred for a psychological evaluation in a U visa case should have a completed *Form I-918, Sup. B* as well as a copy of the police report. These should be reviewed by the MHP prior to interviewing the client. The reasons for this are multifold. Having corroborating evidence of the criminal activity gives more weight to the report, as the examiner will have objective evidence with which to substantiate the applicant's claims. It may also provide details that the client omitted in the interview. When this is the case, find out whether such details were overlooked, forgotten, or intentionally left out.

In addition to immigration forms and police records, go over any other relevant documents that are made available to you, such as affidavits, medical or psychiatric records, and their own written declaration in support of their U or T visa application, where they describe their experiences in detail. Lastly, the U visa certification has an expiration date, and USCIS must receive the petition with the certification within six months of the signature date on the certification for the petition to be viable and not outright rejected, so be mindful of the timeframe.

Explaining inconsistencies between the client's report and the information on the records reviewed is crucial, as not doing so is likely to put the applicant's credibility in question. As always, you are advised to approach the inconsistencies with inquisitiveness as opposed to skepticism.

Assessing the Psychological Impact of Criminal Activity

Because there is no statute of limitations for U visas, an application can be filed at any point in time after the crime occurred. You could be evaluating someone who experienced trauma a few months prior or the victim of a crime that took place 15 years ago. As you can imagine, a person's presentation is very likely to vary depending on how much time has passed since the criminal activity. Keep in mind, however, what the referral question is: how the client was affected by the crime, which is independent of the client's current mental status. One's posttraumatic symptoms are expected to subside over time and after treatment. It is important to keep this in mind when assessing the client's symptomatology—especially if done with the aid of psychological instruments.

How would you go about evaluating the psychological impact of an incident in the past? Asking about the client's emotional reaction immediately following the trauma is one way. I would start with an open question, such as,

"How were you feeling after this incident?" Ideally, they would report their symptoms without any prompting (e.g., "I couldn't sleep"; "I had nightmares every night"; "I was constantly on edge"; etc.). You could then follow by asking about specific symptoms or behaviors. "How was your sleep?" "Did you experience intrusive thoughts or memories of the incident?" Lastly, you will want to assess how long the symptoms lasted. For a diagnosis of post-traumatic stress disorder (PTSD), symptoms must be present for at least one month following the traumatic incident and must have resulted in clinically significant distress or impairment in social, occupational, or other important areas of functioning (American Psychiatric Association, 2013). If symptoms were present for at least three days but less than one month following the trauma exposure, a diagnosis of acute stress disorder is warranted. We will discuss how to report these diagnoses in the following section.

One particularly useful test in these cases is the Trauma Symptom Inventory −2 (TSI-2; Briere, 2010) because it assesses the lasting sequelae of traumatic events as well as the test-taker's defensive avoidance tactics. For those who are still experiencing emotional distress following the trauma, the Posttraumatic Stress Disorder Checklist − 5 (PCL-5; Blevins et al., 2015) is a quick screener for posttraumatic symptoms which, if present, would warrant employing the Clinician-Administered PTSD Scale for DSM-5 (CAPS-5; Weathers et al., 2018). The CAPS-5 is a structured interview considered to be the gold standard in PTSD assessment. In addition to assessing the 20 symptoms in the DSM-5 criteria for a PTSD diagnosis, questions target the onset and duration of symptoms, subjective distress, impact of symptoms on social and occupational functioning, improvement in symptoms over time, overall response validity, and overall PTSD severity.

More important than assessing symptoms is getting a clear idea of how the incident changed their view of themselves, others, and the world in general. It is helpful to explore this from a perspective of *before and after*. In other words, how has this incident changed them? Often people's sense of trust and safety is compromised, leading to modifications in their routine, altered ways of relating with others and establishing close relationships, lifestyle changes, etc. Perhaps there was a silver lining to the trauma they experienced, whereby it prompted them to pursue certain career goals (e.g., law enforcement, counseling, etc.) or to use their own experience to support victims. Regardless of how constructive their changes turned out to be, what is important to assess is the harm they endured as a result of the incident in question. Whether that led to positive changes or not is irrelevant to this case.

Many of the cases we come across are victims of violent or non-violent crimes perpetrated by individuals whom the victim does not know or does not have a familiar relationship with. Some examples are victims of battery, assault, or armed robbery; victims of gang violence; parents of minors who were victims of physical or sexual abuse; or victims of abuse or violence in the workplace, academic settings, or places of religious worship. In some cases, individuals' experiences of abuse in the workplace are similar to those observed in domestic violence settings, such as physical abuse, cruel treatment, abusive sexual contact, intimidation, manipulation, psychological abuse, economic abuse, and exploitation of the victim's immigration status (Cho et al., 2014).

How each individual experiences a traumatic event is influenced by their cultural background, their personality characteristics, and their prior life experiences. We can use the "eggshell skull" rule as an example. The eggshell skull is a legal principle that says the wrongdoer is fully liable for the injuries caused to the victim even if the victim had a pre-existing vulnerability. Even though this is not to assess culpability, we would employ the same concept when considering the damage caused to the victim. For example, a client who had witnessed her father's murder as a child had a sudden reemergence of posttraumatic symptoms when an assailant walked into the store where she was shopping and pointed a gun at the cashier. This is why it is important to obtain a thorough background history with an emphasis on prior traumatic experiences.

Evaluating T Visa Applicants

Evaluating victims of human trafficking poses its own idiosyncrasies. Unlike victims of crime, who often experience an isolated traumatic event, victims of human trafficking have typically been exposed to recurrent and chronic abuse. Moreover, if they were lured into coming to the United States under false promises, they might feel somewhat responsible for their circumstances, and victims who hold themselves responsible or deserving of the abuse tend to endure more negative psychological consequences (Branscombe et al., 2003). Those who were unable to defend themselves or take action against the abuser, or who fear retribution, are also likely to experience more severe psychological distress (Cho et al., 2014).

Victims of human trafficking can be of any gender, age, or cultural background, but the most common victims are women and children. The individuals or organized networks behind these lucrative crimes prey on people who are vulnerable, desperate, or simply seeking a better quality of life. Unlike human smuggling, which is typically voluntary although still bears life-threatening risks, human trafficking is involuntary. A smuggling case can certainly morph into a human trafficking case if the victim is exploited, as in the case of a young woman who arranged to be smuggled into the United States but upon arrival was held captive in a home and forced to prostitute herself until she earned the required "quota" to earn her release.

A study by the United Nations Office of Drugs and Crime (2020) revealed that the most common form of human trafficking is sexual exploitation, followed by forced labor. Sex trafficking survivors tend to have more severe or complex clinical presentations than survivors of labor trafficking although depression is the most common mental health condition among survivors of both sex and labor trafficking (Hopper & Gonzalez, 2018). Evans and Hass

(2018) recommend that the evaluator has some knowledge of the typical experiences of victims of human trafficking, which would not only facilitate the interview process but also mitigate the potential for the MHP's vicarious traumatization.

The National Immigrant Women's Advocacy Project developed a set of questions for interviewing victims of human trafficking. Table 6.1 presents a modified version of it.

Even though sometimes the goal of the evaluation is to determine the quality and severity of harm endured by the victim of human trafficking, what the applicant has to demonstrate is <u>how a return to their country of citizenship would affect them</u>. To do that, it is important to know the circumstances surrounding the abuse and the extent of the harm they endured in order to place it in context with their fear of being removed from the United States. Some cultures shun, marginalize, or even punish victims of human trafficking. In Syria, for example, victims of sex trafficking are treated as criminals and face incarceration. Another factor to take into account is that many victims of human trafficking fled their country in search of safety, so returning to that country would expose them to the very dangers they had hoped to escape.

Considerations When Writing the Report

Since the application for a U visa requires that the applicant submit evidence of the crime they suffered, there is no need to describe the incident in detail in the report. As a matter of fact, it is best to not go into too much detail, as that might open the door for inconsistencies and jeopardize the client's credibility. You will be reviewing records and are likely to encounter some details that are not consistent with the client's description of their experiences. In such cases, it is important to explain such discrepancies.

Focus on the events from the client's background that are relevant to the purpose of the examination, and when describing prior trauma, address how the client coped in its aftermath. Unresolved trauma stemming from adversities early in life predisposes the victim to complex psychological and physiological impairment (Felitti & Anda, 2010). If the client received any type of mental health treatment, it can be described in its own section in the report. Conversely, if the client has not sought counseling following their victimization, you will want to explain why. This could be due to many reasons, including cultural values and beliefs, lack of resources, or language barriers.

Unlike VAWA applicants, U visa and T visa applicants do not explicitly have to demonstrate their good moral character, but be mindful not to include anything that might be misconstrued and jeopardize their case (e.g., their juvenile, sealed criminal record, or the past association but not membership in a local street gang) because applicants do have to demonstrate they merit the discretion of USCIS to waive their inadmissibility and grant them nonimmigrant status.

Table 6.1 Interview Questions for Victims of Human Trafficking

---

Recruitment
- Was the victim recruited by someone?
- What kind of job abroad was offered to the victim?
- How much money was promised to the victim and by whom?
- Did the victim sign a contract? What were the terms?

Migration
- Was the victim kidnapped or coerced into migration? How?
- How did the victim travel to the United States?
- Was a fee paid for organizing the victim's migration? By whom and to whom?

Arrival
- Did the victim have control over their identity documents?
- What happened to the victim's identification documents after arrival?
- Did the employer/trafficker use the victim's identity for another purpose?

Working conditions
- Was the victim placed into debt bondage? By whom?
- Were working conditions different from what the victims expected? How?
- Was the victim's movement restricted? How?
- Was the victim living and working at the same place?
- Was the victim chaperoned, guarded, or incarcerated?
- Was the victim paid? At what rate?
- How many hours a day did the victim work? Did they get time off? Were they allowed to rest?
- Was the victim allowed to communicate with family members? Other workers? Allowed to make friends?
- Was the victim able to quit working for the employer and get a job somewhere else?

Strategies used to coerce the victim

Physical coercion
- Was the victim subjected to pinching, hitting, slapping, punching, kicking, shaking, etc.?
- Was the victim subjected to sexual assault, rape, sexual harassment/abuse?
- Was the victim subjected to torture, beatings, or other physical violence?
- Was the victim subjected to incarceration, imprisoned, or physically isolated? How?
- Was the victim denied medical care, food, clothes, and other basic necessities?
- Did the victim attempt to escape from the traffickers? Why?

Psychological coercion
- Was the victim placed into debt bondage?
- Was the victim subjected to threats of physical abuse, harm, or retaliation?
- Were others abused in front of the victim?
- Were the victim's family members threatened? How?
- Were there threats to report the victim to authorities for deportation/jail?
- Was the victim verbally abused, humiliated, or degraded?
- Did the victim ask their employer if they could leave? Why? Why not? What happened?

Source: Adapted from wcl.american.edu/niwap.

In closing, I want to remind you to convey neutrality and objectivity in your report. Victims' experiences are likely to trigger a strong emotional reaction in MHPs, who are typically compassionate and empathic by nature.[4] Just be careful to not come across as an advocate, as it could compromise the helpfulness of the report.

Notes

1 Domestic violence is a common basis for a U petition. A victim of domestic violence, therefore, may be eligible for "special rule cancellation of removal" (see Chapter 3), a self-petition and adjustment of status (see Chapter 5), or a U visa. There are significant distinctions between each remedy, so each case must be properly analyzed by the attorney to determine which remedy has the best likelihood of success.
2 If the victim is under the age of 16 or unable to provide information due to a disability, a parent, guardian, or friend may assist law enforcement on the victim's behalf.
3 Most grounds of inadmissibility can be waived, except for those related to committing genocide or being a Nazi.
4 We discuss self-care in Chapter 10.

Bibliography

Alien victims of certain qualifying criminal activity. (2021). 8 C.F.R. § 214.14.
American Psychiatric Association. (2013). *Diagnostic and statistical manual of mental disorders* (5th ed.). American Psychiatric Press.
Blevins, C. A., Weathers, F. W., Davis, M. T., Witte, T. K., & Domino, J. L. (2015). The posttraumatic stress disorder checklist for DSM-5 (PCL-5): Development and initial psychometric evaluation. *Journal of Traumatic Stress, 28*(6), 489–498. https://doi.org/10.1002/jts.22059
Branscombe, N. R., Wohl, M. J. A., Owen, S., Allison, J. A., & N'gbala, A. (2003). Counterfactual thinking, blame assignment, and well-being in rape victims. *Journal of Applied Social Psychology, 25*, 265–273.
Briere, J. (2010). *Trauma symptom inventory: Second edition (TSI-2).* Psychological Assessment Resources.
Cho, E. H., Hass, G. A., & Saucedo, L. M. (2014). A new understanding of substantial abuse: Evaluating harm in U visa petitions for immigrant victims of workplace crime. *Georgetown Immigration Law Journal, 29*(1), 1–43.
Evans, F. B., & Hass, G. A. (2018). *Forensic psychological assessment in immigration court: A guidebook for evidence-based and ethical practice.* Routledge.
Felitti, V. J., & Anda, R. F. (2010). The relationship of adverse childhood experiences to adult medical disease, psychiatric disorders and sexual behavior: Implications for healthcare. In R. A. Lanius, E. Vermetten, & C. Pain (Eds.), *The impact of early life trauma on health and disease: The hidden epidemic* (pp. 77–87). Cambridge University Press.
Hopper, E. K., & Gonzalez, L. D. (2018). A comparison of psychological symptoms in survivors of sex and labor trafficking. *Behavioral Medicine, 44*(3), 177–188. https://doi.org/10.1080/08964289.2018.1432551

United Nations Office of Drugs and Crime (2021). *Human trafficking.* www.unodc.
org/unodc/en/human-trafficking/human-trafficking.html.
Weathers, F. W., Bovin, M. J., Lee, D. J., Sloan, D. M., Schnurr, P. P., Kaloupek, D. G.,
Keane, T. M., & Marx, B. P. (2018). The clinician-administered PTSD scale for
DSM–5 (CAPS-5): Development and initial psychometric evaluation in military
veterans. *Psychological Assessment, 30*(3), 383–395.

7 Drafting the Report

Mariela G. Shibley, Psy.D.

In graduate school, most mental health professionals (MHPs) are taught how to write clinical reports. These reports, however, are typically used for diagnostic purposes, treatment recommendations, or academic accommodations, and they are generally read by other MHPs, educators, or healthcare providers who have at least a basic understanding of psychological lingo. Forensic reports are quite different from clinical reports in terms of their purpose and intended audience. The purpose of forensic reports is to answer a psycholegal question to help the trier of fact, or the adjudicator, arrive at a legal decision. The person or persons reading forensic reports are usually attorneys, judges, and—in immigration cases—immigration officers. Consequently, the style, language, and essential content of a forensic report will differ from that of a clinical report.

Length

When writing a report, it is essential to keep the reader in mind. No immigration officer will be too pleased to have to read a 25-page report of a psychological evaluation, and I would bet the absolutely relevant information contained in that report could be easily condensed into just a few pages. In general, immigration reports range between 5 and 12 pages. A shorter report is likely to omit important information, whereas any report over 12 pages probably includes too much information. Unnecessary or convoluted details will only confuse the reader or prompt them to skip sections and run the risk of missing important information.

In short, *How long should the report be?* The answer is, 'as long as it needs to be, and no longer.'

Format

Even though the overall format of the report is entirely based on individual preference, it has to be well organized. Splitting the report into a few simple sections or headings is probably best, as it gives the reader a sense of the report's structure while they are reading it and allows the reader to find specific information, should they want to go back to something. In other words,

DOI: 10.4324/9781003139973-8

clearly defined subsections help minimize effort required of the reader. Some standard sections typically included in a report of an immigration evaluation are the following: the evaluator's qualifications, the client's demographic information, the reason for referral, the client's relevant background history, behavioral observations, impressions and findings, clinical diagnostic impression, and a short summary and recommendations. We will discuss each of these sections in more detail below.

Naturally, you will include other sections or subsections as you see fit. For example, if the client has a history of psychiatric treatment, a psychiatric history section is warranted. In rehabilitation waivers it may be appropriate to include a section on substance use history. Conversely, if the client does not have a history of substance use and the use of substances is irrelevant to the referral question, there is no point in including such a section.

Citing Sources of Information

Including all the sources of information you relied on is essential so that the reader is aware of how you arrived at your conclusions. This includes all psychological measures administered, any records that were reviewed, and any collateral information from a third party, such as a brief conversation with the treating therapist, a relative, a teacher, etc.

There are many different ways to list the records reviewed, and this is ultimately an individual preference. Some writers list the name of the document as it is written (e.g., "San Diego County Arrest Report"). Another way is to provide a descriptive label (e.g., "Police report describing the crime"). Some people include the date of the document in parentheses, whereas others write the date the writer read the document. This is more common in forensic cases that are carried out over an extended length of time, and it is sometimes done to back up their invoice, but there is no black letter rule about it that you are required to observe. In some cases, listing the number of pages of each record reviewed is appropriate. Again, this is mainly done to justify the amount of time spent reviewing records if the evaluator is billing hourly. However, there might be other reasons for specifying the pages of a record. I have come across documents with numbered pages (e.g., "page 1 of 5"), of which only the first three were available to me. Consequently, I clarified that I had only read pages 1–3. Letting the adjudicator know exactly what was considered in terms of record review was important because it provided internal and external corroboration as well as redirected the reader back to the importance of the last two pages for further review.

When reviewing numerous medical records from the same facility, you might want to list the time frame in parentheses rather than listing each document by itself—e.g., "Medical records from Kaiser Permanente (August 2011–March 2015)". Again, you should only list the documents you reviewed that were relevant to your findings. If you sought but were unable to get access to certain documents, it is worth noting that on the report as well. In general, however, there are not many records to review in immigration evaluations.

Style

Use of Jargon

Unlike clinical reports, a report of an immigration evaluation will not be read by someone with a mental health background, so avoiding psychological jargon is key (Harvey, 1997, 2005). Some common words or phrases MHPs are used to writing in clinical reports, such as "oriented times three," "labile affect," or "grossly intact memory," sound like gibberish to someone without a mental health background. Mr. Holt recalled a time when, in reference to a report where an MHP described the respondent as a "poor historian," an immigration judge insisted that he didn't need a "good historian"; he needed the respondent "to have a better memory of what happened to him." The judge could not seem to grasp that the word *historian* could describe someone other than an expert of history.

In keeping the reader in mind, try to use more commonly understood language to describe what you want to convey. For example, "Mr. Smith was aware of the current time, location, and purpose of his visit," or "His emotional expressions fluctuated between crying and laughing depending on the content being discussed," or "Mr. Smith was able to provide a logical, sequential, and intact personal history." It is indeed a longer description, but arguably a necessary and more considerate one.

Other expressions to be mindful of are "congruency between mood and affect." The word *affect* might confuse some readers, as the most common interpretation of that word is as a verb (although, when spoken, the noun and verbs are pronounced differently). A more adequate alternative is *emotional expressions* being congruent with the topics of discussion. Following such a statement with an example such as "He cried when discussing his mother's death" is a great way to bring that statement to life.

Many report writers seem to think that using jargon sounds more professional. In practice, however, it tends to confuse and frustrate the person reading it, unless the reader is a fellow MHP. When in doubt about a particular word, it helps to ask a lay person if they know what that word means. I once asked some attorneys if they knew what *malingering* meant, and one replied, "Yes, it's when something lingers," while another one said, "Isn't it a diagnosis on the DSM?" Try to come up with an alternative word or expression that conveys the same meaning (in this case, *feigning* or *exaggerating* would work well). Alternatively, provide a brief explanation of what the word means. You have surely heard people say something like, "Explain it to me like I'm a 5-year-old." That is a good rule of thumb when reporting on arcane issues that are likely to be outside of the reader's area of expertise. There is no need to sacrifice the formality of your language or the professionalism of your tone, but if you need to resort to jargon to explain something, there is a strong likelihood that you do not comprehend it fully yourself!

Also, when reporting medications, make sure to clarify what it is for (e.g., "Mr. Smith was prescribed bupropion, an antidepressant"), or skip the brand name altogether and just mention the type or purpose of the medication (in this case, *antidepressant*). In some situations, it might be important to include the dose, but always with an explanation. For example, 150 mg of bupropion (Wellbutrin) is very different from 100 mg of alprazolam (Xanax), which would warrant clarifying that the former is a standard dose of the antidepressant whereas the latter is likely to be incorrect, as doses tend not to exceed 10 mg per day.

Redundancies, Repetitions, and Unnecessary Descriptions

As a non-native English speaker, I have developed a strong relationship with my thesaurus, so I understand the temptation to overuse it. I also know what a powerful tool a thesaurus can be, either when I cannot think of the word that exactly captures my thought or when I simply need an alternative to a word I have already used. However, the danger comes when we find an impressive sounding synonym that we are not altogether familiar with. I once edited a report that said, "They had an arduous conversation." It was pretty evident that the writer, perhaps feeling that *difficult* was not smart enough, consulted her thesaurus and discovered a word that was much more impressive. Unfortunately, it was also incorrect, so we changed it back to *difficult*.

On the other hand, redundancies can be just as bad. Be careful not to repeat the same word over and over (and over). Beginning every sentence with "The client reported," for instance, can become tedious for the reader. Otto et al. (2014) cite a report where 61 out of 91 sentences started with "The patient indicated that…" (p. 67). Similarly, overusing the words *said* or *reported* will likely yield an unprofessional report. Diversify your vocabulary by using alternative verbs such as *explained, described,* or *shared.*

Redundancies can be more subtle, though, and, therefore, more difficult to catch. For example, "Mr. Smith has a past history of substance abuse" is not necessarily wrong, but "Mr. Smith has a history of substance abuse" says the same thing. That may seem like a minor quibble, but these things add up, and your reader will appreciate the concision of a more streamlined report.

Similarly, be aware of when you are using more words than you need to get a concept across. You will often find things becoming clearer simply by removing a few words. Compare, for example, the following:

- *He explained that it was very difficult for him during that time to find work, and he reported that he often had to sleep on the streets because he did not have anywhere else to stay.*
- *He reportedly had a difficult time finding work and often slept on the streets.*

The first statement is not incorrect, but it also does not offer any more information than the second. Most of us tend to overwrite our first drafts, so it helps to go over your work a second time looking for unnecessary "padding" in your sentences. Any one instance probably would not make a difference, but enough of them over the course of an entire report certainly can. Here are some typical examples I have recently changed in my own writing:

He came to the United States **in order** to seek better employment.	He came to the United States to seek better employment.
Shortly after that, they had problems with…	**Soon**, they had problems with…
Because of the challenges she will face **in the future**, she…	Because of the challenges she will face, she…
Most of us **have a tendency** to "overwrite" our first drafts…	Most of us **tend** to "overwrite" our first drafts…

Again, there is no grammatically correct choice to make here; these are merely subjective decisions that come down to style. In fact, a certain amount of verbosity is unavoidable and, in some cases, preferable, but overall, concise language makes for reports that are easier to write and easier to read. Ultimately, we need our audience to stay engaged throughout the entirety of our report and swiftly and concisely making our points and findings helps us to ensure that outcome.

Related to our discussion of jargon above, stilted words such as *verbalized* can make your writing sound unnatural and should be avoided. Other words to avoid are those that imply a subtle negative connotation, such as *denied, purported, alleged, claimed,* or *admitted,* all of which might suggest dishonesty on the part of the client. There will also be times when no word is needed at all to introduce information if it is understood that it came from the client. Someone is unlikely to read "Mr. Smith graduated college in 1984" and wonder how you possibly could have known that, so you might not need to say, "Mr. Smith reported that he graduated college in 1984."

In the past, I started my behavioral observations section by commenting on the client's dress style and grooming (i.e., "Mr. Smith was well-groomed and casually dressed") until I realized how irrelevant that was within the context of this type of evaluation. Naturally, if the client has dementia or their ability to maintain proper hygiene is in question, such an observation is warranted, but that is not the case with 99% of my clients. So why comment on something so irrelevant? That is how I was taught to write a report at the psychiatric hospital where I completed a pre-doctoral internship, so I included it when I began writing reports for immigration evaluations. After doing something the same way for long enough, especially if it is a habit we picked up in our formative years, we tend not to question it until either someone else points it out or we have a sudden moment of clarity. Be open to those moments.

Referring to Yourself and the Client

Whether to write in first or third person is ultimately a personal choice, but I have a strong preference for first person, and I am not alone in this (Karson & Nadkarni, 2013; Otto et al., 2014; Resnick & Soliman, 2011). Writing in third person makes the writer sound too far removed from the report. If it is clear that you interviewed the client, you wrote the report, and you signed it with your name, why would you refer to yourself as *this evaluator* or *this writer*? I understand that many people prefer to write that way and that there are reasonable arguments to be made for it, so it will come down to whatever you feel is more effective for your style. Similarly, I prefer to refer to the client by name (e.g., "Ms. Sanchez" as opposed to "the client" or "the examinee") because it is more personable and brings the subject of the report to life. If the client is a minor, we always use their first name only, except in any section of identifying information where the surname is required.

Calling the Grammar Police

Editing a report for typos and grammatical errors prior to submitting it is fundamental, as a report full of careless errors looks unprofessional and can create a negative impression in the reader before they even get to the substance.[1] There are numerous software programs and tools to help with that. Alternatively, hire the services of a skilled editor, which is a much safer option in terms of catching mistakes and procuring a professional writing style, but it will likely come at an added cost and the few extra steps of having to remove all identifying information prior to submitting it to the editor. At the very least, have someone in your office—preferably one who is a strong writer—look over your report.

Using Quotations

Quotations in a report should be used judiciously. Most applicants have to include a personal affidavit with their application, so there will already be a document in their file written in their own words. However, quoting the client directly can go a long way in humanizing the client, allowing you to include certain pieces of information that would come across differently if written in third person. Compare the subtle difference in effect of these sentences:

* Ms. Sanchez described her husband as her best friend and the love of her life. She indicated that she would have considerable difficulty without him.
* When asked to describe her husband, Ms. Sanchez said, "He's my best friend, the love my life. I'd be absolutely broken without him."

As with so many points discussed in this chapter, this is a matter of style and context, so there is no single correct answer as to when to use a quotation or not. However, you should be aware of how your choices affect what you are trying to say.

Report Sections

Evaluator's Qualifications

Usually, a report by an MHP is submitted along with the MHP's curriculum vitae, but a short paragraph within the evaluation itself highlighting the writer's qualifications is still warranted. And by short, I mean short. That is, only as long as it takes you to include your licensure status, relevant clinical experience, and any publications or presentations on related topics. There is no need to include information unrelated to the subject matter. For example, I have specialized training in perinatal mental health, but I do not include that because it has never been relevant to an immigration evaluation.

On the other hand, do not be overly brief. In most cases, the MHP who conducted the evaluation will not get another opportunity to explain their qualifications to the adjudicator. This is because the case is either handled administratively—as with many waivers, VAWAs, and U visa applications—or because the client's attorney did not deem it necessary to have the MHP testify as an expert witness in immigration court (IC). Consequently, this opening paragraph is often your only opportunity to convey to the reader that you possess the education, training, and experience necessary to conduct this type of work.

Identifying Information and Reason for Referral

This is another section of the report that should be brief. Its goal is simply to introduce the client to the reader and to explain the purpose of the report (i.e., the referral question). This can include the client's full name, age, gender, race, marital status, education, and employment. If they are married, it may also include the name of their spouse and their children, if they have any. The paragraph concludes with the referral source and the psycholegal question that the report aims to answer.

Relevant Background History

You can divide the section on background history into subsections or keep it all under one heading, depending on how much information there is. Ultimately, the goal is to create a coherent narrative that leads to answering the psycholegal question. Note the word *relevant* on the section heading. Summarizing a 60-year-old's life in three paragraphs is impossible, so it is understandable that every single detail of their past six decades will not be included on the report. This also lets the reader know that the only information included in this section is that which is absolutely pertinent to the referral question and the information on which you based your professional opinion. One way to think of it is this: aside from foundational identifying information, as in the previous section, any fact you include in your report should have a reason to be there. If it did not factor into your conclusions, you are probably better off leaving it out.

You can start with where the client was born and raised, how many siblings they have, if they were raised in an intact household or if the parents separated, etc. If there was some relevant childhood trauma, this is where you would describe it. This can be followed by a summary of their education and employment history, and if the client is a first-generation immigrant, briefly describe their immigration story. Sometimes that comes before education or employment, so you might want to maintain it in chronological order. Then you can delve into their relationship history and how they met their spouse. In waivers where the client is a qualifying relative parent for their adult child, you should put particular emphasis on the quality of their relationship with that child—especially if they have other children.

To reiterate, the important thing in the background section is that it has to be relevant. Do not bog down the reader explaining that

> Mr. Smith lived in California, but his job transferred him to Tennessee, where he lived for three years, and then his aunt got sick so he decided to move back to California, but since he couldn't find a job, he relocated to Nevada, where his cousin owned a carpet factory, and then a friend offered him a partnership in his business, so he moved back to California, where he eventually met his wife.

Did I lose you? In a case like this, you might write it as something like, "Throughout the following years, Mr. Smith moved around in search of employment until he settled back in California, where he met his wife in 2009." If, however, one of the issues to highlight is the client's need for stability in his life, then the details might actually be relevant because they support why living with his family now is so important to him. Similarly, if the client shares that he was sick a lot as a child, it is probably not a relevant detail to mention. If, however, his health has been an issue most of his life and continues to be, then it becomes a focal point.

In waivers and cancellation of removal cases, the client's relationship with the applicant deserves more real estate because that is at the heart of the evaluation. "They met in 2009, they married in 2012 and had two kids, and now he's worried about a potential separation due to his wife's immigration process," is not detailed enough. The use of a client's quoted statements when they were asked to describe their spouse, the quality of their relationship, any adversities they overcame together, and their family life (among countless other things) brings the report to life and gives voice to the client. As I mentioned when discussing writing style, using quotations prudently and with the main goal of expressing something that can only have its desired impact when told in the client's own words is a hallmark of an effective report.

A brief account of the FN's immigration process is only valuable in order to introduce the client's concerns. It is best to avoid too much detail about the immigration process because (1) the immigration officer is already well aware of those details, and (2) any inaccuracies, even if made unintentionally, could raise doubt as to the client's trustworthiness. We have come across many adjudicators whose reaction to such inaccuracies is along the lines of, "What other lies did you tell the therapist?" This is particularly true when their immigration process has been a complicated one.

In terms of medical or psychiatric history, a safe stance is only to include such sections if there is a substantial history. Writing, "No mental health problems or treatment were reported" might be misconstrued and negatively affect the client. Similarly, a substance abuse history is rarely warranted except for cases involving rehabilitation.

Behavioral Observations

It is important to keep the purpose of the behavioral observations in mind. We have come across a number of reports where this section is thorough but largely irrelevant. For example, why would one need to mention the fact that the client did not display any psychotic features if psychosis was never in the picture in the first place? Going down a laundry list of potential issues only to dismiss them gives the impression of a cookie cutter report that does not really take the client into account, or else that the writer just likes to show off their complex psychological jargon.

In general, this section should describe the client's demeanor (i.e., cooperative, engaging, detached), thought process (i.e., linear, coherent, tangential), thought content (i.e., coherent, well organized, relevant to the subject at hand), speech quality (i.e., pressured, adequately paced, slow), eye contact (i.e., avoided, adequate, intermittent), and memory (i.e., sequential, detailed, logical, struggled to recall, etc.). It should also discuss the client's emotional expressions (i.e., congruent/incongruent with topics of discussion, cried, was fidgeting) and, if appropriate, mention any changes in their expressions (e.g., "She broke down in tears when she recalled___"). The paragraph should close with a statement addressing the client's trustworthiness and the validity of their presentation (e.g., "He appeared to be a reliable historian, and his statements were credible"; "These results appear to be an accurate representation of his current level of functioning").

If you choose to use a template or guide for conducting the interview, it helps to have a section whereby you can note the client's presentation and relevant behaviors. I have a list of descriptive words, and I put a check mark next to the ones that apply to the client's presentation. This not only reminds me to focus on important details but also saves time, and it comes in very handy when I am writing the report several days after the interview.

Impressions and Findings

This section covers the client's subjective report of their current concerns and complaints, followed by objective findings from any test measures administered. For hardship waivers, this is where you detail the client's concerns regarding a current or potential separation from their loved one or a relocation. Making clear the client's concerns are their own and not the evaluator's is crucial to preserve objectivity. That is, "Mr. Smith worries about not being able to find a job in Mexico," is more appropriate than "Mr. Smith is unlikely to find a job in Mexico." This is another instance where clients' direct quotations can be very helpful. Be mindful not to state the client's claims as facts and to make it clear that these are, instead, the client's own thoughts. This is for both maintaining truthfulness and not coming across as an advocate.

It is important to mention every test or questionnaire the client completed, including a simple description of the instrument. There is no need to detail its psychometric properties, however, as that would bog down and potentially confuse the reader. It is your ethical obligation to select tests with adequate validity and reliability and to administer them competently (Turner et al., 2001). The purpose of describing the test is to help the reader, who presumably does not have a mental health background, understand why you chose to employ that measure in your evaluation.

When reporting test results, providing a detailed description in plain language is essential. It may help to think of what would make sense to your spouse, partner, or one of your friends who, though well-educated, does not have a background in psychology. For example, the following paragraph should be easy enough for the layperson to understand without sacrificing formality of language:

> Mr. Smith's responses to the Beck Depression Inventory revealed that he is experiencing a moderate degree of depression. He complained of feeling sad much of the time, not enjoying things as much as he used to, and not having enough energy to do very much. He also reported sleeping a lot more than usual, feeling irritable, and having difficulty concentrating.

Presenting test scores must be done within its pertinent context, such as "He rated his anxiety as a seven on a scale of zero to ten." You should never include raw data in describing test results, which is not only unnecessary—and again, potentially confusing—but also strongly injudicious (American Psychological Association, 2020). It is helpful to tie in the client's background history with the test results and point out where results of one test corroborate results from another. This renders the section more cohesive, and the findings are less likely to be called into question.

Clinical Diagnostic Impression

If the client meets criteria for a DSM-5 diagnosis, this is where it would be discussed. In addition to the diagnostic label, it is very important to describe the diagnosis in terms of its criteria. In other words, explain to the reader why the client's symptoms warrant psychiatric diagnosis. There is no need to include the International Classification of Diseases (ICD) codes, which are used almost exclusively for billing and, even though some might think they make a report look more "technical," can actually create some confusion. I have worked with attorneys who questioned the absence of a code, but only because they had seen other reports that included them (most likely medical records they obtained from a health facility) and not because they were required by law. Not acquiescing to an attorney's request, especially one you know is unwarranted, can be intimidating, but I have learned to stand my ground. Remember, you are the MHP. The attorney is not! For example, I was recently asked to include a GAF score, when GAF scores have not been used since the publication of the latest Diagnostic and Statistical Manual for Mental Health Disorders in 2013! As the MHP, you decide what to include in your written report, and those decisions should be based on current and customary practices, along with your own experience and expertise.

When including a DSM-5 diagnosis, describing it in simple terms is key. While those in the medical or mental health field understand what *adjustment disorder* is, the reader of an immigration report might not. The diagnosis, therefore, has to be accompanied by a detailed description.

> Based on my observations and the symptoms reported by Mr. Smith, he currently meets criteria for *adjustment disorder with mixed anxiety and depressed mood*. This diagnosis, which belongs in the Trauma- and Stressor-Related Disorders category of the DSM-5, is warranted when an individual presents with emotional or behavioral symptoms in response to an identifiable stressor, where such symptoms or behaviors are clinically significant as evidenced by marked emotional distress and significant impairment in social, occupational, or other important areas of functioning. If the stressor or its consequences persist, the adjustment disorder may become persistent and give way to more serious psychiatric conditions, such as major depressive disorder.

One might assume that a client who meets criteria for a DSM diagnosis has a stronger case than one whose symptoms do not warrant a diagnosis. This, as mentioned in Chapter 2, is not the case. McLawsen, McLawsen, and Ruser (2011) found that psychological evaluations that included a DSM diagnosis were just as likely to result in a successful outcome as evaluations that did not. Also, in evaluations where trauma is a factor, such as U visas, the client might not meet diagnostic criteria for a mental disorder currently but, based on their reported symptoms and/or clinical records, had in the past. In such

cases, you would state exactly that, saying, for example, "Based on this information, it appears that Mr. Smith's symptoms following the criminal activity
met criteria for a diagnosis of *acute stress disorder.*" You would then describe
what the symptoms are that warrant such a diagnosis.

Summary and Recommendations

This last part of the report is probably the most important one because it is
where you answer the referral question. Following a brief recap of the most
relevant parts of the client's history, the evaluator presents their conceptual
interpretation of the issue at hand and answers the referral question as stated
at the beginning of the report.

Up until this section, the report only states facts—that is, why the
client sought the evaluation, what the client reported, what measures were
administered, and the results. This is the section where you present your
own conceptualization of the client's presentation as it relates to the referral
question. As MHPs, we can see a client's strengths and weaknesses, and—most
importantly—the characteristics, experiences, and personality structures that
make them particularly vulnerable to suffering. The evaluee will not typically have the self-awareness to determine that their insecurities stem from
their lack of adequate nurturing in childhood, which ultimately impacted
their ways of relating with loved ones and establishing a secure attachment.
And this is why you are the one writing the report and not the client.

Do not introduce any new information about the client in this section, as
it should be what the title says: a summary. Be brief but thorough, backing
up your conclusions with relevant content.

Research

There are some situations where you might want to cite research findings
in your report. In general, I tend to do so only when I make generalizations
or claim facts that clearly came from external sources. For example, I might
cite a study or two on the psychological impact of childhood trauma, or how
a family separation affects children's well-being, summarized in a couple of
sentences. There is no need to write an abstract of a research paper. In addition, be sure to weave it into the text in a way that makes sense and flows
naturally, as opposed to a lone paragraph summarizing the research that might
leave the reader trying to figure out how that relates to the client's case.

Many MHPs include research or analyses of country conditions, availability of medical or psychiatric services in the foreign country, or crime
statistics. Doing so poses a great risk for the MHP, who is unlikely to have the
adequate education, training, and experience to assert such findings. Even
though some cases are adjudicated administratively by a USCIS officer, there
is always the potential that the MHP will have to testify in IC. Having to
uphold their expert opinion on an area that is clearly outside their scope of

practice could impeach their testimony, or worse, result in an ethical violation and a complaint to their professional board.

Writing Tips

Writing the report is, for most people, the least exciting part of the evaluation. But there are many things you can do to ease that burden:

- Write the background section as soon as possible following the interview. You will have all the information fresh on your mind and won't have to rely solely on your notes.
- Starting with a previous report as a template allows you to recycle all the headings, formatting, and sections that remain constant in every report (e.g., your qualifications, the referral question, test descriptions, etc.).
- Since you should always describe the diagnosis in language a reader without a mental health background will understand, it helps to keep a separate document with short paragraphs defining the most popular diagnoses. That way you can just copy and paste it onto the report. The same is true for describing the different tests.
- Always do a spelling check. Some people employ grammar applications to correct their spelling and sentence structure as they go, which is fine, but those shouldn't be relied upon exclusively. Go back and read your report from start to finish to catch typos, repetitions, redundancies, etc. Waiting a day after you finish the report to do so is better, as you are more likely to catch these nuances with a fresh look. If you began by using a previous report from another client, do a read-through just to confirm that you have made all necessary modifications (e.g., changing gender pronouns).
- Click SAVE as you go! Need I say how I learned that lesson?

Note

1 The same applies to any communication you have with your referral sources, which is discussed further in Chapter 10.

Bibliography

American Psychological Association, APA Task Force on Psychological Assessment and Evaluation Guidelines. (2020). *APA guidelines for psychological assessment and evaluation.* www.apa.org/about/policy/guidelines-psychological-assessment-evaluation.pdf.

Harvey, V. S. (1997). Improving readability of psychological reports. *Professional Psychology: Research and Practice, 28*(3), 271–274. https://doi.org/10.1037/0735-7028.28.3.271

Harvey, V. S. (2005). Variables affecting the clarity of psychological reports. *Journal of Clinical Psychology, 62*(1), 5–18. https://doi.org/10.1002/jclp.20196

Karson, M. & Nadkarni, L. (2013). *Principles of forensic report writing.* American Psychological Association.

McLawsen, G., McLawsen, J., & Ruser, K. (2011). Demonstrating psychological hardship: A statistical study of psychological evaluations in hardship waivers of inadmissibility. *Bender's Immigration Bulletin, 16*(10).

Otto, R. K., DeMier, R. L., & Boccaccini, M. T. (2014). *Forensic reports and testimony.* Wiley & Sons.

Resnick, P. J. & Soliman, S. (2011). Draftmanship. In A. Buchanan and M. A. Norko (eds.), *The psychiatric report: Principles and practices of forensic writing* (pp. 81–92). Cambridge University Press.

Turner, S. M., DeMers, S. T., Fox, H. R., & Reed, G. M. (2001). APA's guidelines for test user qualifications: An executive summary. *American Psychologist, 56*(12), 1099–1113. https://doi.org/10.1037/0003-066x.56.12.1099

8 Testifying as an Expert in Immigration Court

Matthew G. Holt, Esq. and Mariela G. Shibley, Psy.D.

Despite having testified in federal and state courts many times for other forensic evaluations, in the 14 years that I have been conducting psychological evaluations I have only testified in immigration court (IC) a handful of times. This is because the mental health professional's (MHP) report of a psychological evaluation is often enough evidence. There are times, however, when inconsistencies in the record, vague descriptions, or a particularly difficult case calls for the evaluator's testimony.[1]

Also, not all immigration cases are adjudicated by an immigration judge (IJ). For example, most waivers of inadmissibility, VAWAs, U visas, some affirmative asylum cases, and rehabilitative waivers are handled by USCIS in a non-adversarial setting. The types of cases that are always decided in IC are cancellation of removal (Chapter 3), defensive or referred asylum and withholding of removal (Chapter 4), and competency and bond hearings, which are not covered in this book. If you, in your professional capacity as an MHP, are particularly anxious about testifying in IC, you might want to limit your scope of practice to cases that are adjudicated administratively. However, I hope that this chapter will alleviate your concerns and provide you with a good understanding of what to expect if you are ever asked to testify as an expert witness in IC.

Court Hearings

There is always a variety of hearings on an IC's docket, including removal hearings where a foreign national (FN) may seek any form of relief, withholding-only hearings in which an FN is limited to applying for withholding of removal and relief pursuant to the convention against torture, and bond hearings to allow an FN to seek a custody review and the setting of bond (bail).[2] In all of these, an FN, whether a lawful permanent resident (LPR) or undocumented, is called a "respondent." Generally, a respondent first attends a master calendar hearing and identifies for the IJ which forms of relief they will seek. Perhaps the respondent requests voluntary departure or termination of removal proceedings, or else indicates they will seek a waiver of inadmissibility, cancellation of removal, or some asylum-related

DOI: 10.4324/9781003139973-9

relief. As applicable, the IJ sets a filing deadline in support of all evidence. All this happens before an MHP becomes involved in the case.

Unlike federal or state courts, there is no jury in IC. The only individuals typically present in the IC are the IJ, the respondent and their counsel, the government attorney, and, if needed, a court interpreter. The respondent can bring witnesses and others to support them in their proceedings. Non-witnesses, so long as the hearing remains open to the public, can observe the full hearing. Witnesses, on the other hand, are usually asked to wait outside (in a waiting room or court lobby) until called to testify. This is meant to minimize how one's testimony could influence another's testimony.

Evidence

As prescribed in INA § 240(b)(4)(B), an FN has the right to due process under the Fifth Amendment of the US Constitution, which means they are entitled to a full and fair hearing with a reasonable opportunity to present evidence on their own behalf.[3] The contributions of MHPs often are—or at least point toward—what an IJ will consider the best evidence and most important considerations. The IJ will then apply the law to those facts to rule on the case.

The threshold issue for evidence in the IC's administrative record is whether the evidence is relevant. As per Federal Rule of Evidence 401, relevant evidence is evidence that "has any tendency to make a fact more or less probable than it would be without the evidence" and "the fact is of consequence in determining the action." For example, relief under convention against torture (CAT, Chapter 4) is nondiscretionary, and an applicant's criminal history cannot cause them to be ineligible for CAT. Thus, a prosecutor cannot enter evidence of prior criminal dealings because that evidence would be irrelevant. Lastly, use of the evidence, in terms of how it was obtained and when it was submitted, must be fundamentally fair.[4]

Relevant evidence that an IJ considers generally includes expert affidavits and records such as a report of a psychological evaluation by an MHP. If the report is well-reasoned and consistent with other evidence in the record, parties will often waive the MHP's testimony. That means "bulletproof" reports often lead to the MHP not even needing to testify! However, if the report or evaluation uncovers information that is inconsistent or incompatible with other evidence in the administrative record of proceedings, the MHP should anticipate being called to testify to clarify and explain. Issues of inconsistency and incompatibility are often the result of less than careful planning and review by the respondent or their counsel or erroneous hearsay evidence provided by the government that simply muddies the record.

The MHP as Expert Witness

Federal Rule of Evidence 702 defines expert witnesses as persons "with scientific, technical, or other specialized knowledge" who can "assist the trier of fact to understand the evidence or to determine a fact in issue." Their testimony can be very persuasive because they testify to conclusions drawn from facts that lay persons are not qualified to make. For example, let's say Marco, a citizen of El Salvador, is the respondent facing removal proceedings and applying for cancellation of removal for certain nonpermanent residents. He has to prove his qualifying family members, such as his US citizen (UCS) wife, Betti, will suffer exceptional and extremely unusual hardship if Marco is removed. Betti has a history of severe depression and is on a kidney transplant waiting list. The family has decided that, if Marco is removed, Betti and their two children will move to El Salvador, too. Marco and Betti can testify to Betti's health, and their church leader can testify to Betti's struggles with depression based on their conversations about it, but none of them is qualified to testify regarding whether Betti will have access to a kidney transplant in El Salvador or how her mental health may decompensate. On the other hand, her medical doctor could testify about the importance of the kidney transplant, the prognosis if the transplant does not occur, and whether there is similar access to a transplant in El Salvador. Moreover, an MHP can testify regarding how Betti's severe depression will be affected without adequate treatment. In these instances, the doctor and MHP are able to draw conclusions as facts, not mere speculations, that lay witnesses cannot. Without testimony of expert-driven factual conclusions, the respondent can fail to meet their burden to prove they are deserving of the benefit sought.

The difference between whether a witness is considered a lay witness or expert witness in the IC is a matter of that witness's qualifications. To accept a witness as an expert in removal proceedings, the IJ reviews evidence of the expert's knowledge, skill, experience, training, or education, as presented by the party who wishes to use their testimony. An expert may testify so long as:

- The testimony is based upon sufficient facts or data.
- The testimony is the product of reliable principles and methods.
- The witness has applied the principles and methods reliably to the facts of the case.

In other words, the expert's testimony—just like a written report—will be admitted if relevant, qualified, and reliable. In practice, qualifying the expert typically includes providing the IC with the expert witness's curriculum vitae (CV) or resume and a brief description of what the expert will testify regarding. There may also be some questioning of the expert during the hearing to establish their qualifications.

MHPs are certainly qualifiable as expert witnesses in IC and are able to testify as expert witnesses not only to facts but also as to their opinions, and to make reasonable inferences. Qualifying an MHP as an expert is fairly simple with the right amount of preparation and the timely filing of the proper documentation. Once the IJ allows the testimony, they will likely rely heavily on it to make their decision of the case, and any concerns the

IJ has about the MHP's reliability will affect the weight they give to the MHP's testimony. Factors such as publication experience, education, and work experience in the relevant field, as well as potential bias, may inform the IJ's view of the weight to give the expert's testimony.

What renders an expert's testimony successful? Kwartner and Boccaccini (2008) identified four basic principles underlying effective testimony by an expert witness, which they refer to as the "Four C's": (1) clarity, (2) clinical knowledge, (3) case specificity, and (4) certainty.

1   *Clarity.* The expert witness's ability to communicate clearly is crucial for ensuring that the trier of fact understands the testimony and can apply it when making decisions. As discussed in Chapter 7, the use of psychological jargon is more alienating than helpful, and in court in particular, judges are more likely to be put off by an MHP who uses terms they do not understand than to be impressed by the MHP's eloquent speech.
2   *Clinical knowledge.* Knowledge that comes from clinical experience is generally given more weight than scientific or research knowledge. In other words, judges prefer to hear opinions based on the expert's clinical observations than statistical probabilities.
3   *Case specificity.* This refers to the expert witness's ability to apply their knowledge to the case in question—for example, explaining to the trier of fact how the respondent's symptoms meet criteria for a diagnosis of PTSD. The more case-specific the expert's testimony, the more persuasive it tends to be.
4   *Certainty.* This has to do with the expert witness's conviction regarding their opinion. Wishy-washy or insecure experts are not as credible as those who can confidently stand behind their opinions.

In summary, when testifying in IC (or any other court, for that matter), MHPs should strive to provide accurate, objective, and informative testimony in a way that is helpful to the trier of fact and to stay within the "four corners" of their report[5] and expertise.

Providing Testimony in Immigration Court

When an MHP is called to testify in IC, either party can call them as their witness. Prior to the hearing, the respondent's counsel should provide the MHP with the date, time, and place of the hearing, a copy of the report and any other evidence that may be considered during direct or cross-examination, and a bit of explanation regarding what the respondent needs to accomplish in order to be successful at trial. However, the respondent's counsel should never coach or rehearse potential questions and answers with the MHP.

At trial, the respondent's counsel will elicit direct testimony from the MHP through open-ended questions. Here are some examples:

- What is your profession?
- What education and formal training have you received relevant to your contact with the respondent?
- When did you first meet the respondent?
- What is your relationship with the respondent?
- Please describe the findings of your evaluation.

The government attorney will then cross-examine the MHP with more pointed questions, often in the form of a leading question with a "yes/no" answer. The prosecutor often attempts to undermine an MHP's findings or downplay the seriousness of a diagnosis. For example, the prosecutor may ask something like:

- So, your entire report is just based on one 3-hour session?
- It is not common for an MHP to diagnose a mental illness within just a couple of hours of meeting the person, is it?
- Your report states the respondent needs medication to improve recollection, but isn't it true that the respondent was not on medication during the evaluation?

After the cross-examination, the respondent's counsel gets an opportunity to clarify any issues raised through cross-examination, and then the government attorney can re-cross examine the MHP. Making things even more interesting, the IJ can raise questions and explore testimony of their own volition at any time. Some IJs are particularly engaging and ask a lot of questions, while others ask no questions and simply allow the parties to present their cases.

When you first arrive at the IC, you will likely have to wait in the lobby or waiting area until it is your turn to testify. As explained earlier in the chapter, that is to avoid undue influence on witnesses' testimony. If you request it, sometimes the attorney can put you first on the witness list so that you do not have to wait for too long. Many times, you will end up not testifying at all, either because the hearing is continued (i.e., postponed) for another date or, most commonly, because there were no objections to your written report and no further explanations necessary. Of course, some attorneys want you to stay around anyway, just in case any questions or concerns regarding the report arise.

Tips for Successful Testimony

Testifying as an expert witness can be daunting, particularly for the MHP who has never testified in court. The following are some things to keep in mind:

- You are not the one on trial, so don't go into it thinking that you have to defend yourself. You are, however, expected to be able to explain your conclusions and to provide information that helps the trier of fact make an informed decision.

- Meet with the respondent's attorney prior to the hearing so that you are better prepared. They will go over the questions they will ask you and what they anticipate the government attorney will want to know.

- Once you have an idea about the line of questioning you can expect, jot down some of the main points you want to cover and commit those to memory. This will ensure that you do not forget important facts or opinions, which tends to happen when we are anxious.

- Bring your report with you but read it thoroughly prior to the hearing, as you will be expected not to rely on the report during testimony.

- Do not bring any documents or any other type of evidence to IC that was not already submitted to the respondent's counsel.

- Answer the question being asked—no more, no less. If it is a "yes" or "no" question, answer "yes" or "no" (it can feel unnatural at first because that is not how everyday conversation usually works). It is absolutely okay to say you don't remember something or that you don't know, if that is the truth. It is better to admit you can't recall something or you did not ask the respondent about something in particular than to guess.

- Don't get snarky with the government attorney if they try to intimidate you. Take a deep breath and continue to behave professionally.

- Do not use any jargon. It will not make you sound any smarter, and it will very likely irritate the government attorney and the IJ. Just like in the report, explain things in terms anyone without a mental health background could understand.

Testifying Telephonically

MHPs may be called to testify in person in court or allowed to testify telephonically. MHPs should coordinate with the respondent and/or counsel to determine which is better. If the MHP wants to testify by phone instead of in person, the respondent must explain in a written motion (or an oral motion at a master calendar hearing) why the witness cannot appear in person, and they must provide the MHP's telephone number and the location from which they will testify.

Testifying over the phone versus in person can have its advantages and disadvantages. It may be less anxiety-provoking than going to IC in person, but any technical glitches or poor sound quality can be frustrating. As when testifying in person, you will be given a time frame for when you can expect to be called, and you will have to be prepared to receive the call at any time during that window. While you wait you can have those bullet points you prepared or any other documents in front of you to facilitate your testimony, and you can be sipping on a cup of hot tea to soothe your nerves. It also saves you from having to drive down to the courthouse and find parking, which can be the most stressful aspect of testifying in court! Ultimately, whether or not to permit telephonic testimony is within the discretion of the IJ.

Procedural Requirements

There are certain procedural requirements parties must follow in IC to submit live or telephonic testimony. These requirements include filing a witness list well in advance of the individual or merits hearing and including the CV or resume for any witnesses on the list that the respondent will attempt to call as an expert. Always make sure the respondent's attorney has put your name on the witness list and that they have your most recent CV.

As an expert witness, you need to be paid for your time. Typically, it is the respondent (i.e., your client) or the respondent's attorney who is responsible for your payment. Because a hearing can take anywhere between minutes (as in the case when it gets rescheduled) and hours, it is best to clear several hours in your schedule. Most MHPs bill for a half day (four hours) or full day (anything over four hours). Whereas for a law firm this is not an outrageous expenditure, it can be so for the respondent. You might want to consider offering a reduced fee to those who need it. Keep in mind, however, that if you are subpoenaed by the IJ to testify, you cannot refuse to do so just because the respondent cannot pay for your time, but it is highly unlikely an IJ will subpoena you.

Keep track of all the cases where you testified as an expert witness, as you will be asked for it either prior to or during your testimony. The government attorney might ask you how much you got paid for the evaluation, hoping to make you look like a "hired gun" whose testimony is not objective (Melton et al., 2007). If this happens, your best approach is to make it clear that you charged what is customary in this type of case and that you bill for your time, not for a specific finding.

Although it is much more common for the MHP to simply file a report as part of the respondent's admissible evidence than to have to testify in court, you must be prepared for anything. I promise it is not as bad as you might think and that it gets easier every time. Reaching out to a colleague for practical or emotional support can be extremely helpful to reduce your anxiety, especially if they have experience testifying as an expert witness. Above all, remember what your role is (you are not on trial!) and that you are there because you have valuable expertise that will assist the IJ to make an informed decision on the case.

Notes

1 MHPs can also be called to testify when the report of the evaluation they conducted was not timely submitted (often the attorney's fault).
2 Violations of federal laws related to immigration may be prosecuted by the US Attorney's Office, but those proceedings occur in federal court, not the IC system.
3 They also have the right to be represented by counsel although they are not provided with one, as a defendant in criminal court would be.
4 See *Matter of Grijalva*, 19 I&N Dec. 713, 721-22 (BIA 1988).
5 When lawyers refer to staying within the "four corners" of something, they mean that you only look at what is contained in the document itself (whether it is a contract, a police report, etc.) and not consider or refer to external factors.

Bibliography

Kwartner, P.P., & Boccaccini, M. T. (2008). Testifying in court: Evidenced-based recommendations for expert-witness testimony. In R. Jackson (Ed.), *Learning forensic assessment* (pp. 565–588). Routledge.

Melton, G. B., Petrila, J., Poythress, N., Slobogin, C., Lyons, P., & Otto, R. K. (2007). *Psychological evaluations for the courts: A handbook for mental health professionals and lawyers* (3rd ed.). Guilford Press.

9 Cultural and Linguistic Considerations

Mariela G. Shibley, Psy.D.

We all identify with multiple cultural and social groups, large and small, each of which exerts its own influences. Because of this complexity, it is never safe to assume a person's cultural background based on any single group to which they belong. A culturally informed mental health professional (MHP) takes into consideration the complexity and intersectionality among and between personal identities. In addition to a person's race and nationality, one must consider a host of background factors that influence a person's view of themselves and the world, such as their age, gender identity and expression, socioeconomic status, religious and spiritual beliefs, sexual orientation, education, developmental and acquired disabilities, and immigration status, among others (American Psychological Association, 2017; National Association of Social Workers, 2015; Ratts et al., 2016). This is essential when conducting psychological evaluations for immigration court and USCIS because MHPs are bound to work with clients whose cultural backgrounds are very different from their own. It is ultimately the MHP's ethical responsibility to attain adequate training, supervision and consultation in cultural diversity issues and to acknowledge the limitations of their expertise (American Psychological Association, 2017; Barber-Rioja & Garcia-Mancilla, 2019; Hays, 2008).

Cultural Competency and Cultural Humility

Cultural competency is the ability to understand and reflect on differing worldviews, customs, and belief systems in relation to one's own. It requires mental flexibility and a commitment to learning and reworking our knowledge about diversity through practice and experience. Cultural competence calls for moving beyond a one-dimensional conceptualization of individuals' behaviors, attitudes, and values (Hays, 2008) and instead reflecting on the influence of different contexts and domains (Clauss-Ehlers et al., 2019; Falicov, 2014). There is no such thing as belonging to one culture; we all belong to various cultural groups, each of which exerts some degree of influence on us as individuals. The intersection of the various cultural groups we identify with and the boundaries that separate us from other cultural groups create a personal map that is both static and constantly shifting. That is, some

DOI: 10.4324/9781003139973-10

of the cultural groups we identify with are constant throughout our life, whereas others are bound to change. Therefore, pretending to understand an individual based on knowledge of one of the cultural groups to which they belong is an outdated and reductionist approach to cultural competency.

If you travel to Thailand, you might hear the phrase "same same but different," a popular catchphrase in tourist areas meaning that, despite having similarities, there are nuances that make one thing different from something else. We as human beings share a number of biological and psychological characteristics that make us, in many ways, the same. And yet we are different in so many others. The concept of cultural universality emphasizes commonalities over differences, but even though focusing on these cultural universals is a great way to connect with others, an overemphasis on sameness runs the risk of imposing one's own values and beliefs on members of other cultures (also referred to as ethnocentrism), and over-pathologizing. For example, in many cultures seeing or hearing a deceased relative during the bereavement period is absolutely normal. Under DSM-5 criteria, however, this behavior might be misdiagnosed as a symptom of a psychotic disorder.

In addition, our beliefs, attitudes, and behaviors are molded within our families, our communities, and the larger society. Many of these also change and evolve throughout our lives. Some cultures place a great deal of value on family kinship, whereas others tend to foment autonomy and independence. Whereas in many Latin countries living with one's parents until well into the 30s or until marriage is the norm, many Americans move out of their home to attend college before they even reach the age of 18. Many families in the United States are spread out in different states, something you will rarely see in Argentina, for example. Considering these differences is important when assessing the impact of a family separation. Also in Latin cultures is the concept of *familismo*, that is, prioritizing the needs of the family over one's own. We see this a lot when it comes to self-care behaviors. When asked why they have not sought mental health treatment, most clients have shared that doing so would take them away from family activities or responsibilities or that spending money on personal therapy would be "selfish." When a family member is forced to depart the country, it creates an immense disruption in the family unit. Similarly, families where all but one or two of the members are living in the United States while the others stayed back in their country of origin feel incomplete or, as one client lamented, "like one of the ducklings was left back on the land."

Someone's position on the individualism–collectivism spectrum can have important implications for psychological assessments. Individuals from collectivistic cultures, which perceive the self as part of a larger whole, consider the effects of their decisions on others and tend to rely on the opinions and views of others when conceptualizing their experiences. The Zulu concept of *ubuntu* ("I am because we are") is a good example of collectivism. By comparison, individualists are motivated by their own preferences and needs, prioritizing personal needs rather than group goals.

In so many ways, not considering cultural influences on individuals' attitudes and behaviors can result in not only misunderstandings and over-pathologizing but also microaggressions. A friend once shared that her therapist had a contemptuous reaction when she, who was 33 years old, told him she still lived with her parents, which the therapist deemed to be an "enmeshed relationship." It took several conversations to reassure her that, despite her therapist's assertions, she was doing nothing wrong in residing with her parents, who had immigrated from the Philippines a few years prior.

What is the best approach when interviewing clients from different cultural backgrounds, then? The concept of *cultural humility* is one worth discussing. Tervalon and Murray-Garcia (1998) coined the term *cultural humility* to contrast *cultural competence*. They stressed the importance of maintaining an interpersonal stance that takes into consideration the provider's beliefs, values, and experiences when attempting to understand aspects of the client's cultural identity. Most importantly, it is setting aside our preconceived knowledge of cultural constructs and accepting the client as the expert of their own cultural identities and experiences.

At a more macro-level, this entails being inquisitive about a client's racial identification, for example. Labeling someone as Black based on the color of their skin is a gross classification that does not take into account the individual's racial identity (consider, for instance, a Nigerian, an Australian aborigine, and a Jamaican—all of whom may have similar shades of skin tone but drastically different cultural perspectives). A forensic psychologist shared that after years of writing reports for the courts, he decided to stop identifying individuals by their race. He said, "I used to start the demographics section with, 'The client is a 46-year-old, African American, male' and then a client told me, 'I'm not African American; I'm Trinidadian.' So, I decided to stop introducing clients by their race."

At a micro-level, inquiring about what something means to the client within their cultural context helps us further bypass our own preconceived constructs. A Guatemalan woman described her mother as "a good woman." As the interview went on, it became evident in her description of her upbringing that her mother was never around. Since my concept of "a good woman" did not seem to fit with her overall description of her mother, I asked her to explain what she had meant by that. She clarified that in comparison to her alcoholic and physically abusive father, her mother was "good, because she didn't hit us."

Cultural humility is not so much about knowledge as it is about openness and curiosity. It entails being willing to learn about our clients' identities and personal experiences and to be able to set aside any preconceptions we were holding onto. Sometimes belonging to the same cultural group can lead us to make assumptions about another person based on our own experiences. As a native of Argentina, I can attest to the differences among the cultural group we refer to as Hispanics. Even though we might speak the same language, Argentine customs are in many ways very different from

Mexican or Peruvian, for example. Conversely, individuals from two totally different cultures can find commonalities in their religious beliefs that overshadow any ethnic differences. A Jew from Argentina can feel a strong sense of connection to an Israeli Jew despite speaking different languages and being radically different in many other ways.

The interaction of cultural and sociopolitical differences between providers and their patients was beautifully conceptualized into a multidimensional framework by Falicov (1995). In her development of the Multidimensional Ecosystemic Comparative Approach (MECA), she advocated for cultural humility by encouraging MHPs and medical providers to explore their own cultural backgrounds and that of their patients, paying particular attention to their differences and similarities. MECA's comparative approach helps providers understand individuals along four universal domains: migration and acculturation (when, why, and how a family migrated and their current immigration status), ecological context (how families, communities, and the larger society shape an individual's beliefs, attitudes, and behaviors), family organization (hierarchies and structure among family members and the family's values, customs, or rituals), and family life cycle (developmental stages, transitions, and rites of passage within the family). Taking such a multidimensional approach when conducting immigration evaluations is extremely helpful because it allows us to gain a better understanding of the client's unique set of identities. It is here where we often find their particular characteristics and vulnerabilities that would make them more susceptible to emotional hardships, or that give context to our understanding of their personal experiences.

How we express cultural humility is also very important. We all sense when a person is asking a question out of genuine curiosity versus a camouflaged condescending attitude with a preconceived notion of the answer. This is very common when interviewing individuals from different cultural backgrounds—especially when the interview is conducted in the client's second (and less proficient) language. We will discuss language in the next section, but what is important to highlight here is the importance of taking an interpersonal stance of humility when working with foreign nationals (FNs).

Some people are known to talk to those who lack command of the English language as if they were intellectually unsophisticated. It is important to acknowledge that just because a person does not have an advanced vocabulary through which to express themselves does not mean they lack experience, knowledge, or maturity. This is also often the case when working with elders, unfortunately. I remember accompanying my grandmother to the emergency room and her turning to me and saying, "Why does the doctor talk to me like I'm an idiot?"

Both cultural competence and cultural humility are indispensable for understanding those from differing cultural backgrounds. The combination of these two abilities results in *cultural attunement* (Falicov, 2014), and this is true both in forensic and therapeutic settings. Being attuned to your client will allow for a more accurate and nuanced understanding of that person's experience.

Acculturation

Acculturation is the degree to which an individual has adapted to the dominant culture where they now reside. The Canadian psychologist John Berry (1997) came up with a model for understanding the process and changes implied in the acculturation process as they affect individuals. He suggested that as a result of exposure to two or more cultures, an individual employs one of four different strategies based on two dimensions: (1) attitude toward keeping heritage culture and identity and (2) attitude toward learning and interacting with new culture. The four strategies are:

Assimilation: When an individual wishes to diminish or decrease the significance of the culture of origin and wants to identify and interact primarily with the other culture.
Separation: Whenever the individual wants to hold onto the original culture and avoids interacting with or learning about the other culture.
Marginalization: When individuals show little involvement in maintaining the culture of origin or in learning about the other culture, often resulting from failed attempts at assimilation combined with experiences of discrimination.
Integration: When a person shows an interest in maintaining the original culture and in learning and participating in the other culture.

Considering where a client is in their acculturation process is very helpful when trying to understand the impact that a return to their country of origin would have on them. A 55-year-old who has been in the United States for 10 years will have a different experience from that of a 25-year-old who was brought here at the age of 2. The less acculturated a client is, the more sensitive one's approach should be when establishing rapport. For example, Stamm and Friedman (2000) commented on an elderly Alaska

Table 9.1 Acculturation Process Model

		Attitude toward keeping heritage culture and identity	
		Positive	**Negative**
Attitude toward learning and interacting with new culture	**Positive**	Integration	Assimilation
	Negative	Separation	Marginalization

Source: Berry (1997).

Native woman who refused to answer the evaluator's questions, reportedly stating, "Why would I tell him anything about me, [*sic*] he just kept asking me questions and never told me anything about himself" (p.78).

If you are thinking about which assessment measure to administer to determine the client's current acculturation strategy, you can try to get a hold of the Stephenson Multigroup Acculturation Scale (Stephenson, 2000). However, I have never used any measures to assess acculturation because that can easily be uncovered in a thorough interview.

Linguistic Differences

Language is an indispensable tool to convey our internal experiences both to the outside world and to ourselves. Words function as schemas of personal experiences. Since every language contains its own set of associations and symbolic representations, experiences that are captured in one linguistic community might not be readily recalled in terms of the schemas of another (Movahedi, 1996). This is true even when two people are speaking the same language but come from different cultural backgrounds. A client from England once recalled being annoyed when her boyfriend came home "pissed." "Why was he pissed?" I asked. "Because he had the night off and went out with his guy friends," she said. With a puzzled look on my face, I asked, "I don't understand. Did something happen to upset him?" Now *she* had the puzzled look on her face as she replied, "No. Nothing upset him. He was *pissed*. He drank too much." Little did I know that in her dialect the word *pissed* means *drunk*! This is a rather insignificant example, but it goes to show that even when speaking the same language, we can form inaccurate interpretations.

For most FNs who come in for a psychological evaluation, English is not their native language. Whether the interview is conducted in English or in their native tongue can have a significant impact on what they share and how they share it. Consistent findings support the notion that the native tongue is directly linked to emotional content, whereas a second language is used in a more rational, intellectual nature (Aragno & Schlachet, 1996; Bloom & Beckwith, 1989; Bond & Lai, 1986; Buxbaum, 1949; Marcos, 1976; Rozensky & Gomez, 1983; Santiago-Rivera & Altarriba, 2002). This impacts the clinical interview in several ways. Javier et al. (1993) found that autobiographical memories recalled in the language of the actual experience show better content organization, detail, and textual vividness than they do when the same event is recollected in another language. This knowledge was very helpful when I testified as an expert on an asylum case and the judge questioned the applicant's credibility based on the fact that during the credible fear interview, he had not shared very important details of the persecution he experienced in his native country. Since the applicant spoke English rather well, that is the language he spoke during the interview. When I evaluated him in Spanish, his native tongue, he was able to recall and describe his experiences in much more detail. "If that indeed happened, why didn't he share that with the immigration officer?" asked the immigration judge. Very reasonable question. Being familiar with the vicissitudes of speaking in a second language myself, I was able to explain to the judge what likely resulted in this discrepancy.

In addition, when individuals are able to recall early traumatic experiences in the same language in which they took place, they can access more intense emotional content (Aragno & Schlachet, 1996; Perez-Foster, 1998). Their narratives, therefore, tend to be more elaborate and emotionally complex (Waisman, 2005).

Allowing clients to express themselves in their native language will therefore likely yield a richer, more poignant discourse. Naturally, this may not be feasible if the evaluator does not speak the client's native tongue, but employing the help of a professional interpreter can facilitate that. More on the use of interpreters will be discussed later.

When people are not very proficient in their second language, they tend to invest more energy in *how* they are expressing themselves than in *what* they are saying. This extra amount of effort may result in suppression of affect (Marcos, 1976; Marcos & Urcuyo, 1979). This is true when either speaking or listening in one's second language, and it is very important to keep in mind when interviewing a client who is not very fluent in English, as it can lead the evaluator to form an inaccurate impression of the client's experience or even question their credibility.

Individuals have also been found to perceive themselves as less intelligent, less confident, and less approachable when speaking in their second language versus their native tongue (Segalowitz, 1976). We often see this when working with clients who are extremely accomplished in their home countries (such as doctors, engineers, and teachers) but who, because they do not have a good command of the English language, are restricted by a rudimentary vocabulary. When compounded with an inability to practice professionally due to legal impediments (e.g., not having a license to practice in the United States), their overall sense of confidence diminishes greatly. Being mindful of this situation will likely lead to a more accurate assessment of the client's presentation.

Conversely, a second language can serve a protective function for the speaker, allowing them to share emotionally charged material that would otherwise be too overwhelming to revisit. Bond and Lai (1986) conducted a study with a group of bilingual Chinese students and asked them to discuss culturally embarrassing topics and non-embarrassing topics in both their native tongue and their second language. Their findings revealed that when the students answered questions on embarrassing topics in their second language, they spoke at a greater length than when they were speaking their native tongue. They concluded that words in the second language are not as emotionally arousing as those in the native tongue, thus allowing a person to disclose material that would otherwise be too upsetting or embarrassing to tolerate.

We have found this to be true in our professional experiences with FNs. It is not uncommon for clients who are aware that we speak their native tongue to prefer to discuss their personal experiences in English despite it being their less dominant language. Sometimes they will say that they feel more comfortable discussing certain material in English, whereas others might justify it (to themselves, even) as an attempt to make it easier for the evaluator. Ultimately, it is the client's choice when it comes to what language they prefer or to switch languages throughout the clinical interview. It is worth noticing, though—and perhaps even mentioning on the written report—the clients' inflections in rate of speech, increases in interjections, and non-verbal behaviors when they are speaking in either language, and to discern whether that is due to anxiety about the content, the process, or their language proficiency.

When individuals are proficient in two languages, especially when the languages were acquired in different contexts, they may develop a "dual sense of self" (Burck, 2004; Katsavdakis et al., 2001; Perez-Foster, 1996). That is, they perceive themselves differently depending on the language they are speaking. This is more prominent for those who are either more proficient in one language than the other or who use one language in a professional context and the other in a more intimate, familiar environment. It is particularly found in second-generation immigrants whose first language is the one their parents speak in the home and who learned English (their second language) when they started attending school. Consequently, they end up being more proficient in English than in their official mother tongue. A study on bilingual MHPs' experiences conducting psychotherapy in their native language revealed that despite being fluent in two languages, speaking with their clients in their mother tongue decreased their confidence level and posed a challenge to their professional identity (Gamsie, 2008). This is something to keep in mind if you are not used to speaking your native language in professional settings!

The Use of Language Interpreters

When a client is not proficient in English and the MHP does not speak the client's language, there are two options: (1) refer the client to an MHP who speaks their mother tongue or (2) employ the help of an interpreter. The latter, although oftentimes very helpful, can present its own hindrances to the evaluation process. In my past life, I worked as a professional interpreter, an experience that now affords me the advantage of having been both the interpreter and the interpreted, as I have hired many interpreters throughout the years when referring clients to another MHP was not a viable option. Even though an online search will produce a number of articles and videos on tips for working with interpreters, there are two very important factors that are frequently overlooked: confidentiality and vicarious traumatization, both of which are crucial when it comes to hiring an interpreter for a psychological evaluation.

Unlike a medical visit to an orthopedist, the information a client discloses in a mental health setting is considerably personal. It is hard enough for some clients to open up to a therapist, and much more so to a non-clinician. When the client belongs to a small cultural community, the likelihood of crossing paths with the interpreter in the future or of having mutual acquaintances is very high. Consequently, it is vital to assure the client that their privacy will be respected. To that end, we have interpreters sign a Confidentiality and Non-disclosure Agreement, and we go over it with the client present. If at any point the client expresses discomfort with the interpreter, we immediately end the interview and make arrangements for how to proceed with the evaluation.

In addition, most interpreters are used to working in medical or legal settings, which is naturally very different from a mental health setting. Listening to someone describe how their pain radiates down their right leg is different from hearing and repeating how a person was brutally raped. Interpreters often have no idea what they are in for in a mental health setting. Consequently, it is crucial to have a meeting with them prior to the clinical interview, warning them that they might have to hear and translate some extremely traumatic experiences, as there is a significant possibility it will result in vicarious trauma (an empathic emotional reaction that results from hearing others' trauma stories and the pain, fear, or terror they have endured). Debriefing with them after the interview is also important to make sure that any emotional reactions to what transpired during the interview are adequately addressed.

In order to save you the trouble of Googling tips for working with interpreters, the most important points are summarized in Table 9.2.

Culturally Sensitive Assessment Procedures and Instruments

One of the challenges of evaluating culturally diverse individuals is the assessment methodology. The DSM-5 Outline for Cultural Formulation (OCF) was specifically designed to help MHPs conduct a culturally sensitive diagnostic interview. This comprehensive approach to clinical diagnosis accounts for cultural influences on mental disorders by addressing the following dimensions: (1) cultural identity of the individual, (2) cultural explanations of the individual's illness, (3) cultural factors related to the psychosocial environment and levels of functioning, (4) cultural elements of the relationship between the individual and the clinician, and (5) overall cultural assessment for diagnosis and care (American Psychiatric Association, 2013). Incorporating some of the questions from the OCF into the clinical interview can be very helpful when evaluating FNs and individuals from cultural backgrounds unfamiliar to the evaluator.

Some MHPs may mistakenly assume that tests can be translated and used along with existing norms. This is not so. When using psychological tests and other measures in immigration evaluations, it is important to employ measures that have been adequately translated and to consider how accurately they assess the constructs measured across distinct cultural groups. The degree to which diagnoses and clinical assessment findings are generalizable

Table 9.2 Tips for Working with Interpreters

---

1. Make sure you hire a professional interpreter—not just someone who happens to speak the client's language. Never, ever have the client's family member do the interpreting. Avoid telephone interpreters.
2. In certain cases, it is important to be mindful of the interpreter's gender and cultural background. Some clients feel very uncomfortable discussing intimate and potentially shameful experiences in front of someone of the opposite gender or from an incompatible cultural group (e.g., an Iraqi refugee recounting the persecution they endured for being Christian in the presence of a Sunni Muslim interpreter).
3. If you meet an interpreter whom you enjoyed working with, keep them in mind for future cases, as they already know how you work and what your expectations are.
4. Meet with the interpreter prior to commencing the interview and explain what the evaluation process will consist of and the importance of maintaining confidentiality.
5. Go over the confidentiality agreement with both the client and interpreter present and have the interpreter sign it. Ask the interpreter to share with the client everything that the two of you discuss, and go over the interview process and your expectations (make sure everything you and the interpreter discuss in front of the client is promptly translated).
6. Ask the interpreter to speak in first person and repeat what the client says verbatim.
7. Instruct them not to summarize, rephrase, or add anything that the client did not say.
8. Decide whether you prefer that the interpreter speak simultaneously (at the same time as the client speaks—as it is done in court) or consecutively (interpreting small bits at a time, having the speaker pause every few sentences).[a]
9. Make seating arrangements so that the interpreter is equidistant from you and the client in a triangular setup, and everyone can see one another.
10. Speak to the client and have the client look at you when they speak. Even though everyone is well aware of the fact that there is a third party involved in the conversation, this will facilitate the development of rapport between you and the client.
11. Be careful if administering psychological tests that are not in the client's language. Having an interpreter read the items aloud may violate the administration protocol. In any event, when modifying the format of the test administration, be sure to note it on the report.
12. Debrief with the interpreter after the interview to address any discomfort they might have experienced as a result of what transpired during the interview. Take this opportunity to have the interpreter offer their observations of any consequential nuances they noticed or educate you on relevant cultural issues (e.g., an interpreter once informed me that the client's description of a political event was inaccurate).

Note: [a]Even though consecutive interpreting takes twice as long (as everything must be repeated twice), some people find it less distracting than hearing two voices at the same time. Nonetheless, if an interpreter is unable to do simultaneous interpretation it might be a sign that they are not professional. All certified interpreters must demonstrate the ability to perform simultaneous interpretation in order to earn their professional certification.

to different cultural groups and multicultural contexts is referred to as "cultural validity" (Leong et al., 2019). It is ultimately the MHP's professional and ethical responsibility to select assessment tools that are adequately validated and appropriate for the population, setting, and context at hand (Turner et al., 2001).

Because we deal with a largely Hispanic population, we have a Spanish version of all of our intake forms and informed consents. In addition, we only select tests and assessment measures that have been normed and/or validated to be used with Spanish speakers. If you work predominantly with a particular ethnic group, it is helpful to have your forms translated into that language.[1]

Assessing the Impact of Trauma

The psychological impact of a traumatic event is mitigated by a person's interpretation of the event, their personality, and their past experiences. Consequently, it is a very personal experience. Being robbed at gunpoint can result in crippling posttraumatic symptoms in one person, and yet it can be a short-lived state of shock for another. Similarly, a miscarriage can scar a woman for life, whereas another woman sees it as an unfortunate setback. It is interesting to note how different women will discuss that experience during an interview, with some breaking down in tears and others mentioning it in passing. Of course, relying on how a person talks about their experiences does not discard the mitigating impact of conscious or unconscious defense mechanisms.

Adding culture to the mix further muddles this assessment. Internalized belief systems and culturally influenced coping methods alter the cognitive processing of traumatic experiences. Women across many cultures in the Middle East endure ostracism following a rape and are often the victims of honor killings by their immediate family. Throughout many countries in Latin America, a husband is believed to have the right to have sex with his wife whenever he so desires as part of the marriage contract, and, as discussed in Chapter 5, marital rape was not considered to be a crime until very recently. In Panama, for example, marital rape was just recently criminalized in 2013, and it was not until 1999 and 2005 when rape perpetrated by a spouse became a crime in Chile and Brazil, respectively. Still, many other countries throughout the world do not consider being raped by one's spouse a crime (e.g., Afghanistan, China, El Salvador, Nigeria, and Jamaica, among many others). Even in the United States, prior to the mid-1970s marital rape was exempted from ordinary rape laws. Although laws have changed and evolved over the years, most states continue to treat marital rape differently from non-marital rape (i.e., more narrow laws, lesser penalties, shorter sentences, etc.), which, in turn, influences the victim's perception of the experience. This is important to keep in mind when evaluating victims of domestic violence who appear inclined to take responsibility for the abuser's conduct or who convey a profound sense of helplessness.

How individuals express their symptomatology can also vary among cultures. For example, Norwegians and Japanese tend to limit and restrain their emotional expressions much more when compared to Italians and Filipinos, even though their subjective distress may be comparable (Stamm & Friedman, 2000). At the same time, it would be reasonable to suspect that a Norwegian client displaying the same acuity of emotion as an Italian is suffering more subjective distress. Malgady and Cortes (1996) found that inner-city Puerto Ricans often use idioms of aggression, assertiveness, and vindictiveness to express psychiatric symptoms such as depression and anxiety. Behind that protective veil of aggression there is likely to be intense sadness and pain. Hispanics are known to somatize their emotional distress (Falicov, 2014; Hulme, 1996; Organista, 2000), as complaining of headaches, neck pain, or gastrointestinal problems is much less stigmatizing than acknowledging they are depressed. A client who denied experiencing any anxiety shared that they had been struggling with gastritis for six months—the exact time when they received a Notice of Intent to Deny from USCIS. Therefore, assessing physical symptoms and their onset is often an important component of an immigration evaluation.

Wilson (2007) astutely posed the question, "If a culture does not have linguistic connotations of a pathogenic nature (e.g., PTSD), how then does the person construe acute or prolonged effects of extreme stress experiences?" (p. 11). This is in line with what is known as the Sapir–Whorf hypothesis (or linguistic relativity), which basically proposes that individuals' worldview is shaped by their language. In Portuguese, for example, there is the word *saudade*, which is loosely translated as longing, nostalgia, or melancholia, yet none of those words exactly convey the meaning Portuguese speakers intended. Does that mean a non-Portuguese speaker does not experience that emotion? I don't think so, and I would be surprised to encounter an immigrant who has not experienced that emotional state.

Lastly, the concept of *insidious trauma*, as coined by Root (1992), refers to the cumulative experiences of degradation, discrimination, and ostracism directed toward individuals whose cultural identities differ from what is valued by those in power. Though not always blatant or violent, these attitudes threaten the sense of safety and overall welfare of those who suffer it and often results in character vulnerabilities. Such vulnerabilities predispose a person to subsequent trauma, even when the event itself may not be deemed to be traumatic by most people. This is a common experience of non-heterosexuals, gender variant individuals, people of color, and individuals with disabilities, among others. Considering the impact of insidious trauma on such individuals helps us understand their reactions to what might otherwise be assumed to be nothing more than an unpleasant experience.

Memory and Trauma

Being able to describe a traumatic experience is the basis for substantiating an asylum claim, a U visa, or any other immigration petitions that are granted on the basis of having suffered physical or psychological harm. Memory, however, is often severely compromised when a person is the victim of a traumatic event. This can put into question the applicant's credibility and potentially ruin their chances of a favorable outcome. There is extensive research on the effect of emotion on the encoding and retrieval of memories of distressing events. As discussed in Chapter 4, memory consolidation (the encoding of autobiographical experiences) is inhibited when the emotional response is too overwhelming, as the pre-frontal cortex (the part of the brain that deals with executive functioning) and the hippocampus (the brain structure in charge of memory storage) are compromised. Consequently, instead of being organized into a unified experience, memories are later retrieved as fragmented images and physical sensations that feel disconnected from other life experiences. As van der Kolk (2007) nicely stated, "Traumatic memories are timeless and ego-alien" (p. 295).

Herlihy et al. (2002) questioned the assumption of lack of credibility when there is inconsistency in the repeated recollection of traumatic memories. In interviewing asylum seekers with posttraumatic stress disorder, they found more discrepancies the longer the time between interviews. This is important when considering the length of the asylum process and the amount of time in between different interviews, court testimony, and any appeals. Furthermore, they found a greater number of discrepancies in the peripheral details of traumatic events as compared to the main event itself, which is consistent with findings from other studies on memory and trauma (Herlihy et al., 2012; van der Kolk, 2007).

Note

1 Google Translate is a wonderful application. Our advice is to run all the text through that application and then go over it meticulously to make sure there are no typos or inaccurately translated words.

Bibliography

American Psychiatric Association. (2013). Cultural formulation. In *Diagnostic and statistical manual of mental disorders* (5th ed.). American Psychiatric Press.
American Psychological Association. (2017). *Multicultural guidelines: An ecological* approach to context, identity, and intersectionality, 2017. https://doi.org/10.1037/e501962018-001
Aragno, A., & Schlachet, P. J. (1996). Accessibility of early experience through the language of origin: A theoretical integration. *Psychoanalytic Psychology*, *13*(1), 23–34. https://doi.org/10.1037/h0079636
Barber-Rioja, V., & Garcia-Mansilla, A. (2019). Special considerations when conducting forensic psychological evaluations for immigration court. *Journal of Clinical Psychology*, *75*(11), 2049–2059. https://doi.org/10.1002/jclp.22863
Berry, J. W. (1997). Immigration, acculturation, and adaptation. *Applied Psychology*, *46*(1), 5–34. https://doi.org/10.1111/j.1464-0597.1997.tb01087.x

Bloom, L., & Beckwith, R. (1989). Talking with feeling: Integrating affective and linguistic expression in early language development. *Cognition and Emotion, 3*(4), 313–342. https://doi.org/10.1080/02699938908412711

Bond, M. H., & Lai, T. (1986). Embarrassment and code-switching into a second language. *Journal of Social Psychology, 126*(2), 179–186.

Burck, C. (2004). Living in several languages: implications for therapy. *Journal of Family Therapy, 26*(4), 314–339.

Buxbaum, E. (1949). The role of the second language in the formation of the ego and superego. *Psychoanalytic Quarterly, 18,* 279–289.

Clauss-Ehlers, C. S., Chiriboga, D. A., Hunter, S. J., Roysircar, G., & Tummala-Narra, P. (2019). APA multicultural guidelines executive summary: Ecological approach to context, identity, and intersectionality. *The American Psychologist, 74*(2), 232–244.

Falicov, C. J. (1995). Training to think culturally: A multidimensional comparative framework. *Family Process, 34*(4), 373–388. https://doi.org/10.1111/j.1545-5300.1995.00373.x

Falicov, C. J. (2014). *Latino families in therapy* (2nd ed.). Guilford Press.

Gamsie, M. (2008). *The function of language for bilingual therapists: Implications for the therapeutic relationship.* Alliant International University, California School of Professional Psychology, San Diego.

Hays, P. (2008). *Addressing cultural complexities in practice: Assessment, diagnosis, and therapy* (2nd ed.). American Psychological Association.

Herlihy, J., Scragg, P., & Turner, S. (2002). Discrepancies in autobiographical memories—implications for the assessment of asylum seekers: Repeated interviews study. *BMJ, 324*(7333), 324–327. https://doi.org/10.1136/bmj.324.7333.324

Herlihy, J., Jobson, L., & Turner, S. (2012). Just tell us what happened to you: Autobiographical memory and seeking asylum. *Applied Cognitive Psychology, 26*(5), 661–676. https://doi.org/10.1002/acp.2852

Hulme, P. A. (1996). Somatization in Hispanics. *Journal of Psychosocial Nursing and Mental Health Services, 34*(3), 33–37. https://doi.org/10.3928/0279-3695-19960301-17

Javier, R. A., Barroso, F., & Muñoz, M. A. (1993). Autobiographical memory in bilinguals. *Journal of Psycholinguistic Research, 22*(3), 319–338. https://doi.org/10.1007/bf01068015

Katsavdakis, K. A., Sayed, M., Bram, A., & Bartlett, A. B. (2001). How was this story told in the mother tongue? An integrative perspective. *Bulletin of the Menninger Clinic, 65* (2), 247–265. https://doi.org/10.1521/bumc.65.2.246.19403

Leong, F., Lui, P., & Kalibatseva, Z. (2019). Multicultural issues in clinical psychological assessment. In M. Sellbom & J. Suhr (Eds.), *The Cambridge handbook of clinical assessment and diagnosis* (Cambridge Handbooks in Psychology, pp. 25–37). Cambridge University Press.

Malgady, R. G., & Cortes, D. E. (1996). Cultural expression of psychiatric symptoms: Idioms of anger among Puerto Ricans. Psychological Assessment, 8(3), 265.

Marcos, L. R. (1976). Bilinguals in psychotherapy: Language as an emotional barrier. *American Journal of Psychotherapy, 30*(4), 552–560. https://doi.org/10.1176/appi.psychotherapy.1976.30.4.552

Marcos, L. R., & Urcuyo, L. (1979). Dynamic psychotherapy with the bilingual patient. *American Journal of Psychotherapy, 33*(3), 331–338. https://doi.org/10.1176/appi.psychotherapy.1979.33.3.331

Movahedi, S. (1996). Metalinguistic analysis of therapeutic discourse: Flight into a second language when the analyst and the analysand are multilingual. *Journal of the American Psychoanalytic Association, 44*(3), 837–862. https://doi.org/10.1177/000306519604400308

National Association of Social Workers. (2015). *Standards and indicators for cultural competence in social work practice.* Author.

Organista, K. C. (2000). Latinos. In J. R. White & A. S. Freeman (Eds.), *Cognitive-behavioral group therapy for specific problems and populations* (pp. 281–303). American Psychological Association.

Perez-Foster, R. (1996). The bilingual self: Duet in two voices. *Psychoanalytic Dialogues, 6*, 99–121. https://doi.org/10.1080/10481889609539109

Perez-Foster, R. (1998). *The power of language in the clinical process: Assessing and treating the bilingual person.* Jason Aronson.

Ratts, M. J., Singh, A. A., Nassar-McMillan, S., Butler, S. K., & McCullough, J. R. (2016). Multicultural and social justice counseling competencies: Guidelines for the counseling profession. *Journal of Multicultural Counseling and Development, 44*(1), 28–48. https://doi.org/10.1002/jmcd.12035

Root, M. P. P. (1992). Reconstructing the impact of trauma on personality. In L. S. Brown & M. Ballou (Eds.), *Personality and psychopathology: Feminist reappraisals* (pp. 229–265). The Guilford Press.

Rozensky, R. H., & Gomez, M. Y. (1983). Language switching in psychotherapy with bilinguals: Two problems, two models, and case examples. *Psychotherapy: Theory, Research, and Practice, 20* (2), 152–160.

Santiago-Rivera, A. L., & Altarriba, J. (2002). The role of language in therapy with the Spanish-English bilingual client. *Professional Psychology: Research & Practice, 33*(1), 30. https://doi.org/10.1037/0735-7028.33.1.30

Segalowitz, N. (1976). Communicative incompetence and the non-fluent bilingual. *Canadian Journal of Behavioural Science, 8*(2), 122–131. https://doi.org/10.1037/h0081941

Stamm B. H. & Friedman M. J. (2000) Cultural diversity in the appraisal and expression of trauma. In A. Y. Shalev, R. Yehuda, A. C. McFarlane (Eds.), International handbook of human response to trauma. Springer Series on Stress and Coping (pp. 279–302). Springer.

Stephenson, M. (2000). Development and validation of the Stephenson Multigroup Acculturation Scale (SMAS). *Psychological Assessment, 12*(1), 77–88. https://doi.org/10.1037/1040-3590.12.1.77

Tervalon, M. & Murray-Garcia, J. (1998). Cultural humility versus cultural competence: A critical distinction in defining physician training outcomes in multicultural education. *Journal of Health Care for the Poor and Underserved, 9*(2), 117–125. https://doi.org/10.1353/hpu.2010.0233

Turner, S. M., DeMers, S. T., Fox, H. R., & Reed, G. M. (2001). APA's guidelines for test user qualifications: An executive summary. *American Psychologist, 56*(12), 1099–1113. https://doi.org/10.1037/0003-066x.56.12.1099

van der Kolk, B. A. (2007). Trauma and memory. In B. A. Van der Kolk, A. C. McFarlane, & L. Weisaeth (Eds.), *Traumatic stress: The effects of overwhelming experience on mind, body, and society.* Guilford Press.

Waisman, P. A. (2005). *Emotional expression of Spanish-English bilinguals in traumatic narratives.* Alliant International University, California School of Professional Psychology, San Diego.

Wilson J. P. (2007). The lens of culture: Theoretical and conceptual perspectives in the assessment of psychological trauma and PTSD. In J. P. Wilson, & C. S. Tang (Eds.), *Cross-cultural assessment of psychological trauma and PTSD.* International and Cultural Psychology Series. Springer.

10 Expanding Your Practice to Include Immigration Evaluations

Mariela G. Shibley, Psy.D.

If you still recall the day you were granted your professional degree as a mixture of excitement and trepidation, you are not alone. You went through years of schooling, unpaid internships and practicums, papers, comprehensive examinations, perhaps what seemed to be an interminable dissertation write-up, and there you were: degree in hand and… now what? The previous nine chapters discussed the nuances that make immigration evaluations unique, the legal elements and procedural aspects of a variety of immigration cases, how to conduct the psychological evaluation, and how to present your findings in a report. Now it is time to put those skills into practice.

Perhaps you are just starting your career, or maybe you already have a thriving practice and are considering expanding to include immigration evaluations. This is also a wonderful opportunity for those who need or want to limit their time away from home, such as new parents or those caring for a loved one, as it allows you to reduce your time at the office by writing the reports from home. After I had my baby, I would go to the office for two or three hours to meet with a client and then return home to score the tests, write the report, and take care of any other administrative tasks. It was a wonderful way to balance work and family life.

Wherever you are in your professional path, incorporating this work is not only a lucrative venture but also an excellent way to help communities that are often disenfranchised and underserved. Research has shown that the number of waiver cases approved on appeal almost doubles when they include written or oral testimony by a mental health professional (MHP) versus when they do not (McLawsen, 2011) and that expert witnesses are "crucial" in asylum cases (Baker et al., 2018).

Reaching Out and Retaining Referral Sources

Advertising your services is key for growing your practice. While you might rely on insurance carriers to promote your therapy services to their members, immigration evaluations are rarely, if ever, a covered benefit under an insurance plan. Consequently, you need to take it upon yourself to market your service. Most clients seeking an immigration evaluation are referred by their

DOI: 10.4324/9781003139973-11

attorneys or by their legal counsel at non-profit agencies. Some might have been advised by others who have been through the process, and other might find you through an online search. If we break it down into percentages, it is safe to estimate that 70% of your clientele will be referred by immigration attorneys, and the other 30% will be split between word-of-mouth and online advertising. Naturally, word-of-mouth, especially among attorneys who network through county bar and other professional associations, will grow as you become better established.

A good place to start would be an online search for immigration attorneys who specialize in removal defense or family-based immigration in your local area. You may consider reaching out to the certified specialists in immigration law in your community, comprised of the more experienced immigration attorneys, to increase the likelihood of reputable feedback as you develop your evaluation practice. You could draft an introductory email to send to their offices, or—better yet—a letter in the mail describing the services you offer.[1] Whatever method(s) you use to make initial contact, you need to follow up with a phone call. Ideally, you would set up a time to talk either over the phone or in person so you could explain to the attorney that you are expanding your practice to incorporate these evaluations and ask if you could be of help to their clients. Surprisingly, many attorneys have never considered the value of an immigration evaluation by an MHP. Perhaps they have included affidavits from treating therapists but were never aware how helpful a well-written report could be. Providing a redacted report that omits all identifying information is useful to show the attorney the quality of your work, and it can be a real eye-opener for an attorney who has not used one before.

When you are starting out, a balance between assertiveness and humility is important. There is nothing wrong with admitting that you are new to this and are still learning from your experience as long as you project confidence. Be assertive enough to convey your professionalism and commitment to quality work but humble enough to acknowledge your room for growth. Immediately after submitting a report, follow up with the attorney to get feedback and suggestions for improvement. It can be difficult to hear sometimes, but we tend to learn more from our mistakes than from our successes. Be careful, however, not to cross the line and become a "hired gun," conceding to the attorney on what to write.

Equally important to securing referral sources is retaining them. Touch base with the attorneys periodically, ask questions about current immigration trends, and network as much as you can. Many of my referrals have come from those who saw me present at conferences, but I have also made many connections by attending conferences or professional presentations geared toward immigration attorneys. You might run into a referral source who will introduce you to one of their colleagues and recommend your work. Remember to always carry business cards with you, or better yet, get their contact information and follow up with them to describe the type of work you do and, if appropriate, send them a sample. Not only could they refer clients for evaluations, but they might also recommend you to those who need mental health treatment.

Just like MHPs, most attorneys need a certain number of minimum continuing legal education (MCLE) hours to renew their professional license. Even among the varying MCLE requirements by state, one or more of those hours must be on "competency issues," which include self-care, preventing substance abuse, and any other topics relevant to maintaining competency to practice law. I have been invited many times to give a lecture on substance use and self-care matters to immigration attorneys. If you are ever asked to present on one of these topics, make sure to mention the type of work you do, either during your presentation or while socializing with attendees. One new referral source is worth a lot more than whatever you might be getting paid for presenting (which is oftentimes zilch, unfortunately). Another way to promote your services is to have a table at a local American Immigration Lawyers Association (AILA) conference. Though pricey, it may yield fruitful results.

One simple way to promote your services is on your professional website. Create a page where you list the type of evaluations you specialize in, the languages you speak (if any), and a brief description of the evaluation process. You do not need to post a sample of a report, but you can offer to produce one upon request.

It is my experience that some attorneys refer their clients in hopes that they will confide in me personal details that would ultimately help their case. The argument that a person might feel more comfortable opening up to an MHP than to an attorney or their paralegal is understandable. However, this gamble often results in there being little to nothing to say in the client's favor. For example, I have come across clients who told me directly, "Honestly, if we have to move to Mexico for ten years it would be fine. I have a business there, and we go there all the time." Or even worse, "Well, my wife and I are separated, and I am in another relationship, but I still want to help her out with her immigration papers." Although I appreciate their honesty, it saddens me to have to say I can be of no help to them—at least when it comes to commenting on their hardships. Consequently, I developed the "Psychological Hardship Screening Questionnaire" (Copyright 2013 by Mariela G. Shibley) for attorneys to give to their clients in order to determine whether they would benefit from a psychological evaluation. The items address most of the potential areas of vulnerability but do not require the client to reveal any specific details about their personal life. This has proven to be extremely helpful in filtering out those individuals who would be better off pursuing a different strategy to substantiate their claim of hardship.

Along those same lines, I designed a referral form that is to be filled out by the referring attorney and submitted either directly to the MHP or given to their client to hand over to the evaluator. The form asks the attorney to indicate the type of evaluation the client needs (e.g., hardship waiver, provisional waiver, U visa, Violence Against Women Act (VAWA), etc.); names of the applicant, beneficiary, qualifying relative, and petitioner; deadline for the completed report (if applicable); and any miscellaneous notes for the evaluator. The form also includes the address with a map to our office. This helps streamline the evaluation process from the start and minimizes misunderstandings and unnecessary back and forth with the referral source.

Sometimes clients contact me without having retained legal representation for their immigration case, which can be problematic. If someone is requesting a psychological evaluation, that is a strong sign that their case is not a straightforward one, they probably should not be going it alone. Following the advice of a friend or family member who has been through a similar process can result in a number of problems because each case is different. Most importantly, you don't know what you don't know. For example, a client ("Tony") came in for an evaluation following the advice of a friend who had been evaluated by me the year before to help get his wife's waiver approved. Tony's wife had come into the country with a student visa, met him, and never left. Since she had stayed past her allowed stay in the United States, she had accrued unlawful presence, and Tony's friend told him she would need a waiver and that he should see me for an evaluation. Unfortunately, it turned out she did not need a waiver because she had never left and re-entered the United States (this is explained in more detail in Chapter 2). By the time they learned this, however, the evaluation and the report had already been finished and paid for.

Having conducted immigration evaluations for well over a decade, I am often sought out by fellow MHPs—or sometimes their clients—for what is, in reality, legal advice. No matter how well-versed I am in this area, I always encourage them to consult with an immigration attorney instead. Many immigration attorneys offer a free consultation, so it is useful to have a short list of names to offer to unrepresented clients. Whatever you do, remember that providing legal advice without a license can get you in serious trouble.

A Word about Notarios *and* Consultants

Immigration processes can be lengthy, expensive, and remarkably complicated. Many individuals in need of assistance seek cheaper alternatives to qualified immigration attorneys. While many legitimate and accredited representatives of organizations recognized by the Board of Immigration Appeals (BIA) can provide immigration-related assistance, unlicensed individuals who advertise themselves as "immigration consultants" or "*notarios*" are not authorized or qualified to offer legal advice, which amounts to the illegal practice of law.

In some Latin countries *notarios* have extensive legal training, but in the United States public notaries (as they are called) are limited to certifying signatures. This is why many foreign nationals (FNs) see the title *notario* and mistakenly assume they are in good hands. I have come across many immigration consultants who are well-versed in immigration law and have their clients' best interests in mind, but they are the exception to the rule. The consequences of someone entrusting their fate to a *notario* or a "consultant" range from being conned out of large sums of money to permanently damaging their immigration case (or both).

Fortunately, many immigration consultants who refer their clients to my practice are themselves former employees of the Department of Homeland Security. In other words, they were the immigration officers who determined the outcome of a case. Naturally, their knowledge and experience would surpass that of other *notarios*, who might be lawyers in another country but never received legal education in the United States. These consultants often attend conferences put on by AILA and stay up to date with current immigration policies. When you prioritize integrity over convenience, you are in a better position to scrutinize the legitimacy of the referral source and decide whether you want to accept the referral or not.

A client was referred by an immigration consultant to document hardship for a provisional waiver application. She was a 23-year-old woman petitioning for her mother's permanent residency, and since her mother had entered the United States unlawfully, she was told by the consultant that she would need to cure her inadmissibility grounds by applying for a provisional waiver, which would be granted based on her ability to demonstrate her daughter's suffering if she were denied prompty admission. What's the problem here?

If you recall from Chapter 2, provisional waivers require a showing of hardship to a qualifying relative (QR). For this type of cases, though, only a USC or LPR spouse or parent of the applicant is considered a QR. After making sure the only ground of inadmissibility in this woman's case was unlawful entry and not something else, I called the consultant for further clarification. However, the consultant was not available. I determined that the best next course of action was to encourage the woman to consult with an immigration attorney and that, if she did indeed need a psychological evaluation, I would discount whatever fee she paid for the consultation. It turned out that the consultant's advice was wrong, but thankfully the attorney was able to find the right avenue to procure her mother's US residency. The mother married her long-time partner, an LPR, and he was the one who eventually came in for a provisional waiver evaluation.

Setting Fees

Deciding how much to charge for an immigration evaluation can be a daunting task, as you want to be compensated adequately for your work but not make it unaffordable to the clients who need your services. Surely, there are some FNs for whom money is not of great concern, but for many more, it is. There are several ways to help you decide on a fair amount. For example, you may be able to find out how much others are charging for this type of work in your area. Many providers list their prices on their website, so this would give you a good starting point.

Another option is to charge your hourly rate. One caveat with this method is that as you are getting started with this type of work, you will naturally move at a slower pace and spend a significant amount of time writing, reviewing, and finalizing your report. Charging by the hour might not only add up to a bill that is unaffordable for your clients, but it would also mean that you will earn less and less as you become more proficient and experienced, which makes no sense.

Alternatively, you could estimate how much time it will take you to conduct the evaluation from start to finish (including report writing) and come up with a flat fee, which can be different for different types of evaluations (i.e., waivers, VAWA, asylum, etc.). There are several things to consider when taking this approach, as the length of the interview can vary due to a number of factors. Taking the background history of a 19-year-old, for example, is unlikely to take as long as that of a 65-year-old. Some people have experienced complex trauma, which might require a more paced interview process and perhaps more than one interview. Administering psychological measures that demand more of your time scoring and interpreting or that need to be scored elsewhere for a fee (like the Minnesota Multiphasic Personality Inventory [MMPI] or Personality Assessment Inventory [PAI]) can increase your overhead costs. In addition, sometimes you will need to evaluate more than one person for the same case, such as two siblings or both parents, which would naturally take longer. If you are employing the help of an interpreter, the duration of the interview basically doubles. Who pays for the interpreter is something you would also have to decide, but it is typically a separate charge. Lastly, the evaluation might require that you obtain collateral information or that you review copious records, adding to the totality of time spent on the case.

A complicated immigration case can cost a client thousands of dollars. Between attorney's fees, immigration filing fees, and other related expenditures, the expense of adjusting someone's immigration status can—and often does—discourage people from pursuing this process. It can be an interminable loop whereby an FN's opportunities for gainful employment are limited due to being undocumented, resulting in never having enough money to start the immigration process (or stretching it out for years, paying for things as they are able). It is worth keeping this in mind when setting your fees.

Most attorneys and MHPs offer clients a payment plan. In my practice, if we are charging a flat fee, we would ask the clients to pay half up front and the rest in either small payments or a lump sum. A side note on payment: clients will occasionally be under the impression that the evaluation and report are included in their attorney's fees. It has a happened a couple times in my own practice that someone came to my office believing that (or, at least, claiming to) and having no money on them to make a payment. In one instance we were never able to recover the fee. Even though we let the clients know, both over the phone and via email, the total cost of the evaluation, when payment is due, and the different types of payment we accept in my office, there is still always the potential for misunderstandings. As a result, we have since been collecting the payment for the evaluation (or half of it, if they are on a payment plan) prior to starting the interview.

"Rush" Fees

In some cases, people are pressed for time and need the report right away. This is often the case when they have to respond to a Request for Evidence (RFE) or a Notice of Intent to Deny (NOID), for which they are given a certain deadline to respond (see Chapter 2 for a description of these letters). Other times it is mere procrastination on the part of the client that puts everything off to the last minute. Most MHPs charge a rush fee if they are asked to submit a report in less time than what is customary. What is customary? Based on feedback from MHPs who conduct immigration evaluations, the average is two weeks. Some people devote one or two days a week to conduct the interviews and spend the rest of the week writing up the reports. Others will set aside an entire day for just one evaluation, conducting the interview in the morning, and spending the rest of the day interpreting test results and writing the report. Naturally, that would result in a quicker turnaround.

Working Pro-Bono

Lastly, a word about *pro bono* work. Because the expense of immigration processes can put the individuals involved at a disadvantage, or even deter them completely, some MHPs choose to do a certain amount of work at no charge to the client, or at heavily discounted rates. Offering *pro bono* services is a personal choice, and not doing so does not mean an MHP is greedy or insensitive. Most attorneys and MHPs who work at non-profit agencies that provide services to immigrants free of charge actually do get paid by means of government funding or grants. If we lived in a world where bartering was the common practice and trading a pail of milk from your cow for a sack of potatoes from your neighbor was how we put food on the table, that would be a different story. The reality is that we need money to pay for our milk and potatoes (not to mention our student loans!), and maintaining our practices and supporting our families are financial burdens we all deal with. For those MHPs who are in a position to do it, though, committing to taking on a limited number of *pro bono* or discounted cases is a nice way to help those who need it the most.

Developing a Streamlined Process

Carrying out an evaluation from start to finish involves several steps and having a system that simplifies the process ensures efficiency and consistency.

In addition, if you have employees who will be handling some aspects of the evaluation, such as scheduling and collecting the payment, having a good system in place makes it easy when you train a new hire.

Scheduling

Everything starts with a phone call from the person wanting to schedule the evaluation. This could be either the attorney, the client, or someone calling on the client's behalf. Although in my practice we welcome input from the attorney or a representative, we always insist on speaking directly with the client before they come in. This ensures that nothing is lost in the chain of communication and that the client is fully aware of what to expect. Once we identify the type of evaluation they need, we describe the process of the evaluation to them and let them know how much time it will likely take, the total cost of the evaluation, and the different forms of payment we accept. We also make sure they know where the office is located.

If the caller does not know exactly what type of evaluation they need to schedule, and if their attorney did not fill out a referral form, it is up to us to decipher what they need. Sometimes it is straightforward, as when they share that their spouse is abroad and needs a pardon to enter the United States (most likely a waiver). Other times, however, it is not so clear. In those situations, ask the client to contact their attorney and either have the attorney send the referral form or clearly state the reason for the referral so the client can relay it to you. I strongly advise against reaching out to colleagues for advice via a social media platform such as Facebook. Invariably, when a person provides the few details they have about a case and asks what kind of case it is, they will get a variety of different responses, and there is no guarantee that any of them is correct.

After scheduling the evaluation, follow up with an email confirmation restating what you went over during the phone call. This further ensures that nothing is missed, and it keeps clients from later complaining, "Nobody told me I would be here for three hours!" We also send them the intake paperwork and the informed consent so that they can fill it out ahead of time. One or two days before the evaluation, we call to confirm the appointment and make sure that they received the email with the forms. Many people are used to having a relative accompany them to their doctors' appointments, but this is a very different type of appointment. If you do not have a comfortable waiting room or a separate private area where the client can complete the psychological measures, instruct the clients to come alone.

Since some interviews take longer than others, allowing some cushion time between the evaluation and your next client prevents you from feeling anxious and your client from feeling rushed. If employing the help of an interpreter, allow for the interview to take double the amount of time. The same is true when evaluating children since you will always need to interview the parents first to get the background information.

Administering Tests

Keep a list of the measures you administer for each type of evaluation. This does not mean that you cannot deviate from the list, but you will find it easier to prepare the materials you need when the client arrives. For my employees at the front desk, who are in charge of greeting the client and handling all the paperwork, I created a chart that lists the tests for each type of evaluation we do, which saves them the trouble of having to come to me each time so I can tell them which tests to give the client. We typically use a tablet to save paper, but if the tests are hard copies, we print them out ahead of time and organize all the paperwork neatly on a clipboard.

Having the clients complete the psychological measures first, either in a private room or in the waiting room, allows you to go over their responses during the interview. Do not ever give clients access to the tests outside of your office and under your supervision. Sharing test materials violates test security and jeopardizes their validity and integrity.

The Interview

There are options for taking notes during the interview. You may want to use a template to help guide your line of questioning and ensure all important areas are discussed. You can handwrite your notes or type your notes onto a blank document and later copy them onto the report. Alternatively, you may feel comfortable enough to type directly into what will become your report. These last two options significantly reduce the amount of time spent writing the report.

I went over the steps for "setting the frame" for the interview in Chapter 2. It is important that clients know that this is an evaluation and not therapy, what to expect during the interview, that they are aware of the limits of confidentiality, and that they are given the opportunity to ask any questions about the evaluation process.

Throughout the interview, I pause every so often and go over the information I wrote down to make sure it is accurate. This frequently results in their adding previously unrecalled information. At the end of the interview, I always ask, "Is there anything I didn't ask you that you think is important for me to know?" Even though I might think I covered everything, there may very well be important information that was inadvertently left out. I also invite them to call me if anything else comes up for them that they did not mention during the interview. If I have a pretty good idea of their diagnosis, I might share it with them in language they will understand. I welcome them to ask me any questions they have, and I assure them that this diagnosis is not going into any type of public record and that I uphold strict standards for safeguarding their privacy.

Whenever possible, write the report immediately following the interview. Writing up the client's background history before moving on to seeing other clients or doing other work means the information is still fresh in your mind, and you will not have to rely exclusively on your notes. Reports also tend to be more detailed and accurate, and the feeling of being done or almost done with one of the more tedious aspects of the evaluation is priceless. Of course, sometimes it is necessary to take a break and give yourself a little distance, especially after listening to a particularly painful or extensive trauma history. More on this is presented below.

Submitting the Report

Most of the time, the report is sent directly to the attorney on the case. Of course, the client will have signed a release of information allowing you to do so. You may email the report to the attorney or send a hard copy, whichever the attorney prefers. If you email it, make sure to do so via a platform that encrypts the messages and/or attachments or to password-protect your document. Some clients prefer to have it sent to them instead, but that is, in my experience, the exception.

Along with your report, you will include your most recent curriculum vitae (CV). If you work with the same attorney on a regular basis, you can ask them to keep your CV on file so that you do not have to include it with every report you send, but make sure they always have a current version.

Telehealth

The coronavirus disease 2019 (COVID-19) pandemic caught us all by surprise and challenged us to adapt to new ways of fulfilling our work obligations. Whereas conducting an immigration evaluation in any way other than in person was not something many of us had ever considered, we were forced to think outside the box and find ways to carry on with the work. Then along came telehealth. The Department of Health and Human Services temporarily waived Health Insurance Portability and Accountability Act (HIPAA) penalties for "good-faith" use of telehealth during the COVID-19 emergency. By "good-faith," they meant the use of technology that offers the highest level of privacy and security possible and ensuring that clients and patients are fully aware of the risks associated with the use of any technology. Even when things opened up and we returned to seeing clients in person, the option to conduct the evaluation remotely remained, broadening our ability to reach clients for whom coming to our office was not a viable or desirable option. If you are interested in offering your services via telehealth, I recommend the following:

- Find an online platform that is HIPAA compliant and reliable. There are many available companies that meet those criteria—some pricier than others. The one requirement is that you have reliable access to the Internet with a strong signal.
- Have clients sign a consent form that thoroughly describes the potential risks to confidentiality, alternative options for conducting the evaluation,

how any emergencies will be handled, and the client's right to discontinue the use of telehealth.

- Ensure the client has privacy. Even though it is not uncommon for patients to do a therapy session from their parked car, sitting for two or three hours in a car to complete an evaluation may not be comfortable for them. When scheduling the appointment, remind them how long it will last and make sure they can be in a quiet, private area where they will not be interrupted. If they have a small child in the home, they will need to have someone look after them, as interrupting the interview to get the kiddo a glass of milk takes away from the flow and efficacy of the evaluation.
- Because you cannot send test materials, you will have to administer the measures orally. Make sure to note on the report that you did so, as it is a deviation from the way the test was intended to be administered. Some tests can be administered online via the test publisher's website, so look into that if you think it would be useful. One concern with that option is that the client might need to have two separate screens: one to administer the test, and the other one where you will be observing them.
- As wonderful as technology is, it can also have its glitches. Make sure to have a back-up plan if you lose connection, such as a phone number where they can call you right away or a different online platform.
- Ask the client to angle their camera so that you get a full view of their face.

Although states vary in the ways they handle rules regarding practicing across state lines via telehealth, most require that the client be present in the state where the MHP is licensed. Keep in mind that, while attorneys licensed to the federal bar can practice immigration law in any state, MHPs conducting evaluations are restricted to the rules of their respective state licensing boards. Therefore, it is generally best to stick to practicing in the state where you are licensed and where both you and the client are physically present at the time of the evaluation. When in doubt, however, consult with your liability insurance and/or your state's professional board.

Other Issues to Consider

Conducting an evaluation via telehealth typically takes longer than in person, in large part because you will most likely have to administer psychological measures by reading the statements on the test and filling in the client's responses. Interruptions due to a poor Internet connection will also extend the length of the interview. Therefore, plan accordingly.

Table 10.1 Do's and Don'ts for MHPs

Do...	Don't...
...be easy to reach and get an appointment scheduled within three weeks of referral.	...put off returning their call and don't assume they will call you again.
...be direct and to the point, and support your conclusions with specific, objective criteria.	...include a bunch of personal opinions or legal conclusions (judges hate that).
...get your report back to me in a timely manner.	...think of this as your "side hustle" and put it on the bottom of your priority list.
...be open to feedback, not only regarding content but also on style and structure.	...think that just because you are highly skilled in your field (which you are, thankfully) you also know what an adjudicator wants to see.

The client will have to sign consent forms. Using an online program is very practical, but many of our clients are unable to use those programs, for a multitude of reasons. An alternative is to mail the documents and have the client mail them back so that they arrive prior to the evaluation date. Similarly, collecting payment for the evaluation can be cumbersome if they are not using a credit card. In such cases, they can either make a direct deposit to your bank account or use a banking app to swiftly send money directly from their account to yours. Alternatively, they can use Paypal or a good ole' check in the mail. Venmo, although very popular, is not HIPAA-compliant.

Advice from an Immigration Attorney's Perspective—By Matthew Holt

My clients are more than just a file to me. They are vulnerable human beings who have turned to me for help, who trust me to guide them through rough waters and into safe harbor. So I'm very discerning when it comes MHPs, and I wouldn't refer my clients to just anyone. As an attorney who has referred clients and their family members to MHPs since the early days of my practice, I have come to look for a few things in an MHP and in their work. I can't speak for other attorneys, but if you want to get on my shortlist, keep these in mind (see Table 10.1).

Self-Care

Immigrants' stories are often loaded with trauma and loss. Bearing witness to such painful experiences can take a toll on an MHP, often leading to vicarious or secondary trauma, so it is vital to incorporate self-care practices when working in this field. The following are tips for mitigating the negative impact of trauma work:

- *Acknowledge and admire the client's resilience.* Some people's trauma stories are truly heartbreaking, but being able to appreciate their ability to pick up the pieces and keep going can help dissolve the bitter aftertaste of taking in their suffering. A woman from Honduras shared the details of witnessing her husband's gruesome murder. When we finished the interview, she thanked me for patiently listening to her agony. As she walked away, I felt the immensity of the weight that had been lifted off her chest as it was unintentionally transferred to mine. I allowed myself to pause for a minute and reflect on this woman's past experiences and her promising future: she is now reunited with her sisters in a safe country, with a job prospect, and learning how to drive. She is nearing the end of the dark tunnel. My sorrow dissipated, and I began to feel hopeful and happy for her, and knowing that I played a part in her journey towards recovery put a smile on my face. She might carry a scar in her heart forever, but it will not keep her from rebuilding her life and finding love again.
- *Debrief with a trusted colleague.* Leaning on loved ones for emotional support is a wonderful thing. However, unless your loved ones are also MHPs, they are unlikely to truly understand your experience or to be able to just listen. Working in a solo practice can be isolating, so it is important to maintain a connection with fellow MHPs who understand the intricacies of your work and who are able to hold space for you to unload your feelings. Undergoing personal therapy can be even more beneficial, as it allows you to process your countertransference within the context of your personal life.
- *Prioritize self-care.* When boarding a plane and the flight attendants go over the safety precautions, they always emphasize that those traveling with a child or someone who needs assistance should put the oxygen masks on themselves first and then help their companion. Why? Because if you run out of oxygen while trying to put the mask on someone else, you can no longer be of any help to others, and now you are the one in trouble. When we give but do not refill our own cup, we end up depleted and have nothing left to give. Some of the most important things to consider when it comes to taking good care of yourself are as follows: getting adequate sleep, eating healthy meals at suitable times, doing some sort of physical exercise to counteract the long hours of sitting at the office, and engaging in a pleasurable activity (e.g., a hobby, a good book, spending time with friends, or going to church). Taking good care of ourselves needs to be a priority. When people say, "I don't have time," what they are really saying is, "I don't consider it very important."

Always remember: Self-care is not a luxury; it is an essential need for those in a helping profession.

Furthering Your Training

To reiterate what I mentioned in Chapter 1, having a solid understanding of the legal concepts guiding a psychological evaluation is an MHP's ethical obligation (American Psychological Association, 2013, 2020; Heilbrun et al., 2009). Speaking a second language does not in and of itself qualify an MHP to conduct an immigration evaluation. It might open up doors to more referrals, but it does not bestow upon an MHP any special ability to do this work without the adequate training.

As you learned in the previous chapters, immigration law is exceptionally complex, full of exemptions, special considerations, and nuances, and there is a great deal of room for error when a case is not properly handled. Even though MHPs are not expected to be experts in immigration law, it is fundamental that they receive adequate training and that they continue their education by keeping abreast of the most current immigration trends as they relate to an MHP's work.

My intention was to make this book as thorough and practical as possible. However, just like with most things we learn throughout our career, there are no shortcuts and there is no substitute for hands-on practice. You are strongly advised to seek consultation and to attend workshops and trainings to sharpen your assessment skills. Mr. Holt and I chose to focus on just a handful of the most typical immigration cases an MHP is likely to come across, but there are many other areas of immigration law where a report or expert testimony by an MHP is called for, such as waivers to cure crimes involving moral turpitude, risk and dangerousness assessments, relief under the Adam Walsh Child Protection and Safety Act,[2] evaluating minors for Special Immigrant Juvenile Status,[3] and evaluating competency for self-representation in immigration court. Evans and Hass (2018) and Meyers (2020) reference such types of evaluations, some of which can only be carried out by licensed psychologists.

Immigration evaluations, while not new to the United States Citizenship and Immigration Services and immigration court, are not typically included in forensic assessment trainings. However, there has been a recent surge of MHPs interested in conducting these evaluations and many who offer workshops or online trainings. As with most things, the quality of such trainings will likely vary, but it is worth exploring what is out there, including my own (www.psychevalcoach.com).

As we get to the end of this book, Mr. Holt and I want to thank you for reading. Both of our lives have been richly and forever rewarded by our clients and their stories. We are grateful to share in their journeys and know that we, in our own ways, help not only them but also their families and, potentially, future generations. Your evaluations will support clients in unlocking doors to benefits they dream of obtaining but are terrified they will never receive. It is a responsibility we take on gladly, but with humility, with gratitude, and with great care.

Notes

1 Make sure that when communicating with potential referral sources, your letters or emails are professionally written and do not contain any typos. From an attorney's perspective, if an MHP was not careful enough to ensure their writing contained no errors, how can they trust the quality of their reports?
2 Individuals who have been convicted of any specified offense against a minor are restrained from filing a family-based visa petition on behalf of any beneficiary, unless the DHS Secretary finds that the petitioner poses no risk to the beneficiary of the visa petition.
3 A type of immigration relief available to certain undocumented immigrants under the age of 21 who have been abused, neglected, or abandoned by one or both parents.

Bibliography

American Psychological Association. (2013). Specialty guidelines for forensic psychology. *American Psychologist, 68*(1), 7–19.

American Psychological Association, APA Task Force on Psychological Assessment and Evaluation Guidelines. (2020). *APA guidelines for psychological assessment and evaluation.* www.apa.org/about/policy/guidelines-psychological-assessment evaluation.pdf.

Baker, K., Freeman, K., Warner, G., & Weissman, D. M. (2018). *Expert witnesses in U.S. asylum cases: A handbook.* https://law.unc.edu/wpcontent/uploads/2019/10/expertwitnesshandbook.pdf.

Evans, F. B., & Hass, G. A. (2018). *Forensic psychological assessment in immigration court: A guidebook for evidence-based and ethical practice.* Routledge.

Heilbrun, K., Grisso, T., & Goldstein, A. M. (2009). *Foundations of forensic mental health assessment.* Oxford University Press.

McLawsen, G., McLawsen, J., & Ruser, K. (2011). Demonstrating psychological hardship: A statistical study of psychological evaluations in hardship waivers of inadmissibility. *Bender's Immigration Bulletin, 16*(10).

Meyers, R. (2020). *Conducting psychological assessments for U.S. immigration cases.* Springer.

Appendices

Appendix A

The following are samples of the different types of cases discussed in this book. For the sake of brevity, I only included the section on my qualifications in the Provisional Waiver sample, but the same information goes at the beginning of all of my reports. The same goes for the heading of the reports.

Note that all identifying information has been changed to preserve the clients' confidentiality. Consequently, some of the contents may not be historically accurate.

Sample Affidavit of Support

July 9, 2018

To Whom It May Concern,

I was asked by Ms. Patricia Guerrero to write a letter confirming her mental health treatment. I have been seeing Ms. Guerrero for weekly individual psychotherapy since September 25, 2017. Based on the stressors and symptoms she reported, she meets diagnostic criteria for *persistent depressive disorder*. This disorder is diagnosed when an individual presents with depressed mood that lasts for most of a day, continues for more days than not, and persists for over two years. The main clinical presentation is the presence of chronic and persistent symptoms of depression, such as low mood, low self-esteem, feelings of hopelessness, low energy, poor concentration, irritability, and sleep difficulties. These symptoms cause clinically significant distress in many areas of the individual's life.

The abusive quality of her relationship with her estranged husband appears to be the principal source of Ms. Guerrero's emotional distress. The main goal of her present treatment is to help her gain coping skills to decrease her symptoms and effectively deal with her life stressors independently. Most importantly, Ms. Guerrero needs a safe setting where to process the years of emotional and physical abuse she has endured and the torment she continues to experience as her marriage approaches legal dissolution.

Since the onset of her psychotherapy treatment, Ms. Guerrero has shown some improvement in her psychiatric condition. She has been consistent in her attendance and has demonstrated increased awareness with regard to her feelings, thoughts, and behaviors. Her improvements have been evidenced both by her verbal report and by clinical observations made during the course of her treatment. Despite such positive progress, it is recommended that she continue weekly psychotherapy sessions until her symptoms resolve. In addition to mental health treatment, a consistent source of emotional support and stability in her present life circumstances are key for Ms. Guerrero's positive therapeutic prognosis.

If you have any further questions, please do not hesitate to contact me.

Sincerely,

Mariela G. Shibley, Psy.D.
Licensed Clinical Psychologist, PSY23239

Appendix B

Sample Provisional Waiver Report

Report of Psychological Assessment

★★ CONFIDENTIAL ★★

The contents of this report are considered a legally protected medical document. Psychological evaluations and reports are by nature confidential and should, therefore, be made available to select and authorized persons only.

Client's Name: Anne Juarez
Date of Birth: 05/28/1993
Date of Assessment: 01/19/2020
Date of Report: 01/22/2020
Assessment Procedures: Biopsychosocial History Interview
Structured Clinical Interview for DSM-5 Disorders –
Clinician Version
Experiences in Close Relationships – Relationship
Structures
Sentence Completion Test
Recent Life Changes Stress Test
Personality Assessment Inventory

Evaluator's Qualifications and Assessment Methodology

I am a clinical psychologist licensed in the states of California and Nevada. Since 2007, I have conducted and supervised over two thousand reports for United States Citizenship and Immigration Services and for Immigration Court. I have a private practice in San Diego, where in addition to my forensic work; I provide psychotherapy to adults, couples, and families, specializing in issues around acculturation, immigration, and trauma. I have published a number of articles and op-eds on cultural diversity and immigration, and I have been a guest speaker at conferences put on by the American Immigration Lawyers Association.

Forensic evaluators, such as myself, are specifically trained to carry out psychological evaluations that answer a psycholegal question and to conceptualize and focus on the legally relevant aspects of the client's presentation. Accordingly, this report is based on a one-time visit and a thorough assessment of this client's mental health status within the context of the legal issue at hand. Its conclusions and recommendations are based on my professional education, training, and experience and any limitations to my findings will be clearly noted, if applicable.[1] For further qualifications, please refer to my curriculum vitae.

Identifying Information and Reason for Referral

Mrs. Anne Juarez (formerly Ms. Anne Smith) is a 26-year-old, self-identified Caucasian female. She is married to Mr. Juan Juarez, and she does not have any children. Mrs. Juarez is pursuing a master's degree in education and works as an elementary school teacher at Very Good Elementary School. She also works as a caregiver to a disabled woman on the weekends. She resides with her husband, her brother, and a roommate in a house she owns in San Diego, California.

Mrs. Juarez was referred for an evaluation to assess her current psychological status. She has reported experiencing emotional distress associated with her husband's immigration status and the potential hardships she might endure if he were forced to leave the country for an extended period of time. She is seeking evidence of how a lengthy separation from her husband or a relocation might affect her and whether it would be beyond what is typically expected when separating from a loved one.

Relevant Background Information

Mrs. Juarez was born and raised in Vista, California. She comes from an intact family and is the second youngest of five siblings. She described a childhood marked by her father's violent outbursts and witnessing repeated instances of domestic violence. Mrs. Juarez explained that her parents separated when she was 4 years old but that her father continued stalking them and physically and verbally abusing her mother. Approximately one year after separating from her father, Mrs. Juarez's mother became romantically involved with a man she had met at church. By the time Mrs. Juarez entered kindergarten, this man was living in the house with them and had begun sexually abusing Mrs. Juarez on a regular basis. She painfully recalled how he would molest her whenever her mother was not around and would threaten that she would be punished if she ever told her mother. When Mrs. Juarez eventually confided in her older brother, he convinced her to tell their mother, who subsequently ended her relationship with her boyfriend. Mrs. Juarez cried as she shared that her mother later rekindled the relationship and allowed the man to move back into the house with them. This was a profound betrayal for Mrs. Juarez, who has continued to live with the pain to this day. The couple eventually separated, but since he had fathered one of Mrs. Juarez's younger sisters, he continued to be involved with the family until he was deported to Mexico several years ago.

Mrs. Juarez reported a strained relationship with her father, whom she perceived as emotionally absent throughout her upbringing. She described her mother as "cold and strict" and reported that even though they have a cordial relationship, she has never felt particularly close to her. "She's a hard worker and has had a rough life, so I can see why she was like that with us," she said. Mrs. Juarez reported having a very good relationship with all her siblings and being closest to her older brother, who recently moved in with her.

Mrs. Juarez recalled a traumatic loss in her life when her babysitter was killed in a motor vehicle accident. She painfully recalled, "I loved her so much. She was like a mom to me and did the things my mom didn't do. She lived with us, so I was devastated when she died. But my mom got mad at me because she didn't like that I loved her so much. So, I went outside to cry and just tried to keep it all in. I think that's why I cry so much now."

Mrs. Juarez started working at a fast-food restaurant while finishing high school, and it was there that she met her first partner. They dated for three years before Mrs. Juarez felt safe enough to be sexually active with him. However, shortly before they were to get married Mrs. Juarez found out that he had been unfaithful and had gotten another woman pregnant. When they separated in 2014, Mrs. Juarez recalled being very lonely, saying, "I had no friends because he was so controlling that he wouldn't allow me to hang out with friends. I just focused on school to cope."

In 2015, Mrs. Juarez met Mr. Juan Juarez. She recalled that initially she was not attracted to him because he was three years her junior. However, as they developed a friendship, Mrs. Juarez felt he was the only person she felt truly safe with and whom she could trust. "He knows everything about me, including the abuse, and he doesn't judge me and supports me unconditionally," she said. They eventually started dating and moved in together in 2017. They married in December 2018. Mrs. Juarez described her husband as "hard working, loving, faithful, and a good family man," adding, "He's really close to his family, and I admire that so much about him. I know he's gonna be a great dad." According to Mrs. Juarez, they have plans to start a family in approximately two years.

Mrs. Juarez continued to describe a positive relationship with Mr. Juarez despite the stress of his immigration status. Mrs. Juarez explained that Mr. Juarez was brought to the United States from Mexico when he was only 3 months old and has not left the country since. Keenly aware of her husband's immigration status, Mrs. Juarez is petitioning for his U.S. residency, but she now worries that he will have to serve a lengthy ban outside of the United States, which would be emotionally devastating for her. "I'm trying to stay positive, but it's really hard," she cried.

Behavioral Observations

Mrs. Juarez arrived on time to her appointment. She was overall engaging, cooperative, and forthcoming. She was able to provide an intact, detailed, sequential, and logical personal history. She spoke clearly and coherently and maintained appropriate eye contact. Based on her overall cognitive faculties and range of knowledge, Mrs. Juarez is estimated to be of average intellectual ability for her age.

Throughout the evaluation, Mrs. Juarez's emotions were appropriate and congruent with the subjects of discussion. She cried throughout most of the clinical interview, and her pent-up anguish was noticeable. She became visibly distraught when she discussed her worries over her husband's immigration process and the uncertainty of her future, fidgeting with her hands and biting her lip. Mrs. Juarez appeared to be a reliable historian, and her accounts of her personal experiences were believable. Overall, she provided sufficient information for diagnostic purposes, yielding valid clinical impressions of her current functioning.

Impressions and Findings

During the clinical interview, Mrs. Juarez described the ways in which an extended separation from her husband would create emotional and practical hardships for her. She reported experiencing anxiety, worry, and stress due to her husband's immigration status and the uncertainty of their future. According to Mrs. Juarez, finding out about her husband's potential departure has brought to light her dependence on him for emotional and practical support. She acknowledged her depressive state, saying, "Since I found out that his DACA wouldn't get renewed [because of his conviction for DUI], I've been freaking out. I've had like six panic attacks; I can't breathe, and everything starts spinning, and I think I'm dying. I tell him to call an ambulance, but he tells me to relax and that everything's fine, and it eventually goes away."

Mrs. Juarez stated that she disclosed some of her distress to her brother, who encouraged her to seek psychiatric treatment. However, Mrs. Juarez is apprehensive about seeking help out of fear that she will be medicated. "I lean on my faith in God, and I go to church every Sunday. I need it," she said.

When asked how an extended separation from her husband would affect her, Mrs. Juarez stated, "I'm already a hot mess right now, so I can't imagine it getting worse. I'm scared that this will affect me when I'm in school. I love my work and my students, and I don't want this to affect me and ruin what I've worked so hard for."

According to Mrs. Juarez, her husband is her main source of emotional support, as he is the only one who knows the full extent of her suffering. "He's always there, and I just cling on to him," she said. In addition, she expressed concern about her husband's welfare in Mexico, as he has no ties to that country since being brought to the United States as an infant. She cried, "I don't know how he would survive. And there's so much violence and drug trafficking there, and they're gonna tell immediately that he's from here, so they'll take advantage of that."

Relocating to Mexico to be with her husband is not a viable option, according to Mrs. Juarez. "There's nothing there for me," she stated, explaining that she has no ties to that country and does not speak Spanish. She said she is unwilling to sell her home or to quit her job and her studies, as she expects to earn her master's degree at the end of the year. She also lamented being far away from her family of origin, as well as not being able to continue looking after the disabled woman she cares for on the weekends. "I can't, I just can't. I don't think I can handle it emotionally. Being far away from my church and my family, it would just be too hard," she said. She reiterated her fear of the indiscriminate crime in Mexico and highlighted how disruptive a relocation would be for her professional career.

To assess her psychological symptoms further, Mrs. Juarez was evaluated by following the guidelines of the Structured Clinical Interview for DSM-5 Disorders – Clinician Version (SCID-5-CV). The SCID-5-CV is a semi-structured guide designed to evaluate a broad range of psychological problems and symptoms of psychopathology according to the diagnostic criteria established by the Diagnostic and Statistical Manual of Mental Disorders – Fifth Edition (DSM-5). Mrs. Juarez complained about various anxiety symptoms, such as being worried about a number of things in her life and having difficulty controlling her worry, a persistent sense of angst, recurrent panic attacks, difficulty concentrating, ruminative thoughts, and trouble sleeping. She also indicated depressive symptomatology, such as feeling sad most of the time, having decreased interest in things she used to enjoy, feeling hopeless, and lacking motivation. She complained of tension headaches and gastrointestinal problems and reported worrying about her physical health.

Mrs. Juarez completed the Experiences in Close Relationships – Relationship Structures (ECR-RS). The ECR-RS is a self-report questionnaire that assesses an individual's attachment style, a personality dimension that describes attitudes about relationships with loved ones. Test-takers can be classified into one of two attachment pattern groups: *secure* or *insecure*, based on their scores along the dimensions of anxiety and avoidance. The ECR-RS revealed an *insecure* global attachment classification with others and a *secure* attachment classification with her husband. Her way of relating to others is characterized by a strong desire for closeness in relationships while at the same time avoiding close relationships due to fear of being rejected or mistreated. Thus, she is likely to maintain distance as a means to protect herself from others. When faced with stressors or feelings of vulnerability, Mrs. Juarez tends to seek less intimacy and support from others and frequently suppresses and hides her feelings of despair or distress. Her *secure* attachment classification with her husband, however, corroborates how her relationship with him functions as an emotional buffer that contributes to an overall sense of security and psychological stability. This evidences their ability, as a couple, to establish and maintain an open and trustworthy relationship with each other. People in *securely* attached relationships feel comfortable expressing their emotions to their partners and are able to rely on their partners when feeling troubled. These relationships tend to be honest, loving, and supportive.

Mrs. Juarez's anxiety regarding a potential separation from her husband was also demonstrated on several of her responses to the Sentence Completion Test (SCT). The SCT provides respondents with beginnings of sentences, referred to as "stems," and respondents then complete the sentences in ways that are meaningful to them. The responses help shed light into an individual's attitudes, beliefs, motivations, or other mental states. The general scope of Mrs. Juarez's responses on this instrument revealed her pervasive sense of worry and anxiety and her fear of being alone.

The Recent Life Changes Stress Test (RLCST) is a validated measure of stress and illness. Events in the past year of an individual's life are registered and tabulated to give a rough estimate of how stress affects health. The overall results from the RLCST indicate that Mrs. Juarez is experiencing significant levels of distress, which are highly predictive of serious physical or psychological deterioration. In particular, Mrs. Juarez reported struggling with work stressors, academic demands, and her husband's immigration process. Strain on the body from important life changes and stress can impair normal immune system function. Sources of further distress, such as a major change in her life, may result in an increase in potential for illness in the near future and a worsening of any physical complaints.

To better understand Mrs. Juarez's more enduring personality characteristics and ways of relating with others, she completed the Personality Assessment Inventory (PAI). The PAI is a self-administered, objective test of personality and psychopathology designed to provide information on critical client variables in professional settings. It consists of a number of scales that measure the respondent's overall approach taking the test, psychopathological traits, treatment considerations, and interpersonal functioning. Mrs. Juarez's scores indicate that she attended appropriately to item content and responded in a consistent fashion to similar items. She answered in a reasonably forthright manner and did not attempt to present an unrealistic or inaccurate impression that was either more negative or more positive than the clinical picture would warrant. Her PAI clinical profile depicted a person with prominent distress and ruminative worry. Mrs. Juarez appears to be withdrawn and isolated, feeling estranged from the people around her. As a result, she probably has few, if any, close interpersonal relationships and tends to become anxious and threatened by such relationships. She is tense and pessimistic about what the future holds and appears to be harboring specific fears or anxiety surrounding certain situations, resulting in her life being severely constricted by psychological turmoil. Her pattern of responses revealed that she is likely to display a variety of maladaptive behavior patterns aimed at controlling anxiety. Phobic behaviors are likely to interfere significantly in her life, and it is probable that she monitors her environment in a vigilant fashion to avoid contact with the feared object or situation. She ruminates about matters to a degree that impairs her ability to concentrate and make even simple decisions. Changes in routine, unexpected events, and contradictory information are likely to generate untoward stress. Mrs. Juarez's life is probably severely constricted by her tension and her proclivity to feeling overwhelmed, as relatively mild stressors can precipitate a major crisis. Overt physical signs of tension and stress, such as sweaty palms, trembling hands, complaints of irregular heartbeats, and shortness of breath, are also present.

Mrs. Juarez reported a number of difficulties consistent with a significant depressive experience. Although she does not appear to feel hopeless and her self-esteem seems largely intact, she does manifest affective and physiological signs of depression. She admits openly to feelings of sadness, a loss of interest in normal activities, and a loss of pleasure in things that were previously enjoyed. She also demonstrated an unusual degree of concern about her physical functioning and health matters in general.

Clinical Diagnostic Impression According to the Diagnostic and Statistical Manual of Mental Disorders – 5 (DSM 5)

Based on the symptoms she endorsed, along with the results of the psychological instruments administered during this evaluation, Mrs. Juarez meets criteria for the following DSM-5 diagnosis:

• Generalized anxiety disorder with panic attacks

Individuals with this type of disorder typically experience excessive anxiety and worry which they find difficult to control. In addition, they experience a range of symptoms, such as restlessness, irritability, difficulty concentrating, and sleep disturbances, where such symptomatology causes clinically significant distress or impairment in important areas of functioning.

In addition, Mrs. Juarez experiences recurrent unexpected panic attacks. A panic attack is an abrupt surge of intense fear or intense discomfort that reaches a peak within minutes, and during which time a number of other symptoms occur, such as palpitations, accelerated heart rate, sweating, trembling or shaking, shortness of breath, nausea, fear of losing control or fear of dying. The disturbance is not attributable to the physiological effects of a substance or another medical condition or mental disorder.

Summary and Recommendations

Mrs. Anne Juarez was referred for an evaluation to assess her current psychological functioning and the degree to which an extended separation from her husband due to his immigration process would affect her. She underwent a thorough psychological assessment consisting of a face-to-face clinical interview and the administration of empirically validated instruments. Overall, she provided a candid account of her current struggles, yielding valid clinical impressions of her current functioning.

Mrs. Juarez described a traumatic upbringing, marked by domestic violence and sexual abuse. Trauma early in the lifecycle, particularly when it is recurrent and when it occurs in the context of an inadequate caregiving system, has pervasive effects on cognition, socialization, and the capacity for affect regulation. A significant amount of research has shown that adverse childhood experiences, specifically abuse and emotional trauma, affect neuroregulatory systems, which can have profound and enduring effects on physical and psychiatric health.[2] In particular, rape and childhood sexual abuse are known to cause significant psychological damage. One occurrence of sexual aggression may be sufficient to create long-lasting negative effects, especially if the child-victim does not subsequently receive appropriate support. The disabling effects of such traumatic experiences can carry over into adult life. Given her history of trauma, it is remarkable that Mrs. Juarez has been able to form a secure attachment to her husband. However, her ways of coping with life stressors and her propensity for psychological deterioration are consistent with what one would expect of individuals with similar trauma histories.

It appears that Mr. Juarez's departure would cause great upheaval for Mrs. Juarez and would unequivocally pose practical and emotional hardships for her. She highlighted her dependence on her husband for emotional support and feared decompensating emotionally in his absence. Mrs. Juarez also described the reasons why relocating to Mexico in order to live with her husband is not a viable option for her. She highlighted her lack of ties to Mexico and not being able to speak Spanish, her inability to pursue her career, and her concerns for her safety. In particular, she feared being away from her loved ones and her psychological functioning severely deteriorating. Mrs. Juarez also explained how such a move would hinder her professional development.

It is unlikely that Mrs. Juarez would be able to adequately adjust to an extended separation from her husband or to a major change in her living environment due to a relocation without experiencing a significant deterioration in her psychological functioning. A forced separation from her husband, the man she has come to trust and on whom she leans for emotional support, would compound with her history of trauma and loss, resulting in potentially irreparable psychological damage. Given her current clinical diagnosis of *generalized anxiety disorder with panic attacks,* along with her trauma history, her personality characteristics, and her strong dependency on her husband, Mr. Juarez's departure from the United States will likely affect Mrs. Juarez beyond what is considered a normal response to a separation from a loved one. Therefore, an extended separation from her husband or a relocation outside of the United States is highly inadvisable. Although she has thus far been able to lean on her loved ones for emotional sustenance, Mrs. Juarez would greatly benefit from mental health treatment to process her childhood trauma and to learn healthy ways to cope with her emotional distress.

If you have questions regarding this report, feel free to contact me at your convenience. I declare under penalty of perjury that all statements contained in this document are true and correct to the best of my professional judgment.

Notes

1 The Specialty Guidelines for Forensic Psychology and the Ethical Principles of Psychologists and Code of Conduct set forth by the American Psychological Association state that "Providing forensic and therapeutic psychological services to the same individual or closely related individuals involves multiple relationships that may impair objectivity and/ or cause exploitation or other harm" (American Psychological Association, 2013. Guideline 4.02.01: Therapeutic- Forensic Role Conflicts). In other words, evaluating a patient whom the evaluator also treats

with regular therapy sessions compromises the integrity of the evaluation and therefore is highly discouraged.

2 Felitti, V. J. & Anda, R. F. (2010). The relationship of adverse childhood experiences to adult medical disease, psychiatric disorders and sexual behavior: Implications for healthcare. In R. A. Lanius, E. Vermetten, & C. Pain (Eds.), *The Impact of Early Life Trauma on Health and Disease: The Hidden Epidemic* (pp. 77–87). Cambridge University Press.

Appendix C

Sample Follow-Up Affidavit

February 25, 2020

RE: Jason McCarthy

Mr. Jason McCarthy underwent a psychological evaluation in April 2018 to assess his psychological status and how an extended separation from his wife, Mrs. Silvia McCarthy Flores, would affect him—psychologically and emotionally. At that time, Mr. McCarthy's symptoms did not meet diagnostic criteria for a mental health disorder. However, the evaluation specifically highlighted Mr. McCarthy's anxiety pertaining to his wife's immigration process.

Mr. McCarthy was referred for a follow-up evaluation to assess his current psychological health and comment on any further developments pertaining to his symptoms. To assess his current symptoms, I conducted a thorough clinical assessment and re-administered some of the same instruments used during his previous evaluation. The following is a summary of Mr. McCarthy's most current psychological status, as well as my professional recommendations.

Update on Background Information

Mr. McCarthy is now 52 years old, and he lives with two of his daughters, his son-in-law, and his grandson in San Diego, California. He continues to work full-time as a quality control specialist for Renegade Appliances.

According to Mr. McCarthy, his wife attended her consular interview in Ciudad Juarez, Mexico, around March 2019. At that time, she was reportedly told that she needed to submit more evidence of her husband's current hardships in order to waive her grounds of inadmissibility. Mr. and Mrs. McCarthy then made the necessary arrangements for Mrs. McCarthy to travel to her relatives' house in Culiacan, while Mr. McCarthy returned to San Diego. For the past nine months, Mr. McCarthy has continued to work and live in San Diego and has visited his wife three times. He stated, "I wish I could spend more time with her, but my job is extremely demanding."

Mr. McCarthy described how his separation from his wife has been affecting him. He stated that he has been under great financial strain since he has to send money to his wife in Mexico while continuing to pay for his own expenses here. He added that because she was the one in charge of keeping track of their bills, he often falls behind on his payments due to being distracted and disorganized. Mr. McCarthy also lamented that he had started attending Grossmont College in pursuit of a degree in engineering but quit following his wife's departure. He explained, "I just couldn't concentrate, and my grades went down almost immediately after she left." In addition, Mr. McCarthy described how his daughters and his young grandson struggle to cope with Mrs. McCarthy's absence. He became tearful as he stated that his grandson, who has medical issues, asks about his grandmother daily. "It just breaks my heart. When we FaceTime with her, he thinks she's in the house and starts going around looking for her," he said. Most importantly, Mr. McCarthy highlighted his pervasive fear for his wife's safety in Mexico, explaining that he does not want his wife to leave the house. He stated, "Last week they shot and killed a man three blocks from where she lives. When I talk with her on the phone, I sometimes hear shots in the background, and I've had to tell her to get down on the ground. It's terrible there. Even when I went to visit, at night we could hear gunshots."

Mr. McCarthy's stressors stemming from his prolonged separation from his wife have resulted in a number of depressive symptoms. According to Mr. McCarthy, he has been struggling with lack of appetite, and he went down two sizes in clothing. He stated, "My daughters and my co-workers force me to eat." He reported that whereas he used to be more stoic and in control of his emotions, he now cries almost daily. He also stopped doing things that he used to enjoy, explaining, "I used to like working on my car. That's what I did as a hobby. Now my car is parked on the street, dirty. The other day my neighbor washed it for me."

Mr. McCarthy explained that his symptoms have been interfering with his performance at work. He said he recently received a warning when he made a mistake using a dangerous chemical. "I had never ever been in trouble at work before," he said, adding, "The customers have been complaining about missing parts, and that's my responsibility. Even though my boss understands my situation, I'm worried because I don't know how much longer he'll put up with it." Mr. McCarthy attributed his oversight to his difficulty concentrating. He also stopped volunteering at church, stating, "I just don't have the interest or the energy." Worrying about his wife has reportedly kept him up at night, which results in his getting an average of four hours of sleep. When asked how he has been coping with his symptoms, he stated, "Nothing really makes me feel better. Sometimes I'll go for a drive and try to clear my mind, but my wife is all I think about." Although Mr. McCarthy said he has been trying to start psychotherapy, he explained that he has been unable to find a therapist with openings and who accepts his health insurance.

Relocating to Mexico to be with his wife is not a viable option, according to Mr. McCarthy. He reiterated not wanting to quit his job of over seven years and his only source of income, anticipating that he would not be able to find gainful employment in Mexico because he does not speak Spanish. Most importantly, he explained that moving to Mexico would entail separating from his daughters and grandson, which he is unwilling to do. He also explained why his wife living closer to San Diego in order to facilitate his visits would be unsustainable, primarily because he would not be able to afford paying for her rent and also because he would worry about her welfare in a dangerous area where neither one has any contacts.

Current Findings

To assess Mr. McCarthy's current symptomatology compared to his psychological status during his previous evaluation, I again followed the guidelines of the Structured Clinical Interview for DSM-5 Disorders – Clinician Version, a semi-structured guide designed to evaluate a broad range of psychological problems and symptoms of psychopathology according to the diagnostic criteria established by the Diagnostic and Statistical Manual of Mental Disorders – Fifth Edition (DSM-5). Mr. McCarthy reported a significant increase in his symptoms of anxiety and depression. He struggles with a pervasive sense of angst and ruminates about his problems to a point that interferes with his ability to concentrate. He reported sad mood, hopelessness, and a noticeably decreased interest in things he used to enjoy. He also complained of difficulty sleeping, forgetfulness, and lack of appetite leading to weight loss.

Mr. McCarthy also completed the Recent Life Changes Stress Test, a validated measure of stress and illness. On this instrument, he received a much higher score than during his previous evaluation, indicating that based on Mr. McCarthy's current stressors and recent life changes, he has a 30 percent chance of developing an illness over the following year, as the immune system is significantly compromised by high stress levels. Mr. McCarthy identified his current stressors as his strained financial situation, the recent changes in his household responsibilities due to his wife's departure, his wife's welfare, and the uncertainty of his future.

Summary and Recommendations

Mr. Jason McCarthy attended a follow-up clinical assessment to evaluate his current psychological status. Results from this evaluation indicate that Mr. McCarthy has had a noticeable increase in his psychological symptoms when compared to the results from April 2018. He attributed his depressive symptoms to his sudden and prolonged separation from his wife. The quality, frequency, and severity of his symptoms currently meet criteria for a diagnosis of *major depressive disorder*. Symptoms of this disorder include persistent depressed mood, markedly diminished interest in most activities, insomnia, lethargy, diminished ability to think or concentrate, hopelessness, worthlessness, and irritability, where such symptomatology causes clinically significant distress or impairment in important areas of functioning.

It is evident that Mrs. McCarthy's departure from the United States has significantly impacted Mr. McCarthy's overall well-being, and his condition appears to be worsening with the passing of time and his inability to see his wife. Although Mr. McCarthy reportedly attempted to seek mental health treatment to learn healthy ways to deal with his symptoms, he has thus far been unsuccessful. Unless his wife's immigration process is resolved in a timely fashion and his stress and depression levels decrease, Mr. McCarthy's prognosis is poor. Given that Mr. McCarthy considers his wife to be his most important source of emotional support, a prompt reunification with her is of utmost importance to avoid further deterioration of his mental health status.

If you have further questions, feel free to contact me at your convenience. I declare under penalty of perjury that all statements contained in this document are true and correct to the best of my professional judgment.

Appendix D

Sample Cancellation of Removal Report

<u>Clients' Names:</u> Oscar Perez; Juancito Perez
<u>Date of Birth:</u> 10/05/1971; 09/06/2004
<u>Date of Assessment:</u> 02/24/2020
<u>Date of Report:</u> 03/02/2020
<u>Assessment Procedures:</u> Biopsychosocial Clinical Interview
       Structured Clinical Interview for DSM-5
       Disorders – Clinician Version
       Sentence Completion Test
       Personality Assessment Inventory (Mr. Perez)
       Millon Adolescent Clinical Inventory (Juancito)
<u>Collateral Information:</u> Brief interview with Ms. Maria Sanchez
<u>Records Reviewed:</u> Psychoeducational Evaluation Report (01/2020)
       Psychiatric notes from Dr. Smith (08/2019–10/
       2019)
       Clinical records from Neighborhood Healthcare
       (3/2017–01/2020)

Evaluator's Qualifications and Assessment Methodology

(Please refer to Sample Provisional Waiver Report for this introductory section)

Identifying Information and Reason for Referral

Mr. Oscar Perez is a 49-year-old, self-identified Hispanic male. He is married to Ms. Maria Sanchez, with whom he has one son, Juancito. Juancito is a 15-year-old male who is currently attending tenth grade at Riverside High School. Mr. Perez works as a warehouse attendant at Jimmy's Holdings. He resides with his wife and their son, along with a roommate, in Riverside, California.

 Mr. Perez and his son, Juancito, were referred for an evaluation to assess their current psychological status and how Ms. Sanchez's forced removal from the United States due to her current immigration proceedings would affect them—practically and emotionally—and whether their suffering would be beyond what is typically expected following a separation from a loved one.

Relevant Background Information

Mr. Perez was born and raised in Chiapas, Mexico. He comes from an intact family and is the second youngest of seven siblings. Mr. Perez described an unremarkable childhood although he lamented that his parents struggled to raise their large family on his father's income. He denied having experienced any trauma or abuse growing up. Upon graduating from high school, Mr. Perez decided to join some of his older siblings, who had been residing in California. He started working at a restaurant but eventually returned to Mexico to pursue a degree in law. Five years into his studies, Mr. Perez reportedly realized that making a life as a lawyer in Mexico would be very difficult. "There is so much corruption in Mexico. Everything is about money, and you solve everything with money. That is not what I wanted for myself," he said. It was around that time when he married Ms. Maria Sanchez, and the couple decided to settle in California to raise a family.

Mr. Perez initially worked at restaurants and was eventually hired at Jimmy's Holdings, where he has been working for the past 15 years. In 2004, their son, Juancito, was born. Mr. Perez described an uneventful birth but stated that, although he had not noticed any difficulties in Juancito as a toddler, he was told upon Juancito's entering elementary school that he had some odd behaviors. Juancito was evaluated and ultimately diagnosed with autism. Mr. Perez stated, "I still have difficulty accepting it. He looks normal to me. I don't think there's anything wrong with not having friends, but I guess it isn't normal. They gave him medication, but I don't know why he needs it." He did acknowledge that he is well aware of his son's erratic behavior and volatile temper. "He does not like to lose at games. One time he lost, and he was so enraged that we almost had to call the police because we couldn't calm him down," he said. Mr. Perez reported that Juancito would bang his head against the wall repeatedly and started punching the walls. "He had a tendency to do that, so I had to buy him some boxing gloves, and I enrolled him in boxing," he said.

When Juancito was interviewed alone, he shared that "school is too hard," explaining that he has "a problem keeping up," and adding, "I'm a slow learner." He shared that he has been diagnosed with attention deficit hyperactivity disorder (ADHD), which is why he struggles academically. According to Juancito, he has a handful of friends but they don't spend time together outside of school. "I don't know why," he said, adding that he likes to watch TV in his free time. He reportedly enjoyed his boxing classes but said he "just didn't want to go anymore. I don't know why." He denied having ever dated or being attracted to anyone in particular. When asked about his plans for the future, Juancito said, "I don't bother thinking about the future. It's too far in advance, and I can't predict the future. There's really no point because we're not there yet." Juancito continued to describe his role in the family as sheltered, sharing that he does not get an allowance, has never handled money, and depends on his parents for most of his basic needs. He does not have any chores around the house, explaining, "We really don't have that much trash or anything."

According to Mr. Perez, Juancito has been receiving mental health treatment for some time, but he has recently been refusing to see his therapist. "The only thing that works when disciplining him is to promise him rewards for his actions, and it works," he stated. Mr. Perez held back tears as he shared, "My son is my everything. I am one of seven children, so I definitely wanted to have just one child so I could give him my best. I wanted him to have everything he needs." Mr. Perez described his role as the family's breadwinner. "It's important to me that nothing is lacking at home. I work hard for that," he said. He and his wife have established a household based on mutual support and collaboration, whereby both Mr. Perez and Ms. Sanchez work to afford their family's expenses. He reported that his wife is the one who is most in charge of their son, she being the one to drive him to and from school and attend all of Juancito's parent-teacher conferences. "She's definitely the one who takes better care of him," Mr. Perez stated. This information was corroborated by Ms. Sanchez during her interview.

When describing his relationship with his son, Mr. Perez stated, "We're more like friends. I always talk with him, and I always told him that I wanted to be his friend. We have good times together because we both like cars. I like soccer, but he never liked it. So I prioritize what he likes. I tell him, 'I'm your friend, not your dad. You tell me what you need, and if it's within my ability, I will get that for you.' I ask him what he needs and how I can help him."

Around 2003, Mr. Perez initiated the process to adjust his wife's immigration status, and he updated his petition once he became a naturalized U.S. citizen in 2009. Upon learning that she would have to serve a lengthy penalty outside the country, the couple decided not to follow through with the immigration process paperwork. Mr. Perez was unable to explain how or why his wife is currently in removal proceedings, but he is aware that she might be forced to return to Mexico, which would result in a number of hardships for him and their son.

Psychiatric History

Juancito recalled that he was "very stressed out in fourth grade because of a super strict teacher," and that prompted his being referred to a counselor. He then shared that he has had a number of counselors in the past, but he never liked them. "They just treated me like a child, so I just stopped going with them," he said, adding, "I just didn't want to go to a counselor anymore. I felt good."

A review of the psychiatric records available revealed that Juancito has been receiving special education services at school since the fourth grade and that based on a thorough assessment, he meets criteria for specific learning disability[1] and attention deficit hyperactivity disorder (ADHD).[2] Most recently, Juancito was re-evaluated to determine if he continues to qualify for special education services. Results from that evaluation revealed that in addition to these diagnoses, Juancito meets diagnostic criteria for autism spectrum disorder.[3] In addition, his intellectual functioning is significantly below what is expected of a child his age.

Psychiatric records from Neighborhood Healthcare indicate that Juancito has been receiving mental health treatment at their clinic since

June 2017, when he was treated for ADHD. Throughout the years, he has been treated for anxiety, depression, and symptoms associated with autism spectrum disorder. Notes from Dr. Alexa Smith revealed a progressive worsening of Juancito's mental health, which is maintained under control by psychotropic medications. She noted his bizarre behavior and, based on her observations and Juancito's mother's description of his behaviors at home, Dr. Smith suspects Juancito has some type of psychotic disorder. Juancito's dependence on his mother was evident on the doctor's notes, as she was always the one to bring him in for therapy and meet with the doctor.

Behavioral Observations

Mr. Perez and Juancito arrived at their appointment on time, accompanied by Ms. Sanchez. Ms. Sanchez was interviewed briefly in order to corroborate some background details that Mr. Perez was unsure of and to elaborate on the quality of Juancito's condition and current treatment. Mr. Perez was overall engaging, cooperative, and forthcoming, and he was able to provide a sequential and logical personal history. Based on his overall cognitive faculties and his range of knowledge, Mr. Perez is estimated to be of average intellectual ability for his age.

Throughout the evaluation, Mr. Perez's emotional expressions were appropriate and congruent with the subjects of discussion. He appeared anxious as he spoke about his worries over his wife's immigration process and when describing his concerns about his son's mental health. He spoke clearly and coherently and maintained appropriate eye contact. Mr. Perez appeared to be a reliable historian, and his accounts of his personal experiences were believable.

Juancito required some prompting to engage in conversation and was at times incoherent, making contradictory statements. For example, he struggled to recall some details from his past, claiming only that something was "a long time ago" although he later stated, "I remember every detail from my past." His emotional expressions were restricted, and his eye contact was intermittent. Juancito's intellectual functioning appeared to be lower than average when compared to same-age individuals, and he struck me as immature for his age. No unusual gestures, mannerisms, or postures were observed during the interview.

Impressions and Findings

During the clinical interview, Mr. Perez described how his wife's forced removal from the United States would create emotional, practical, and financial hardships for him and their son. He stated, "My main concern is my son. He would not want to go to Mexico. I took him to Tijuana once, and after two hours we had to come back because he got so anxious and he refused to eat. He was afraid of people and very uncomfortable. He gets very anxious and angry due to his condition, so I had to turn around and come back home".

Being left alone to raise his son without his wife's support would be "unbearable," according to Mr. Perez. He explained that his son is very dependent on his mother and that he would not be able to fulfill her role in her absence. "She's the one who takes him to the doctor and who is involved with his school," he said, admitting that he feels ill equipped to handle such responsibilities. "Also, with my work, I don't know how I would do it," he said. In addition, Mr. Perez worried about not being able to cover his living expenses without his wife's financial contributions, and he anticipated having to support her in Mexico because he doubted she would be able to find gainful employment at her age. He also lamented having to separate from his wife of 19 years, on whom he relies for emotional and practical support. "Especially now that I have cholesterol problems and arthritis, and she's the one who cooks healthy meals for me," he added.

While interviewing Juancito, he disclosed that his mother's removal from the United States would result in "complete hell." He elaborated on how stressful it would be for him to be apart from his mother, stating, "It would be horrible, as horrible as someone dying." He shared that he depends on his mother for most of his practical needs and acknowledged that his father would not be able to adequately fulfill her obligations. "He works a lot, and he doesn't even cook. He comes home from work, and he goes to sleep because he's very tired," he said. Juancito described a loving relationship with his mother, stating, "We've never fought, we've never been separated, and we're always very close. She made a ton of sacrifices for us, and she dedicates a lot of her well-being for us." He shared that he enjoys spending time with his parents on their days off from work and recalled brief trips they have taken together.

To assess his current mental state further, Mr. Perez was evaluated by following the guidelines of the Structured Clinical Interview for DSM-5 Disorders – Clinician Version (SCID-5-CV). The SCID-5-CV is a semi-structured guide designed to evaluate a broad range of psychological problems and symptoms of psychopathology according to the diagnostic criteria established by the Diagnostic and Statistical Manual of Mental Disorders – Fifth Edition (DSM-5). Mr. Perez reported being worried about a number of things in his life and having great difficulty controlling his worry. He reported a pervasive sense of angst and fear, physical tension, difficulty sleeping, and various stress-related physical complaints.

Mr. Perez's most pressing concerns were evident on his responses to the Sentence Completion Test (SCT). The SCT is an instrument that provides respondents with beginnings of sentences, referred to as "stems," and respondents then complete the sentences in ways that are meaningful to them. The responses help shed light into an individual's attitudes, beliefs, motivations, or other mental states. The overall theme of Mr. Perez's responses on this measure highlighted the importance of his relationship with his son, whom he referred to as his "best friend," and his anxiety regarding a potential forced separation from his wife.

Juancito was administered the Millon Adolescent Clinical Inventory (MACI), which is the most widely used personality assessment test for adolescents. It was designed to provide information about an adolescent's personality, as well as the unique concerns, pressures, and situations of the adolescent test-taker. Juancito's responses to this test revealed a marked naiveté and significant deficits in self-insight. He fails to recognize, or to admit recognizing, his deeper social insecurities and his persistent need to garner attention and be well liked.

Juancito's social dependency and strong need for attention and security were prominent on his responses to the MACI. His fear of being on his own leads him to seek someone among his peers to lean on and to assume an overly compliant and obliging manner with others. He may often act in a socially gregarious and charming way, seeking attention through immature, self-dramatizing behavior. More extreme reactions, such as impulsive acting out, may emerge when his need for dependency is genuinely threatened. Also notable is a naive attitude about life, and he may demonstrate rather immature and scattered thinking. When faced with interpersonal difficulties, he is likely to try to portray an attitude of adeptness and enthusiasm, denying disturbing emotions and concealing his true discomfort with superficial comments. This is consistent with Dr. Smith's observations, as she remarked that Ms. Sanchez had described Juancito being anxious about her upcoming surgery and her having to spend one night at the hospital, yet Juancito verbally disavowed such fears while at the same time seeming very concerned about his mother's welfare.

Summary and Recommendations

Mr. Oscar Perez and his 15-year-old son, Juancito Perez, were referred for an evaluation to assess their current psychological level of functioning and how Ms. Maria Sanchez's forced departure from the United States due to her immigration proceedings would affect them. Mr. Perez and Juancito underwent a thorough psychological assessment consisting of a face-to-face clinical interview, a review of scholastic and mental health records, collateral information from Ms. Sanchez, and the administration of empirically validated instruments.

Mr. Perez and his wife have developed a family unit based on rather delineated roles, whereby Mr. Perez is the main breadwinner while Ms. Sanchez is the one in charge of their son's welfare. Juancito is a child with significant cognitive and emotional problems who requires special education services and medications to reduce his symptoms of anxiety and depression. Although his father is well aware of Juancito's limitations, his tendencies to minimize their severity and to normalize Juancito's deficiencies were notable. Mr. Perez's good intentions and undisputable love for his son are commendable; however, he lacks the ability to set boundaries and follow treatment guidelines that are indispensable for this child's welfare. In my opinion, Mr. Perez is unfit to care for Juancito on his own. Ms. Sanchez, on the other hand, prioritizes her son's well-being and tends to feel overly responsible for his shortcomings. Juancito's dependency on his mother would make a separation from her extremely detrimental to his mental health and could result in potentially irreparable damage. Relocating to Mexico in order to live with her would also result in exceptionally negative consequences. Juancito does not adapt well to change, which is likely to result in a severe decline of his mental status. Most importantly, Juancito requires special education and ongoing psychiatric treatment. Not being able to access these critical services will unquestionably result in a significant deterioration of his mental health.

It is well established that children who are separated from their parents due to immigration proceedings are prone to develop anxiety, depression, troubled behaviors, and academic difficulties. Many factors can further complicate this transition, including family dynamics and the circumstances surrounding the separation.[4] Ms. Sanchez's forced departure from the United States would be extremely damaging to this family, her son in particular. Based on his most recent symptoms and his psychiatrist's observations, Juancito's condition not only is unlikely to improve, but might actually become more complicated. Juancito would therefore benefit from continued mental health treatment and close monitoring of his psychiatric conditions.

If you have questions regarding this report, feel free to contact me at your convenience. I declare under penalty of perjury that all statements contained in this document are true and correct to the best of my professional judgment.

Notes

1 Specific learning disorder is diagnosed when an individual has significant difficulties learning and using academic skills. This is evidenced by inaccurate or effortful word reading; difficulties understanding the meaning of what is read; difficulties with spelling; difficulties with written expression; difficulties mastering number sense, number facts, or calculation; and/ or difficulties with mathematical reasoning. The affected academic skills are substantially and quantifiably below those expected for the individual's chronological age and cause significant interference with academic or occupational performance.
2 Attention-deficit hyperactivity disorder (ADHD) is a brain disorder marked by an ongoing pattern of inattention and/ or hyperactivity-impulsivity that interferes with functioning or development. Individuals with this condition often experience difficulties staying focused and paying attention, difficulty controlling behavior, and hyperactivity (over-activity).
3 Autism spectrum disorder is a condition related to brain development that impacts how a person perceives and socializes with others, causing problems in social interaction and communication. The disorder also includes limited and repetitive patterns of behavior. The range and severity of symptoms can vary widely.
4 Suarez-Orozco, C., Todorova, I., & Louie, J. (2002). Making up for lost time: The experience of separation and reunification among immigrant families. *Family Process*, 4 (4).

Appendix E

Sample Asylum Report

<u>Client's Name:</u> Fabiola Guritan
<u>Date of Birth:</u> 02/23/1982
<u>Date of Assessment:</u> 08/15/2020
<u>Date of Report:</u> 08/19/2020
<u>Assessment Procedures:</u> Biopsychosocial History Interview
                                       Structured Clinical Interview for DSM-5
                                       Disorders – Clinician Version
                                       Posttraumatic Stress Disorder Checklist – 5
                                       Clinician-Administered PTSD Scale for DSM-5
                                       Trauma Symptom Inventory – 2
<u>Records Reviewed:</u>   Ms. Guritan's written declaration in support of her
                                       asylum application

Evaluator's Qualifications and Assessment Methodology

(Please refer to Sample Provisional Waiver Report for this introductory section)

Identifying Information and Reason for Referral

Ms. Fabiola Guritan is a 38-year-old, self-identified Haitian female. She is single and has no children. Ms. Guritan lives with a friend from church in an apartment they rent in San Diego, California. She has the equivalent of a high school education and is currently unemployed.

Ms. Guritan was referred by her attorney for an evaluation to determine her current psychological status and the benchmarks of her current functioning. More specifically, this evaluation aims to assess the extent to which having been the victim of torture at the hands of Haitian government officials has affected her, emotionally and psychologically.

Background Information

Ms. Guritan was born and raised in Saint Marc, Haiti. She comes from an intact family and is the middle child of five siblings. She described her parents as hardworking, explaining that her father was a farmer and her mother was a housewife who was in charge of caring for the children. Ms. Guritan recalled a mostly happy childhood, attending public school and helping her mother care for her younger siblings; however, she became tearful as she recalled her experience being circumcised at the age of 4, apologizing for not wanting to discuss it further.

Around 2015, there were presidential elections in the country, and it was a time of great political unrest. Ms. Guritan painfully recalled how one night as she was finishing dinner at home with her family, three national police officers came to the door and demanded that her father come outside. "All of a sudden, we heard gunshots, and when we ran outside, we saw my dad lying dead on the ground," she tearfully recalled. According to Ms. Guritan, the officers said that her father was shot as he tried to run away. They reportedly accused him of being a member of the Liberation Front (LF) party, which opposed the current political regime. She explained that she did not believe her father was indeed involved with any political party and that he never discussed his political views at home; however, he had been arrested a few times in the past for being an alleged member of the LF. "All I know is that my dad was a farmer and a family man. I never heard him speak about politics, or anything," she said.

Approximately one week after her father's murder, officers came back to the house and demanded that she come outside. She stated, "My mom opened the door, and she begged them not to take me. My mom was crying, and the men took me to the police station." Throughout the month she spent in confinement, she was repeatedly tortured and questioned. She described how she was hung from the ceiling and shocked continually on the soles of her feet as she was asked about her father's membership in the Liberation Front and whether he had been hiding LF fighters in his home. "The whole month, they kept asking me the same questions, and I kept giving them the same answers," she stated. She reported that an officer promised her that if she had sex with him, she would be released. Ms. Guritan refused to have sex with the officer, who subsequently raped her and threatened to kill her if she ever told anyone. She was eventually released, and she was threatened that if she had contact with anyone opposing the government, she would be put back in jail and her cousin, who had signed her release paperwork, would be forced to pay a large sum of money.

Upon her release, Ms. Guritan returned home, wounded and in pain. She explained that she had difficulty walking from all her injuries and that her physical recovery took many weeks. Emotionally, however, Ms. Guritan felt "destroyed." She was still grieving the tragic death of her father, and she was constantly on edge, fearing for her safety even when at home. She reportedly struggled sleeping and suffered nightmares almost daily. According to Ms. Guritan, a relative strongly advised her to leave the city, as he had heard that someone had been detained and told government officials that her father was indeed a member of LF. Consequently, Ms. Guritan was deemed to have lied to the officers and was at great risk of being arrested again. "My mom was crying, and she said she'd rather have me leave than be killed in front of her," she stated. Ms. Guritan then relocated to Port-au-Prince, where she began working as a maid for a family.

"Life was very hard," Ms. Guritan lamented, who recalled the three years she spent in Port-au-Prince as "meaningless." She explained that she was always working at the house, had no friends or family nearby, and isolated most of the time except for when she went to church. Her mother passed away in 2018, which was another painful loss for Ms. Guritan, as she was unable to return home to see her or to attend her funeral. Ms. Guritan continued attending church, which was her safe haven. Some members of the congregation asked the family she worked for to help her apply for a passport so she could leave Haiti. With their assistance, she was able to secure an employment opportunity in Mexico and applied for a work permit at the Mexican embassy. She explained, "I had no life in Haiti. I barely left the house because I was always scared. I didn't feel safe there. All I did was stay home with the family, and I only left the house to go to church. I was always in hiding, afraid of getting killed."

She cried as she recalled finding out about the murder of one of her best friends by government officials, as the political unrest continued and intensi-fied in 2017, culminating in a large-scale riot in April of that year.

In Mexico, she spent four months working for a family, which she recalled as "very difficult." She explained that even though she had been promised a monthly salary of 1,000 dollars for eight hours of daily work, she was only paid 500, of which she was only given 250 and told that the other 250 were being put in savings. She was reportedly forced to sleep on the floor of an exercise room and to pay for her own food. "I felt I had no choice. I couldn't say or do anything," she stated, explaining that she was afraid that she would be sent back home to Haiti. She recalled crying daily, feeling hopeless and helpless as she worked from 6 in the morning until 9 in the evening. "She always threatened to send me back to Haiti and that if I left the house to go to church, she would pay me less," she stated. Ms. Guritan was eventually allowed to attend church services on Saturdays, where she met a man who subsequently helped her make her way to the United States, where one of her cousins lived. On July 4, 2019, Ms. Guritan arrived at the U.S. international border and asked to be allowed to enter the country as an asylee. She was subsequently transferred to another immigration detention center where she was interviewed again and offered to either pay bond and be released or find an attorney. She asked her cousin for financial help and was subsequently released.

Ms. Guritan moved in with her cousin, who introduced her to the Haitian community and has been instrumental in helping Ms. Guritan rebuild her life. "I feel safe now," she stated, adding, "It's a new life for me." However, Ms. Guritan fears that if her asylum petition is denied, she will be deported back to Haiti, where she is certain that she will be killed. She said that she had heard of a person who fled to the Bahamas and, as soon as he was deported back to Haiti, was murdered. "The minute I land in Haiti and go through the immigration checkpoint, they'll have all of my information. And that's it. They'll kill me for sure," she stated.

If allowed to stay in the United States, Ms. Guritan plans on continuing to learn English and further her education. "I would like to find a job," she stated, adding, "I know I can't ever undo everything I've been through, but I can try to put it behind me." Ms. Guritan stated that although she has not been receiving any mental health treatment, she tries to cope with her dis-tress by leaning on her church and reading the Bible.

Behavioral Observations

Ms. Guritan arrived at her appointment on time. The clinical interview was conducted in English with the help of a professional Creole interpreter, Mr. Joseph Word, who provided simultaneous translation between Creole and English. The interpreter was made aware of the purpose of this evaluation, and he signed a confidentiality and nondisclosure agreement.

Ms. Guritan was overall engaging, cooperative and forthcoming. She was able to provide an intact, sequential, and logical personal history. She spoke clearly and coherently and maintained appropriate eye contact throughout the interview. Based on her cognitive functioning and her range of knowledge, Ms. Guritan is estimated to be of average intellectual ability for her age.

Throughout the evaluation, Ms. Guritan cried openly as she discussed the trauma she experienced in Haiti. She was hyperventilating at times, needing to take breaks to regain composure. It was evident that recalling her traumatic past was very painful for Ms. Guritan. Nonetheless, she answered every question posed and her accounts of her personal experiences were believable. Overall, she provided sufficient information for diagnostic purposes, yielding valid clinical impressions of her current functioning.

Impressions and Findings

During the clinical interview, Ms. Guritan discussed how having been raped and tortured by Haitian officials has affected her. She specifically complained of experiencing a pervasive sense of insecurity and mistrust, self-loathing, and helplessness, as well as sudden, repeated, unwanted memories of the abuse she endured, sleep disturbances, and random nightmares. She admitted that her experiences in Port-au-Prince and Mexico further intensified her suffering and prevented her from beginning her healing process. Based on her account of her experiences, it appears that Ms. Guritan suffered significant emotional distress as a result of the trauma she endured in Haiti.

Her self-report was consistent with the results from the psychological instruments she was administered during this psychological evaluation. Ms. Guritan completed the Posttraumatic Stress Disorder Checklist – 5 (PCL-5), which is a brief assessment that helps identify the presence and symptom severity of posttraumatic stress disorder (PTSD). On the PCL-5, she received scores on all four categories of DSM-5 symptom criteria (intrusive symptoms, avoidance, negative symptoms, and arousal behaviors). This warranted the administration of the Clinician-Administered PTSD Scale for DSM-5 (CAPS-5). The CAPS-5 is a structured interview considered to be the gold standard in PTSD assessment. In addition to assessing the 20 DSM-5 PTSD symptoms, questions target the onset and duration of symptoms, subjective distress, impact of symptoms on social and occupational functioning, improvement in symptoms through time, overall response validity, and overall PTSD severity. Ms. Guritan reported repeated, disturbing memories and dreams about the trauma she endured in Haiti, physical reactions such as heart palpitations and sweating when something reminds her of the trauma, feeling emotionally numb, and avoiding anything that triggers memories of her traumatic experiences. This was both evident in her responses to the tests administered and observed during the clinical interview. She also reported feeling fearful, losing interest in activities she used to enjoy, and having difficulty sleeping.

To further assess Ms. Guritan's psychological symptoms, I followed the guidelines of the Structured Clinical Interview for DSM-5 Disorders – Clinician Version (SCID-5-CV). The SCID-5-CV is a semi-structured guide designed to evaluate a broad range of psychological problems and symptoms of psychopathology according to the diagnostic criteria established by the Diagnostic and Statistical Manual of Mental Disorders – Fifth Edition (DSM-5). Ms. Guritan reported a number of anxiety and depressive symptoms, including persistent worry that she has difficulty controlling, sad mood more days than not, crying easily, impaired sleep, and feelings of worthlessness, hopelessness and loneliness. She reiterated her recurrent, distressing thoughts and dreams about traumatic experiences in her past, such as her father's murder, her subsequent arrest, and having been the victim of torture and rape. She stated, "I just want to move past all this, but it haunts me." In addition, Ms. Guritan complained of a number of physical symptoms, such as headaches (migraines) and back pain.

Ms. Guritan was administered the Trauma Symptom Inventory-2 (TSI-2), a multi-scale instrument used to evaluate posttraumatic symptoms related to rape, spousal abuse, assault, combat experiences, major accidents and natural disasters, as well as the lasting sequelae of childhood abuse and early traumatic events. Ms. Guritan's responses on the TSI-2 yielded particularly high scores on the *intrusive experiences (IE)* scale and the *defensive avoidance (DA)* scale. Her elevated *IE* score indicates that Ms. Guritan experiences intrusive posttraumatic reactions and symptoms, such as nightmares, flashbacks, upsetting memories that are easily triggered by current events, and repetitive thoughts of unpleasant previous experiences that intrude into awareness. The presence of elevated *IE* scores is often, if not implicitly, linked to a previous experience of psychological trauma. High scores on this scale, therefore, typically reflect the intrusion of such traumatic material into current awareness, with subsequent distress. Individuals with elevated *DA* scores often report attempts to suppress or eliminate painful thoughts or memories from awareness, and they frequently attempt to avoid events or stimuli in their environment that might restimulate such thoughts or memories. In many cases, a high *DA* score reflects a need to avoid recall or triggered memories of a specific traumatic event. Such avoidance is generally a conscious, effortful process for managing posttraumatic distress.

Ms. Guritan also received a high score on the *posttraumatic stress (TRAUMA)* factor. Individuals with an elevation on the *TRAUMA* factor tend to report some combination of flashbacks, nightmares, intrusive or triggered memories, cognitive or behavioral avoidance of reminders of previous traumatic events, sympathetic hyperarousal (e.g., sleep disturbance, jumpiness, irritability, and hyperalertness) and various dissociative symptoms. Although *TRAUMA* factor items do not explicitly refer to a specific traumatic event, in almost all cases respondents with an elevated *TRAUMA* score have undergone one or more major traumas in their lives. Lastly, Ms. Guritan's high score on the *Anxious Arousal (AA)* scale indicates that she is experiencing symptoms of anxiety, such as fears, phobias, and panic, and/or autonomic hyperarousal symptoms such as hyperalertness, tension, or jumpiness. An elevation on this scale is often present in individuals who have been abused, assaulted, or exposed to disasters or serious accidents. At high levels, these symptoms may be associated with a diagnosis of posttraumatic stress disorder (PTSD), acute stress disorder (ASD), or another anxiety-related condition or disorder. More specifically, Ms. Guritan endorsed symptoms such as worry, irrational fears, nervousness, and fear of death or injury. Generalized anxiety, fearful preoccupations, and a specific tendency toward panic attacks are not uncommon among people with high *AA-A* scores.

Diagnostic Impression According to the Diagnostic and Statistical Manual of Mental Disorders – 5 (DSM 5)

Based on the symptoms reported by Ms. Guritan, as well as the results of the psychological instruments administered during this evaluation, Ms. Guritan meets criteria for the following mental disorders:

• Posttraumatic Stress Disorder (PTSD)

A diagnosis of PTSD is warranted when an individual experiences direct exposure to a threatening event or events; experiences recurrent involuntary and intrusive memories, nightmares, or flashbacks of the events; makes a strong effort to avoid trauma-related thoughts and feelings; has persistent negative beliefs and expectations about oneself and others, persistent distorted blame for causing the traumatic event, persistent negative trauma-related emotions, and/or feelings of detachment and estrangement; and experiences irritable or aggressive behavior, reckless behavior, hypervigilance, and/or sleep disturbance. Such symptoms must have persisted for more than one month. Ms. Guritan reported that her symptoms have worsened since the onset of her immigration process, as she has had to recall very painful memories.

Summary and Recommendations

Ms. Fabiola Guritan was referred for an evaluation to assess her current psychological status and the extent to which having been the victim of rape and torture in Haiti has affected her psychologically. She underwent a thorough psychological assessment consisting of a face-to-face clinical interview and the administration of a series of empirically validated instruments. Overall, she provided a candid account of her struggles and sufficient information for diagnostic purposes, yielding valid clinical impressions of her current functioning.

Having been a victim of rape and torture by Haitian government officials and witnessing the murder of her father has resulted in long-lasting negative consequences for Ms. Guritan. The intensity and chronic quality of the symptoms she is currently experiencing meet criteria for a diagnosis of *PTSD*. It is important to note that PTSD typically waxes and wanes throughout life, and its symptoms tend to re-emerge or be exacerbated by subsequent trauma or specific reminders of the trauma. There is no cure for this type of disorder, but symptoms can be effectively managed through timely mental health treatment. In addition, stability and a safe, supportive environment are crucial for fostering her well-being.

Ms. Guritan has been struggling greatly in trying to rebuild her life practically and emotionally in the aftermath of her traumatic experiences. According to Ms. Guritan, if she were to return to her native country, she fears that she would be recognized and killed by government officials, despite the fact that she does not intend to partake in any political associations. "The government has all my information—my arrest, my father, everything. There is no question that they will kill me if I return," she asserted. Returning to Haiti would clearly subject Ms. Guritan to unbearable psychological distress, as well as real, objective dangers. Remaining lawfully in the United States and being able to find gainful employment with which to support herself and be a contributing member of society therefore appears to be the optimal setting to foster her healthy emotional and psychological well-being.

If you have questions regarding this report, feel free to contact me at your convenience. I declare under penalty of perjury that all statements contained in this document are true and correct to the best of my professional judgment.

Appendix F

Sample VAWA Report

<u>Client's Name:</u> Musa Achebe
<u>Date of Birth:</u> 09/10/1992
<u>Date of Assessment:</u> 01/20/2019
<u>Date of Report:</u> 01/30/2019
<u>Assessment Procedures:</u> Biopsychosocial History Interview
Structured Clinical Interview for DSM-5
Disorders – Clinician Version
Posttraumatic Stress Disorder Checklist – 5
Abuse in Relationships Questionnaire
Trauma Symptom Inventory – 2

Evaluator's Qualifications and Assessment Methodology

(Please refer to Sample Provisional Waiver Report for this introductory section)

Identifying Information and Reason for Referral

Ms. Musa Achebe is a 26-year-old, self-identified African female. She is legally married to Mr. Jonathan Jay Weber, but they have been separated since January 2018. Ms. Achebe has the equivalent of a bachelor's degree in nursing, and she volunteers at a nursing home. She lives in an apartment with her cousin in San Diego, California.

Ms. Achebe was referred by her attorney for a psychological evaluation to assess her current psychological status and the extent to which the domestic violence that she was a victim of by Mr. Jonathan Jay Weber has affected her—emotionally and psychologically. She is currently undergoing an immigration process to obtain permanent legal residency in the United States.

Relevant Background History

Ms. Achebe was born and raised in Nasarawa State, Nigeria. She was raised in an intact household along with her two older brothers. Ms. Achebe recalled a positive childhood and denied any history of trauma or abuse growing up. She lamented, however, that her father worked in a different state and that she would go for long periods of time without seeing him. Ms. Achebe reported having always had good relationships with both of her parents as well as her siblings.

Upon graduating high school, Ms. Achebe attended nursing school. She then found employment in her field at a local hospital. She was involved in two serious relationships that lasted about a year each. In 2015, Ms. Achebe met Mr. Jonathan Jay Weber, a United States citizen, on an online dating site. They developed a friendship and maintained contact via the Internet for approximately one year. "We talked about culture and our cultural differences. He was very interested in the African culture and music," Ms. Achebe said. In September 2016, Ms. Achebe came to the United States with her mother to visit her cousin, who had been residing in San Diego since 2012. Three days into her visit, Ms. Achebe decided to contact Mr. Weber. Unbeknownst to her, Mr. Weber lived in San Diego. The two met up, and they developed a romantic relationship a few weeks later.

Ms. Achebe described Mr. Weber as "sweet and compassionate" initially, explaining that even though she had no intention of developing a romantic relationship, she "fell in love." As the date for her return to Nigeria approached, Mr. Weber proposed that she stay in the United States, and they get married. She stated, "I thought about it a lot because I was very happy [in Nigeria], and I never intended on coming here to stay. But I was in love and felt so loved that I didn't want to let it go." The couple married in January 2017 and moved into an apartment they shared with one roommate.

Ms. Achebe described the first few months of marriage as "beautiful" but lamented that it was a very short-lived period before their problems started. She said that Mr. Weber began complaining that she was "lazy" because she did not work. She explained that she did not have authorization to work in the United States, so she mostly stayed home while Mr. Weber worked two jobs. Ms. Achebe reported that she soon realized that Mr. Weber had a "drinking problem." "He would come home drunk and sometimes not come home for days," recalled Ms. Achebe, adding, "I tried to get him to stop drinking because he had to work at night, but he got so mad at me. He would yell, 'You don't tell me what to do, bitch!' No one had ever treated me that way before."

She shared that Mr. Weber's abuse went from verbal (calling her profanities such as *bitch, asshole, lazy pig*) to physical, recalling that around September 2017 they had an argument and Mr. Weber slapped her across the face. "He had not been home for days and he wasn't answering my calls, so I confronted him, and he got mad and slapped me," she said. Over the following months, Mr. Weber reportedly became increasingly physically violent with Ms. Achebe, throwing "anything within his reach" at her, hitting her, and once punching her in the face.

According to Ms. Achebe, Mr. Weber would often take away her cell phone so that she could not call her cousin, and the few times she tried to call the police, he threatened her that she would be deported because she was "an immigrant and nobody listens to an immigrant." Feeling helpless and hopeless, Ms. Achebe succumbed to depression. "I just stayed home and felt like I lost my freedom. I couldn't do anything on my own because he had to approve it." Mr. Weber also controlled whom Ms. Achebe spent time with. She explained that she started attending continuing education classes and met a few friends, but Mr. Weber would tell her that she "did not need any people [other than] him" and dissuaded her from contacting others, including her cousin. When asked why she did not leave Mr. Weber, Ms.

Achebe cried, "I didn't feel I could. I had nowhere to go, and there was no way out."

Ms. Achebe last saw Mr. Weber a few days before Christmas in 2017. Since Mr. Weber had not answered his phone for several days, Ms. Achebe spent the holidays alone, as her cousin was visiting family back in Nigeria. After days went by with no signs of Mr. Weber's whereabouts, Ms. Achebe decided to look at the transaction history on their credit card, where she noticed that the card had been used in jail. She subsequently found out that Mr. Weber had been arrested for possession of a firearm. Ms. Achebe attended three of Mr. Weber's court hearings, where Mr. Weber was sentenced to 32 months in prison. "I found out he had a long criminal history, which he never told me before," Ms. Achebe said.

Unable to pay rent, Ms. Achebe moved into her cousin's house. In March 2018, Ms. Achebe had her adjustment interview, but her green card was denied because Mr. Weber was in prison and thus unable to attend the adjustment interview with her. "It was devastating. I was arrested by ICE, and I was treated like a criminal," she tearfully stated. She was subsequently released with an ankle monitor and placed in removal proceedings. Ms. Achebe struggled greatly to rebuild her life on her own in a foreign country. She explained, "There's nothing to go back to in Nigeria. When I left, I left my job and everything. And I'm not the same person anymore, and that's going to hurt my parents even more." Ms. Achebe shared feeling ashamed about her failed marriage and not wanting people in Nigeria to find out about it. "Where I'm from, a divorce is like taboo; they treat you like an out-cast. Nobody is going to want to have anything to do with me," she stated.

Ms. Achebe reported a profound sense of despair and hopelessness. If she were forced to return to Nigeria, she fears that her "life would be over." She said, "It would be such shame, going back to my country." If allowed to stay in the United States, Ms. Achebe hopes to start a homecare business with her cousin. She stated, "I love being a nurse. I want to help people."

Behavioral Observations

Ms. Achebe presented on time to her scheduled interview. Prior to commencing this evaluation, Ms. Achebe was fully informed of its nature and purpose. She was also informed that any information she provided was subject to inclusion in the evaluation report, which would be available to her attorney. Ms. Achebe indicated that she understood the purpose of the evaluation and limits of confidentiality. She readily agreed to participate in all of the assessment procedures.

Ms. Achebe was overall engaging, cooperative, and forthcoming. She was able to provide an intact, sequential, and logical personal history. She had a soft voice, but she spoke clearly and coherently, and she maintained appropriate eye contact. Even though English is her second language, she did not have difficulty expressing her thoughts. Based on her overall cognitive faculties and range of knowledge, Ms. Achebe is estimated to be of average intellectual ability for her age.

Throughout the evaluation, Ms. Achebe's emotional expressions were appropriate and congruent with the subjects of discussion. She became tearful when recalling the abuse she endured while married to Mr. Weber, but she quickly regained her composure, apologizing for her display of emotions. Ms. Achebe appeared to be a reliable historian, and her accounts of her personal experiences were believable. Overall, she provided sufficient information for diagnostic purposes, yielding valid clinical impressions of her current functioning.

Impressions and Findings

Throughout the clinical interview, Ms. Achebe described in detail the emotional, physical, and psychological abuse she endured at the hands of Mr. Weber. She reported feeling "like a different person," when compared to the time before she met Mr. Weber. She stated, "I'm not myself anymore. I feel like nothing really matters anymore and I can't trust anybody." Despite her pervasive sense of hopelessness, Ms. Achebe denied any intention to end her life or harm herself. She reported that she feels so ashamed about her failed marriage that she had not told her family she was no longer living with Mr. Weber until last week. She stated, "My mom has high blood pressure, so I don't want to upset her. I didn't tell them he's in prison, just that I needed time to myself." Ms. Achebe reported that she copes with her despair by overeating and said that she has put on over 20 pounds since last year. She reported that she has never considered seeing a therapist because it is often looked down upon in her culture and "it's not something one thinks about. I wouldn't know how to go about it."

To assess her current psychological symptoms further, I followed the guidelines of the Structured Clinical Interview for DSM-5 Disorders – Clinician Version (SCID-5-CV). The SCID-5-CV is a semi-structured guide designed to evaluate a broad range of psychological problems and symptoms of psychopathology according to the diagnostic criteria established by the Diagnostic and Statistical Manual of Mental Disorders – Fifth Edition (DSM-5). Ms. Achebe's responses revealed that she is experiencing symptoms of anxiety, including worrying about a number of things in her life and having great difficulty controlling her worries; feeling irritable, restless, and on edge; and having difficulty sleeping. She also reported symptoms of depression, such as a pervasive sense of sadness, hopelessness, low self-worth, and a profound sense of loneliness. Ms. Achebe reported experiencing recurrent, intrusive thoughts and dreams about her abusive relationship with Mr. Weber. She expressed undue guilt over the dissolution of her marriage and wondered aloud if there was anything she could have done to prevent it.

Ms. Achebe completed the Posttraumatic Stress Disorder Checklist – 5 (PCL-5), which is a brief assessment that helps identify the presence and severity of symptoms characteristic of posttraumatic stress disorder (PTSD). Even though Ms. Achebe endorsed a number of posttraumatic symptoms related to the abuse she experienced, the frequency and severity of such symptoms did not reach the threshold required for a diagnosis of PTSD at this time.

Ms. Achebe completed the Abuse in Relationships Questionnaire. This instrument was designed to identify various typical abusive behaviors in relationships and the frequency of such behaviors. Out of the 33 abusive behaviors listed on the measure, Ms. Achebe endorsed 30, most salient of which were Mr. Weber's physical aggression, controlling behaviors, irrational jealousy, and hurtful, insulting, and degrading comments with the intent to humiliate her. In addition, Ms. Achebe reported feeling scared of Mr. Weber's unpredictable temper, avoiding certain topics so as not to upset him, and being blamed for things she did not do. Ms. Achebe also reported that Mr. Weber repeatedly used her immigration status to control her and humiliate her, and he threatened that if she ever called the police, she would be the one to get arrested.

To gain a better understanding regarding the impact of the trauma she endured, Ms. Achebe was administered the Trauma Symptom Inventory-2 (TSI-2), a self-report measure that is globally used to assess a variety of symptom domains related to trauma. Ms. Achebe's responses on the TSI-2 revealed a faulty perception of herself and others, along with a relative inability to access a stable, internal sense of self or identity from which to interact with the external world. This combination of difficulties may lead to ambivalent, insecure, and often problematic interactions, a tendency to rely on other people for information about herself, and a greater susceptibility to influence by others. This relative lack of a stable, ongoing model of self or identity, in combination with disturbed relationships with others, has clearly contributed to her depression. Ms. Achebe appears to have developed a largely unconscious, defensive alteration in awareness as an avoidance response to overwhelming—often posttraumatic—psychological distress. Her attempts to suppress or eliminate painful thoughts or memories from awareness, and to avoid events or stimuli that might restimulate such thoughts or memories, were also evident. Ms. Achebe has a profound fear of rejection and abandonment. She now deals with such fears by avoiding relationships altogether and maintaining emotional distance from others. Lastly, the combination of intrusive traumatic memories, cognitive and behavioral avoidance of reminders of previous traumatic events, sympathetic hyperarousal (e.g., sleep disturbance, jumpiness, irritability, and hyperalertness) and various dissociative symptoms indicate that Ms. Achebe has experienced a major trauma in her life. Upon inquiry, she identified such trauma as the abuse she endured from Mr. Weber.

Clinical Diagnostic Impression According to the Diagnostic and Statistical Manual of Mental Disorders – 5 (DSM 5)

Based on the symptoms reported by Ms. Achebe, as well as the results of the psychological instruments administered during this evaluation, Ms. Achebe currently meets criteria for the following mental disorder:

- Major Depressive Disorder

Symptoms of *major depressive disorder* include persistent depressed mood, markedly diminished interest in most activities, insomnia, lethargy, diminished ability to think or concentrate, hopelessness, worthlessness, and irritability, where such symptomatology causes clinically significant distress or impairment in important areas of functioning.

Summary and Recommendations

Ms. Musa Achebe was referred for a psychological evaluation to assess her current psychological level of functioning, the emotional impact of being the victim of domestic abuse by Mr. Jonathan Jay Weber, and the potential implications that being forced to return to her country of origin would have on her well-being. She underwent a thorough psychological assessment consisting of a face-to-face clinical interview and the administration of empirically validated psychological instruments. Overall, she was a good historian and provided a candid account of her struggles, yielding valid clinical impressions of her current functioning.

Being the victim of verbal, emotional, and physical abuse by her estranged husband has resulted in long-lasting negative consequences for Ms. Achebe. The intensity and chronic quality of the abuse she endured, paired with her current stressors, has resulted in symptoms that meet criteria for *major depressive disorder*.

Results from this psychological evaluation clearly demonstrate that the abuse she experienced in her marriage with Mr. Weber has resulted in emotional and psychological trauma for Ms. Achebe and has compromised her overall level of functioning. The symptoms and personality characteristics that Ms. Achebe is exhibiting are consistent with those typically observed in victims of domestic violence (e.g., self-blame, low self-esteem, and learned helplessness). Domestic violence is the willful intimidation, physical assault, battery, sexual assault, and/or other abusive behavior as part of a systematic pattern of power and control perpetrated by one intimate partner against another. It can include physical violence, sexual violence, psychological violence, and emotional abuse, and the frequency and severity of domestic violence can vary dramatically; however, the one constant component of domestic violence is one partner's consistent efforts to maintain power and control over the other. It is important to note that domestic violence does not always manifest as physical abuse. Emotional and psychological abuse can often be just as extreme as physical violence. Lack of physical violence does not mean the abuser is any less dangerous to the victim, nor does it mean the victim is any less trapped by the abuse.

Ms. Achebe has struggled greatly trying to rebuild her life in a foreign country in the aftermath of the abuse and torment she endured while married to Mr. Weber, and although her resilience is noticeable, so is her profound despair. A forced return to her country of citizenship would be detrimental to her, as her compromised mental state would undoubtedly deteriorate. Ms. Achebe expressed her overwhelming sense of shame and her fear of being ostracized and mistreated if she were to return to Nigeria.

Based on my knowledge of the Nigerian culture, her fears seem rational and credible. Ms. Achebe would, therefore, greatly benefit from stability in her living environment, as well as mental health treatment to process the trauma she has experienced and to learn ways to cope with her psychological symptoms.

Appendix G

Sample U Visa Report

Client's Name: Carina Beatriz Silva
Date of Birth: 03/07/1982
Date of Assessment: 07/09/2020
Date of Report: 07/16/2020
Assessment Procedures: Biopsychosocial History Interview
Structured Clinical Interview for DSM-5 Disorders – Clinician Version
Personality Assessment Inventory
Clinician-Administered PTSD Scale for DSM-5
Trauma Symptom Inventory – 2
Records Reviewed: Los Angeles Regional Crime/Incident Report (01/2006)
Santa Monica Police Department Crime Report (01/2006)
Santa Monica Police Department Supplemental Report (01/2006)
Psychiatric Evaluation by Dr. John Ortiz, Ph.D. (10/2014)

Evaluator's Qualifications and Assessment Methodology

(Please refer to Sample Provisional Waiver Report for this introductory section)

Identifying Information and Reason for Referral

Ms. Carina Beatriz Silva is a 38-year-old, self-identified Hispanic female. She is married to Mr. Jesus Justo Sanchez, and she has two daughters from her first marriage: Maria (age 19) and Misty (age 13). Ms. Silva is a certified public accountant and is self-employed. She lives with her husband and her daughters in San Diego, California.

Ms. Silva was referred for an evaluation to assess her current psychological status. More specifically, she is seeking evidence of the extent to which having been the victim of a crime in 2006 has affected her—emotionally and psychologically.

Relevant Background Information

Ms. Silva was born and raised in Guatemala City, Guatemala. She has one older brother, and both were raised by their maternal grandparents. She explained that she never met her biological father and that her mother moved to the United States when Ms. Silva was about 3 years old. Her mother would visit her children back in Guatemala periodically, and despite the distance, they developed a close relationship. Ms. Silva recalled an otherwise unremarkable childhood, denying any history of trauma or abuse.

At the age of 18, Ms. Silva met Mr. Carlos Munguia, who was her neighbor and approximately 10 years her senior. The two developed a friendship and eventually a romantic relationship. They had their first daughter, Maria, in 2001. Ms. Silva described a positive relationship with Mr. Munguia, and the two married around 2003. Mr. Munguia reportedly insisted that they move to the United States in search of a better quality of life, and they settled in Los Angeles, California, in 2005. Mr. Munguia found work in construction while Ms. Silva looked after their young daughter. According to Ms. Silva, her husband then started drinking heavily and was involved in a car accident that resulted in the death of one of his coworkers. Mr. Munguia was convicted of voluntary manslaughter and sentenced to six years in custody. Ms. Silva, who was three months pregnant with their second daughter at the time of her husband's arrest, applied for a job at a deli near her house. She explained, "I didn't have a work permit, and they didn't ask me for a social security card or anything, so I was happy to be able to work and support my daughter." On her third day at work, Ms. Silva was raped by her manager, Mr. Eduardo Esposito.

Ms. Silva described in detail the incident on January 23, 2006.[1] She stated that she was working alongside another female employee, whose shift ended in the afternoon. In the evening, after closing down the store with her store manager, both went to the back of the store to get some fruit when a man entered the store and pointed a gun at Ms. Silva. She stated, "He was wearing like a stocking over his head, and he told us not to look at him. He gave us orders to kneel down on the floor and for the manager to tie me up. He tied me with a cord or something and then covered my head, so I didn't see anything else."

She recalled begging to be let go because she was pregnant and had a little girl at home. Ms. Silva shared how her manager, Mr. Esposito, took off her pants and raped her. At one point, he lifted what was covering her head and began kissing her in the mouth. She said she did not hear anyone else's voices or footsteps even though Mr. Esposito told her he was being forced to rape her. Once it was over, he ordered Ms. Silva to wash herself off. According to Ms. Silva, the supposed assailant was no longer around by the time Mr. Esposito uncovered her head. She shared that Mr. Esposito dissuaded her from calling the police, saying that she would get in trouble because she was undocumented. "I just wanted to get out of there, so I promised him I wouldn't call the police," she said. Once she was able to leave the store, Ms. Silva ran to the home of her sister-in-law, who promptly called the police.

Following a thorough investigation, Mr. Esposito was arrested and convicted of rape. Ms. Silva painfully recalled having to attend the court hearings and retell her story, stating, "I was pregnant, and my husband was still in jail, so I was basically alone." Mr. Esposito, who turned out to have raped other female employees in a similar manner, was sentenced to 20 years in prison.

Ms. Silva described how she struggled to rebuild her life in the aftermath of the crime. She lamented that her first husband blamed her for the rape, and the two divorced while he was still serving time. Their second daughter, Misty, was born in 2006. Ms. Silva started making and selling tamales with her mother to make ends meet, and she enrolled in adult school to learn English. Upon his release from prison, Mr. Munguia was deported back to Guatemala, and Ms. Silva lost track of his whereabouts. She raised her daughters as a single mother until she met Mr. Jesus Sanchez at a church in 2012. After a three-year courtship, she agreed to marry him in September 2015.

Being the victim of rape has continued to affect Ms. Silva in all aspects of her life. She stated, "It's like something was taken from me. I can't explain it, but it's like you don't feel complete. I carry a lot of anger, and I have a hard time trusting people." She moved from Los Angeles to Riverside and subsequently to San Diego in hopes of escaping any reminders of the trauma. "I keep looking for a fresh start, to put it all behind me," she said. Ms. Silva added that she has always struggled with intimacy, stating, "I feel terrible because I want my husband to be happy, but I sometimes still go for months without being able to be intimate with him. I feel dirty and weird."

Despite the passing of time, Ms. Silva continues to suffer from post-traumatic symptoms, which are exacerbated every time she has to recount details of the rape. She tearfully stated, "It's been 14 years, and it doesn't go away. It's like I can't get over it. Anything that reminds me of [the rape] just makes me fall apart. I start to cry, to shut down, and I just can't function."

Because of this, she explained, she was so reluctant to apply for a U visa. Ms. Silva reportedly initiated the process to apply for a U nonimmigrant visa in 2014, but she did not follow through. She said, "I had to tell the attorney everything that happened, and I saw a [psychologist], but it was too hard. I didn't want to have to relive it, and I especially didn't want anything that was in any way related to that man."

Ms. Silva recently sought the help of an immigration attorney with the hopes of adjusting her immigration status. She lamented that one of her best friends was deported a few months ago, and she fears the same could happen to her. "I need to do this for my daughters and for my husband," she said.

Psychiatric and Medical History

Ms. Silva first saw a mental health provider shortly after the rape, which she found somewhat helpful. She explained, however, that she discontinued her treatment out of concern for her unborn baby. "I just felt like I didn't want her to sense my distress, or to hear the things I was talking about," she said.

A few years later, Ms. Silva began receiving mental health treatment at the encouragement of her daughter's school counselor. She saw a therapist weekly and was prescribed psychotropic medication. She cried as she stated, "It helped for a while, but then I would go through phases when I just didn't want to take chemicals to feel better. Why should I have to depend on pills to feel normal? Seeing the pill and knowing I have to take them to feel better was humiliating. It's because of [Mr. Esposito]'s fault that I have to still take medication. It's not fair."

Ms. Silva reportedly continued to struggle with posttraumatic symptoms for years. She acknowledged her need for mental health treatment but said, "It's like I have this heaviness take over me, and I have no energy. I just want to go to sleep and just wake up and feel better." She reported that keeping busy and "reaching exhaustion" is what keeps her depression at bay. She said she does not like to socialize and tends to keep to herself. "I like being with my husband and our daughters. We love going to church, making crafts, or baking sweets. That's my only joy in life."

In a psychological evaluation report dated October 23, 2014, Dr. John Ortiz detailed the long-term effects of the rape on Ms. Silva. He determined, based on her symptoms at the time, that Ms. Silva met criteria for a diagnosis of posttraumatic stress disorder and major depressive disorder. He mentioned the different periods of time when Ms. Silva received mental health treatment, and he concluded that despite the passing of time, Ms. Silva's severity and frequency of her symptoms significantly interfered with her functioning.

Ms. Silva has reportedly been suffering from gastrointestinal problems since the birth of her second daughter and was diagnosed with irritable bowel syndrome. She reported that her symptoms tend to worsen when under stress, and that she takes herbal remedies to feel better.

Behavioral Observations

In light of the social distancing mandate imposed due to the current global pandemic, Ms. Silva and I wore protective masks during the clinical interview. This, however, did not impair our ability to establish rapport and pick up on non-verbal communication. The interview was conducted in Spanish, Ms. Silva's native language. She spoke clearly and coherently and maintained appropriate eye contact. Overall, Ms. Silva was engaging, cooperative, and forthcoming. She was able to provide an intact, detailed, sequential, and logical personal history. Based on her overall cognitive faculties and range of knowledge, Ms. Silva's intellectual ability appears to be in the average range for her age.

Throughout the evaluation, Ms. Silva's emotional expressions were appropriate and congruent with the subjects of discussion. Despite her attempts to maintain her composure, she cried while describing the rape and its lingering effects on her mental health. Ms. Silva appeared to be a reliable historian, and her accounts of her personal experiences were believable. Overall, she provided sufficient information for diagnostic purposes, yielding valid clinical impressions of her current functioning.

Impressions and Findings

Ms. Silva reported going through "phases" throughout the years since 2006. She stated, "I might feel better, start taking care of myself, but then something happens, and I just fall apart. I have to force myself to do things I need to do, and it's taking me more and more effort to do that."

She reported that she visited the hospital emergency department several times due to severe stomach pain and that she was eventually diagnosed with gastritis. "I would just run and exercise, and I didn't want to eat. Or if I ate, I would throw up afterwards because I felt bad about it." Ms. Silva reported engaging in these behaviors for years following the birth of her second daughter in July 2006, six months after the rape. She also reported suffering from posttraumatic symptoms. "That was something that stuck with me for a long time. I couldn't stand anyone touching my head or my neck."

To further assess Ms. Silva's psychological symptoms, I followed the guidelines of the Structured Clinical Interview for DSM-5 Disorders – Clinician Version (SCID-5-CV). The SCID-5-CV is a semi-structured guide designed to evaluate a broad range of psychological problems and symptoms of psychopathology according to the diagnostic criteria established by the Diagnostic and Statistical Manual of Mental Disorders – Fifth Edition (DSM-5). Ms. Silva endorsed most symptoms presented to her, revealing her profound need to be heard and taken seriously. She complained of a pervasive state of angst, sadness, and worry, and reported having difficulty sleeping and trouble concentrating. She also reported still experiencing intrusive thoughts that she cannot control and overall difficulty managing her overwhelming emotions. Ms. Silva expressed concern about her physical health, acknowledging how her emotional distress tends to manifest physically, such as in gastrointestinal problems, headaches, and chronic pain.

The Personality Assessment Inventory (PAI) is a self-administered, objective test of personality and psychopathology designed to provide information on critical client variables in professional settings. It consists of various scales that measure the respondent's overall approach taking the test, psychopathological traits, treatment considerations, and interpersonal functioning. Ms. Silva's responses on this test indicated a tendency to present an unfavorable impression or represent particularly bizarre and unlikely symptoms. Although this raises the possibility of exaggeration of complaints and problems, response styles of this type often indicate a "cry for help," or an extremely negative evaluation of oneself and one's life. Despite such general level of negative distortion, there are some areas where Ms. Silva described problems of greater intensity than are typically obtained, even among respondents with similarly negative response styles. The configuration of the PAI clinical scales suggests a person with marked anxiety and tension. Ms. Silva may be particularly uneasy and ruminative about her personal relationships, some of which are an important source of her current distress, and she may be responding to these circumstances by becoming socially withdrawn. The disruptions in her life have left her uncertain about her goals and priorities, and tense and fearful about what the future may hold. Her life is probably severely constricted by her tension, and she may not be able to meet even minimal role expectations without feeling overwhelmed. Relatively mild stressors may be sufficient to precipitate a major crisis. She is likely to be plagued by worry to the degree that her ability to concentrate and attend is significantly compromised.

Ms. Silva reported a number of difficulties consistent with a significant depressive experience. She is likely to be plagued by thoughts of worthlessness, hopelessness, and personal failure. She admits openly to feelings of sadness, a loss of interest in normal activities, and a loss of sense of pleasure in things that were previously enjoyed. She feels that her health is not as good as that of her age peers and likely believes that her health problems are too complex and difficult to treat successfully. Ms. Silva is reportedly uncomfortable in social situations, appearing to have little interest in or need for interacting with others, and she likely takes a passive, submissive stance when dealing with other people. Her responses indicate that she experiences her level of social support as being lower than that of the average adult. She may have relatively few close relationships or be dissatisfied with the quality of these relationships, often questioning and doubting the motives of those around her. It was evident from her responses to the PAI that Ms. Silva has experienced a traumatic event that continues to distress her and produce recurrent episodes of anxiety, which she identified as the rape in 2006.

Ms. Silva's posttraumatic symptoms were further assessed through the Clinician-Administered PTSD Scale for DSM-5 (CAPS-5). The CAPS-5 is a structured interview considered to be the gold standard in PTSD assessment. In addition to assessing the 20 DSM-5 PTSD symptoms, questions target the onset and duration of symptoms, subjective distress, impact of symptoms on social and occupational functioning, improvement in symptoms through time, overall response validity, and overall PTSD severity. It is evident from her answers to this instrument that Ms. Silva was very much affected by the rape in 2006 and that she developed posttraumatic symptoms as a result. Even though so much time has passed since the traumatic incident, she continues to experience several posttraumatic symptoms, which get exacerbated every time she has to revisit this trauma. She reported having repeated, intrusive memories and dreams about the assault and becoming hypervigilant as a result. She stated, "I'm always watching out for attackers and coming up with plans for defending myself. I tell my daughters to expect the worst, to not trust others, and to always protect themselves." She reported feeling overwhelmed with emotion when recalling details of the rape—which were observed during the interview—and thus making effortful attempts to avoid any reminders of the trauma.

Ms. Silva was administered the Trauma Symptom Inventory-2 (TSI-2), a multi-scale instrument used to evaluate posttraumatic symptoms related to rape, spousal abuse, assault, combat experiences, major accidents and natural disasters, as well as the lasting sequelae of childhood abuse and early traumatic events. Similar to the PAI, Ms. Silva endorsed several items that are uncommon in clinical populations. The results of this test were thus uninterpretable. However, it is possible that her difficulty concentrating and overwhelming emotional distress resulted in her faulty responses.

Clinical Diagnostic Impression According to the Diagnostic and Statistical Manual of Mental Disorders – 5 (DSM 5)

Based on the symptoms reported by Ms. Silva, as well as the results of the psychological instruments administered during this evaluation, Ms. Silva currently meets criteria for the following mental disorders:

- Posttraumatic Stress Disorder
- Major Depressive Disorder

A diagnosis of *posttraumatic stress disorder* is warranted when an individual experiences direct exposure to a threatening event or events; experiences recurrent involuntary and intrusive memories, nightmares, or flashbacks of the events; makes a strong effort to avoid trauma-related thoughts and feelings; has persistent negative beliefs and expectations about oneself and others, persistent distorted blame for causing the traumatic event, persistent negative trauma-related emotions, and/or feelings of detachment and estrangement; and experiences irritable or aggressive behavior, reckless behavior, hypervigilance, and/or sleep disturbance, where such symptoms have persisted for more than one month.

Symptoms of *major depressive disorder* include persistent depressed mood, markedly diminished interest in most activities, insomnia, lethargy, diminished ability to think or concentrate, hopelessness, worthlessness, and irritability. Such symptomatology causes clinically significant distress or impairment in important areas of functioning.

Summary and Recommendations

Ms. Carina Beatriz Silva was referred for an evaluation to assess her current psychological status and the extent to which the rape she was a victim of in 2006 has compromised her well-being. She underwent a thorough psychological assessment consisting of a face-to-face clinical interview and the administration of psychological instruments to assess her current mental health and more enduring characteristics of her personality. Overall, she was a good historian and provided a candid account of her experiences, yielding valid clinical impressions of her past and current functioning.

Ms. Silva recounted a mostly unremarkable upbringing despite her parents' notable absence. Having been the victim of rape, however, undoubtedly affected Ms. Silva's life in exceptionally negative ways. She demonstrated her resilience in adapting to a new culture, learning a new language, and pursuing a career while raising two young daughters as a single mother. It is remarkable that she has been able to accomplish her professional achievements and build a home with her husband in the aftermath of such tremendous trauma. It is unfortunate, however, that her posttraumatic symptoms have interfered in other areas of her life and have continued to affect her daily functioning.

A significant amount of research indicates that rape and violence against women can lead to multiple detrimental effects. When compared with non-abused women, women who have suffered any kind of violence are more likely to experience serious health problems and to endure long-lasting negative effects and psychological suffering.[2] Ms. Silva's specific fears about being victimized again and the changes she has made in her lifestyle clearly demonstrate that the rape she was a victim of in 2006 has significantly compromised her overall level of functioning. Even after so much time has passed, she continues to be affected by posttraumatic symptoms and to meet diagnostic criteria for posttraumatic stress disorder and major depressive disorder. Posttraumatic stress disorder typically waxes and wanes throughout life, and its symptoms tend to re-emerge or be exacerbated by subsequent trauma or specific reminders of the trauma. There is no cure for this type of disorder, but symptoms can be effectively managed through timely mental health treatment. In addition, stability and a safe, supportive environment are crucial for fostering her well-being. Ms. Silva would, therefore, greatly benefit from mental health treatment so she can continue to process her trauma and learn healthy ways to cope with her symptoms.

Notes

1 A review of law enforcement records confirmed Ms. Silva's report and no inconsistencies were noted.
2 World Health Organization (1997). Violence against women: Health consequences. Retrieved from www.who.int/gender/violence/v8.pdf.

Index

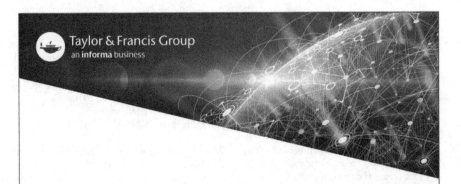